D0082851

TO PROMOTE THE GENERAL WELFARE

Market Processes vs. Political Transfers

By
Richard E. Wagner

PACIFIC RESEARCH INSTITUTE FOR PUBLIC POLICY
San Francisco, California

Copyright © 1989 by Pacific Research Institute for Public Policy. All rights reserved.
No part of this publication may be reproduced, stored in a retrieval system, or
transmitted in any form or by any means, electronic, mechanical, photocopy, recording,
or otherwise, without the prior written consent of the publisher.

Cloth ISBN 0–936488–25–5
Paperback ISBN 0–936488–26–3

Library of Congress Catalog Card Number 88–64203

Printed in the United States of America.

Pacific Research Institute for Public Policy
177 Post Street
San Francisco, CA 94108
(415) 989-0833

Library of Congress Cataloging-in-Publication Data

Wagner, Richard E.
    To promote the general welfare: market processes vs. political transfers / by
Richard E. Wagner.
        p. cm.
    Includes bibliographies and index.
    ISBN 0–936488–25–5 : $29.95. — ISBN 0–936488–26–3 (pbk.) : $12.95
    1. Social choice.   2. Welfare state.   3. Income distribution.
4. Democracy.   I. Title.
HB846.8.W34 1989
361.6—dc19   88–64203
                                                                          CIP

PRESIDENT
William H. Mellor III, J.D.

SENIOR ECONOMIST
Terry L. Anderson, Ph.D.

BOARD OF ADVISORS

Charles W. Baird
California State University, Hayward

Yale Brozen
University of Chicago

James M. Buchanan
Nobel laureate in economics
George Mason University

Steven N. S. Cheung
University of Hong Kong

Robert W. Clower
University of South Carolina

Richard A. Epstein
University of Chicago

John Gray
Oxford University, England

Steve H. Hanke
Johns Hopkins University

Friedrich A. Hayek
Nobel laureate in economics
University of Freiburg, Germany

George W. Hilton
University of California, Los Angeles

Jonathan R. T. Hughes
Northwestern University

Michael C. Jensen
University of Rochester

John Kaplan
Stanford University

Israel M. Kirzner
New York University

Gary D. Libecap
University of Arizona

Stephen C. Littlechild
University of Birmingham, England

Fred McChesney
Emory University

Chiaki Nishiyama
Rikkyo University, Japan

Ellen F. Paul
Bowling Green State University

Anna J. Schwartz
National Bureau of Economic Research

Julian L. Simon
University of Maryland

Edwin G. West
Carleton University, Canada

Leland B. Yeager
Auburn University

The Pacific Research Institute produces studies that explore long-term solutions to difficult issues of public policy. The Institute seeks to facilitate a more active and enlightened discourse on these issues and to broaden understanding of market processes, government policy, and the rule of law. Through the publication of scholarly books and the sponsorship of conferences, the Institute serves as an established resource for ideas in the continuing public policy debate.

Institute books have been adopted for courses at colleges, universities, and graduate schools nationwide. More than 175 distinguished scholars have worked with the Institute to analyze the premises and consequences of existing public policy and to formulate possible solutions to seemingly intractable problems. Prestigious journals and major media regularly review and comment upon Institute work. In addition, the Board of Advisors consists of internationally recognized scholars, including two Nobel laureates.

The Pacific Research Institute is an independent, tax exempt, 501(c)(3) organization and as such is supported solely by the sale of its books and by the contributions from a wide variety of foundations, corporations, and individuals. This diverse funding base and the Institute's refusal to accept government funds enable it to remain independent.

iii

The Pacific Research Institute for
Public Policy gratefully
acknowledges the grants from the
J.M. Foundation and the
Dean Witter Foundation
which made this book possible.

CONTENTS

6

Regulation and the Welfare State   107

7

The Market for Legislation in a Republican Polity   133

8

The Transfer Society and the Welfare State   155

LIST OF FIGURES

LIST OF TABLES

PREFACE

While a market economy is generally acknowledged to be an efficient institutional arrangement for promoting the general prosperity of a people, it is also widely believed that the very onrush of an economy's progressive forces leaves a wake of unfortunate people who do not share in that prosperity. The various programs that constitute what is commonly called the welfare state are typically justified as being necessary to provide for those people. That provision requires some transfer of income from those who do well to those who do poorly.

Wishing something were so doesn't make it so, of course, and several bodies of scholarship suggest that the reality of the welfare state conflicts significantly with the justificatory arguments advanced in its support. The economic aspect of this conflict concerns what happens when the programs of the welfare state confront human nature and the unceasing efforts of people to replace what they value less with what they value more. In consequence, there may exist very little ability to redistribute income and wealth, almost as if there were some natural distribution of income and wealth. Furthermore, there is a growing body of scholarship on public choice that explains that political processes follow an economic logic, in which political outcomes—public policies, including those relating to the distribution of income—are constrained and shaped by the constitutional rules within which contemporary politics unfolds. Once it is recognized that the production of public policy follows an economic logic and reflects the operation of political incentives, it becomes problematic to speak meaningfully of piecemeal economic reform, for alternative policies would seem to require alternative sets of incentives for their creation and implementation, which, in turn, require constitutional reformation.

This book, I should perhaps note at the outset, is *not* about the transfer programs of the welfare state per se. Its central concern is democracy and the operation of democratic institutions. The programs of the welfare state are considered as illustrations of the operation of democratic institutions, as that operation is explained through the literature on public choice. The reader seeking detailed descriptions and analyses of particular programs will find numerous citations to other works. My central purpose here is to illustrate how the operation of the welfare state fits sensibly within the rapidly developing literature on the economic theory of politics. This book, then, looks at the welfare state from a different perspective.

What is unique about this book is not the material it examines, but the *constitutional perspective* it brings to bear on that material. The entire set of political outcomes, ranging from food stamps designed to make food less expensive for some people to price support programs that make it more expensive—both of which burden the general taxpayer for the benefit of subsets of the population—follow naturally from the incentives contained within a particular constitutional regime. Consequently, it is illegitimate to conclude that the transfer programs of the welfare state benefit the poor, simply by comparing those programs with what would happen if those programs were eliminated, because the entire range of outcomes that emerge from a particular constitutional regime are inseparable components. Hence, proper analysis is not so much a matter of examining alternative policies and recommending better ones as it is a matter of comparing alternative constitutional regimes. In particular, I characterize two alternative regimes: (1) a limited government or contractarian regime, in which the legislature cannot abrogate rights of property and contract but is itself bound by them; and (2) an unlimited or majoritarian regime, in which legislative majorities can do as they choose, limited only by the vicissitudes of electoral necessity, with at most a requirement that the legislature declare that it has some "public interest" in mind when it acts.

As applied to the welfare state, this book has two primary themes, one predominantly economic and one mainly political. The economic theme is that government has little ability to change the distribution of income, at least within the framework of what remains essentially a self-organized economy, because efforts to do so will be largely offset as people interact through various market processes. The political theme is that benevolence is unlikely to dominate collective choices anyway, and that the reality of collective choices will diverge sharply from the justifications commonly given for the transfer programs of the welfare state.

Although I am an economist, I have written this book not just for economists but for everyone who is interested in political economy and public policy in relation to income transfers and the provision of personal security. I have tried to limit my use of technical economic argumentation and concepts; where I could not avoid such usage, I have tried to present it in a generally understandable fashion.

I am deeply grateful to Professors Terry L. Anderson (Montana State University), Gregory B. Christainsen (California State University, Hayward), and James D. Gwartney (Florida State University) for sharing with me, through their comments on an earlier version of this book, their considerable knowledge spanning both public choice and income transfer programs and to Brenda Curts, who typed several versions of the manuscript speedily and accurately with graciousness and good humor. Finally, I wish to thank William H. Mellor III and the Pacific Research Institute for their support and encouragement throughout this project.

1

CONTRACTARIAN STATE, WELFARE STATE, AND CONSTITUTIONAL ORDER

Before the mid-1960s, when the War on Poverty began, public assistance programs were generally limited to people who for one reason or another were outside the labor force. With that war there began an earnest effort to use public assistance to supplement the incomes of people who were working but whose earnings were low. And since 1974 the public assistance and social insurance programs that constitute what has come to be called the welfare state have been the largest category of expenditure in the federal budget, replacing national defense as the federal government's most significant activity.

Even in times when public assistance programs were relatively small, they were magnets for controversy.[1] This controversy concerned the perceived terms of the trade-off between the promotion of the wealth of a nation and the alleviation of poverty. While the wealth of a nation is based on work and capital accumulation, the alleviation of poverty through transfers of income generally discourages work and capital formation and so undermines, or at least impedes, the promotion of the common wealth. The offer of aid to the unfortunate may demonstrate the better side of human nature, but the lower side of human nature exploits such offers: as aid becomes more generous and more

---

1. For an examination of this controversy in Great Britain from the late eighteenth through the nineteenth century, see Gertrude Himmelfarb, *The Idea of Poverty* (New York: Alfred A. Knopf, 1983).

easily available, the number of people seeking aid increases. Much of the controversy surrounding the history of public assistance and poverty relief has reflected the tension inherent in such assistance: we wish to share our good fortune with the less fortunate, but as we do so the amount of "misfortune" increases. The central issue for public assistance has been how to provide for humane treatment of those whom we regard as genuinely unfortunate, without at the same time extending that provision to those who are merely improvident, foolish, lazy, or cunning. There is no escape from this tension, and the effort to deal with it always has—and probably always will—involve controversy.

The role of government in providing personal security and in transferring income has grown massively over the past half-century and especially over the past two decades. The consequences of this growth are, of course, a topic of continuing controversy. Although relatively neglected to date, the constitutional basis for this extension in governmental activity deserves attention. Richard Epstein, for instance, argues persuasively that most transfer programs of the welfare state are constitutionally infirm within our system of constitutionally limited government.[2] A government that did not engage in transferring income among the citizenry but was concerned only with maintaining order and providing services that could not be provided through ordinary market processes would obviously be a much smaller government than ours. Such a government can be called a *contractarian state*, in contrast to government as a *welfare state*. Although this book is centrally concerned with government as a welfare state, it will be useful to consider briefly the idea of a contractarian state, to which the welfare state will be compared throughout the book.

THE CONTRACTARIAN STATE

Justifications for the redistributive activities of the welfare state can be approached by first considering the nature of government policies in a state that does not redistribute income. Such a state can be called a *contractarian state*, meaning that the state undertakes only activities that its members agree to and only to the extent that they are willing to pay for them. In such a state there would be two main categories

2. Richard A. Epstein, *Takings: Private Property and the Power of Eminent Domain* (Cambridge, Mass.: Harvard University Press, 1985).

of activity. One would involve government as an umpire or referee, a policing agent to maintain order through protecting people's rights. The other would involve government as a participant in the economic process, acting as an agent of the members of society by helping them do things they could not otherwise do for themselves. These two categories of activity correspond to what James Buchanan has described as the *protective* and the *productive states*.[3]

The Protective State

In its protective manifestation, government maintains a framework of security and order within which liberty can reign. The activities of the protective state include the enforcement of laws against theft and fraud, so the state requires expenditures on police and courts. The state also provides security against foreign aggression, which requires expenditures on military forces. The provision of security and order promotes economic activity, for it is the guarantee of a stable framework of rules that makes it possible for people to undertake long-term investments. After all, people will not invest in the construction of houses if they do not feel secure in their rights of ownership to those houses.

The protective state is involved in the *enforcement* of laws, not in their *enactment*. Government is not the source of rights, but rather is one reflection or manifestation of people's use of their rights. People and their rights of person and property are treated as normatively prior to government, as standards that take precedence. Governments are instituted among people so as to secure and protect those rights. Government, ideally, represents a compact among people to control the predatory proclivities that would otherwise erupt, both among themselves and through the instigation of outsiders. The protective state refers to government as a night watchman—as a rule enforcer and not as a rule creator.

It is certainly possible, indeed likely, that even a purely protective state would involve some redistribution of income. The central idea behind the protective state is that everyone stands to gain by escaping from the Hobbesian anarchy that would exist in the absence of some rule-enforcing entity. However, there can be many different ways of

3. James M. Buchanan, *The Limits of Liberty* (Chicago: University of Chicago Press, 1975), pp. 68–70.

distributing the expenses of the protective state among the members of society—ways that would leave all of them better off than under anarchy. Hence, the particular way of financing the escape from anarchy may alter the distribution of income, as compared with some alternative distribution of cost. This is, of course, only one illustration of the proposition that when an exchange process offers gains-from-trade to the participants, there are many different ways those gains can be shared.

Suppose that in the predatory world of Hobbesian anarchy, Jennifer Goeasy and Sally Hardwork each has a net income of $100. Further suppose that if Jennifer and Sally jointly spend $100 for protective activities, Jennifer's gross income will rise to $200 and Sally's will rise to $300. By spending $100 on the protective state, Jennifer and Sally increase their combined net income from $200 to $400. But the distribution of this gain will depend on how Jennifer and Sally share the cost of the protective state. If the expense of the protective state is borne wholly by Jennifer, the entire $200 increase in net income will accrue to Sally. If the entire expense is borne by Sally, each will have gained $100 from the creation of the protective state, with Sally capturing 50 percent of her potential gain and Jennifer capturing 100 percent of hers. And for each of the other possible distributions of the expense of the protective state, a different distribution of net income will result. So even the purely contractarian world of the protective state entails distributional considerations dealing with the sharing of the joint gains that are created through escaping from a regime of Hobbesian anarchy.

The Productive State

Even though government fulfills its protective function, there will be other activities that people cannot undertake effectively for themselves through ordinary market transactions. In its productive state manifestation, government conducts these activities. These activities cannot be organized through market transactions because, at least within the present limits of knowledge and technology, it is not possible (or perhaps not feasible) for a producer to prevent people from consuming without paying. A brewer can easily prevent merchants from taking the beer he has made, so a society can establish and police the property relations that buyer-seller relationships require to organize beer production and distribution.

But what about protection against floods and communicable diseases? A network of buyer-seller relationships may not be able to organize production under such conditions because there may be no feasible way to develop a set of property rights that would allow producers to sell protection against communicable diseases or floods. One could, of course, sell insurance against losses, but this is not the same thing as selling protection against the event's occurrence in the first place. Even though a network of buyer-seller relationships may not develop to organize production, people are interested in protection against flooding, communicable diseases, and other problems. The provision of such services is a province of the protective state, which acts to bring about those outcomes that would have resulted had the buyer-seller relationships been able to organize production.

The activities of the productive state have been characterized by the theories of externality and public goods. The essence of these theories is reflected in Abraham Lincoln's famous dictum: "The legitimate object of government is to do for a community of people whatever they need to have done, but cannot do at all, or cannot do so well themselves, in their separate and individual capacities."[4] The theories of externality and public goods represent efforts to reason systematically about the range of things people might not be able to do so well for themselves acting individually as acting collectively. As a result of such "market failure," the participants in a market economy may not fully exploit the gains-from-trade that exist among themselves. If these participants could reach a consensus about the desirability of collective action, they could correct what otherwise would be market failures. The theories of externality and public goods describe those failures and the corrective policy measures that constitute the productive state.

Externality refers to those consequences, beneficial or detrimental, of an agreement that are borne by others than those who make the agreement. Pollution has long provided examples of detrimental externalities, although many of those examples are inapt, misleading, or wrong.[5] Some common illustrations are air pollution from auto-

---

4. Quoted in Peter G. Sassone and William A. Schaffer, *Cost-Benefit Analysis: A Handbook* (New York: Academic Press, 1978).

5. See the essays collected in Tyler Cowen, ed., *The Theory of Market Failure: A Critical Examination* (Fairfax, Va.: George Mason University Press, 1988). For a presentation of many of these issues with respect to pollution, see Paul B. Downing, *Environmental Economics and Policy* (Boston: Little, Brown, 1984).

mobile exhaust, noise pollution from aircraft and power lawn mowers, damage to wildlife and fish from oil drilling and chemical manufacturing, and the cluttering of the landscape through the dropping of rubbish alongside highways. If a lumber mill deposits its wastes in a river, fish may die downstream. If the lumber mill does not have to include the value of the fish killed in its cost of production, that value will not be reflected in the terms of trade between the lumber mill and its customers.[6] Nonetheless, that damage is part of the resource cost of operating the lumber mill: fish are, as it were, one of the inputs used in producing lumber. Although the contract between the lumber mill and its customers incorporates the cost of such inputs as lumber and saws, it excludes the fish and the fishing opportunities that are destroyed.

To describe this situation as one of possible market failure is to claim that the network of trades that constitute a market economy will fail fully to move resources from less valuable to more valuable uses. The river may be valued by people more highly as a source of fish than as a dumping ground for wastes from the lumber mill. But the wastes may be dumped nonetheless, perhaps because there are no acknowledged ownership rights to the water or fish. Such ownership rights might not exist for many reasons, ranging from technological inabilities to monitor the use of some resources to refusals by actual governments (as distinct from idealized protective states) to allow ownership rights to emerge despite their feasibility. In any event, the productive state would be devoted primarily to undertaking those activities that cannot be undertaken through market transactions.

Many of these activities are described as *public goods*. The theory of public goods is really an extension of the theory of externality, for public goods are an extensive type of beneficial externality. One attribute of a public good is that it can be consumed by many people at the same time. A cup of coffee can be drunk by only one person, but a flood control project that protects one person in an endangered area simultaneously protects all people in that area. One person's consumption of protection does not preclude someone else who lives in the affected area from being protected.

---

6. To be sure, if people can acquire ownership rights to the river, the value of the fish can be reflected in the lumber mill's cost of production. The operation of ownership rights to fishing streams in Great Britain is examined in Jane S. Shaw and Richard L. Stroup, "Gone Fishin'," *Reason* 20 (August 1988): 34–37.

There are, of course, many market-provided activities for which this is true. For instance, one person's attendance at a theater performance does not preclude others from attending that performance, so long as the capacity of the theater has not been reached. However, it is easy to prevent people who do not pay from entering the theater. With flood control, it would be difficult and perhaps impossible to preclude people who do not pay for it from consuming the service anyway. The creation of a flood control project, such as a dam, a levy, or a network of drainage channels, provides protection to all people who live in the area. Someone who might build a flood control project if it were possible subsequently to sell flood protection to people would be unlikely to do so if people can receive protection whether or not they pay for it. Under such circumstances, it would be difficult or even impossible for people to make and enforce the contractual arrangements needed to organize economic activity through ordinary market processes and institutions.[7] Market failure would thus result. Hence, governmental action to provide such goods can be a value-enhancing activity for everyone.

The *benefit principle* of public economics represents this idea of the contractarian state. Under this principle, people would pay for the support of government activities according to the value they place on those activities. Of course a wide gap may separate the statement of a principle from the actual institutional implementation of that principle.[8] But the normative point of departure for the productive state is that it would serve as a substitute for market transactions, with the amounts that people pay for public goods reflecting the values they place on those goods. As with the protective state, so long as there are gains-from-trade from the activities of the productive state, the choice of one form of financing those activities over others will entail distributional consequences. The productive state, like the protective

---

7. For a careful examination of such free-rider arguments about the failure of contractual processes and the need for government provision, along with an explanation of why economists may have exaggerated the force of those arguments, see Earl R. Brubaker, "Free Ride, Free Revelation, or Golden Rule?" *Journal of Law and Economics* 18 (April 1975): 147–61; Harold Demsetz, "The Private Production of Public Goods," *Journal of Law and Economics* 13 (October 1970): 293–306; and Thomas E. Borcherding, "Competition, Exclusion, and the Optimal Supply of Public Goods," *Journal of Law and Economics* 21 (April 1978): 111–32.

8. The distinction between principle and practice is examined in Richard E. Wagner, "*The Calculus of Consent:* A Wicksellian Retrospective," *Public Choice* 56 (February 1988): 153–66.

state, will inescapably be involved in income redistribution. However, that involvement is incidental and not intentional; it is a by-product of consensus among the participants. The redistributive actions of a contractarian state would be sharply restrained because the state would be limited to undertaking activities generally beneficial to the members of society.

THE WELFARE STATE

In contrast to the contractarian state, in the welfare state income redistribution is regarded as an intentional activity. To be sure, a variety of arguments support government activities that aim to influence the distribution of income. But regardless of the lines of argument chosen, the redistribution of income is viewed as an activity government should be directly involved in. Whereas in the contractarian state government would be involved in securing people's rights and providing services people cannot provide for themselves through ordinary contractual processes, in the welfare state government would be involved, in addition, in redistributing income and rearranging people's rights.

The welfare state is made up of two kinds of programs—public assistance programs and social insurance programs. *Public assistance programs* are means-tested, essentially antipoverty programs, designed to provide support for the poorer residents of the nation. The main programs that fit under this rubric, sometimes referred to as the "safety net," include Aid to Families with Dependent Children (AFDC), which provides support for children in poor families; the Food Stamp Program, which subsidizes the food purchases of poor people; Supplemental Security Income (SSI), which awards cash payments to various categories of the aged, the blind, and the disabled; and Medicaid, which supports the medical expenses of those who are relatively poor.[9]

The social insurance programs, also commonly considered part of the welfare state, provide general, universal support, regardless of income. The main programs of social insurance are unemployment insurance and the various components of the social security program. Unemployment insurance provides income for people who have lost

9. For a collection of essays examining the impact of the Reagan administration on the programs of the safety net, see John C. Weicher, ed., *Maintaining the Safety Net* (Washington, D.C.: American Enterprise Institute, 1984).

their jobs but are seeking work. The social security programs (Old Age, Survivors, Disability and Health Insurance, OASDHI) provide payments to elderly retirees who are surviving spouses or children of covered decedents, who are disabled, and who have medical expenses while retired.

Some ambiguity is necessarily present in defining what programs constitute the welfare state, as well as in measuring its size. Reasonable people could enumerate those programs differently and hence arrive at different budgetary magnitudes. For Thomas Wilson, the welfare state is characterized by a situation "in which benefits in cash or kind are provided by the state and do not correspond to any contribution to production over the same period of time on the part of the beneficiaries."[10] In a related vein, Jonathan R. Hobbs and Charles D. Hobbs refer to the welfare state as a mélange of programs characterized by the taxing of earned incomes so as to provide unearned incomes.[11]

The general idea is clear even if the specific content is sometimes ambiguous: the welfare state refers to what alternatively can be called the *transfer* or the *redistributive state*.[12] There are, of course, hundreds of transfer programs that might be included in a listing of welfare state programs, which would include, in addition to those already mentioned, rent and mortgage interest subsidies, school lunches and breakfasts, low-income energy assistance, and earned-income tax credits. Granted, many of these programs are not properly viewed solely as transfer programs. Although the distinction between programs of social insurance, which are designed to provide security for everyone, and programs of public assistance, which are designed to alleviate poverty, is clear conceptually, it is quite blurred in practice.

Unlike the benefits from true insurance, the benefits that people can expect to receive under the social insurance programs generally have little relation to the payments they make to support the program.

10. Thomas Wilson, "The Finance of the Welfare State," in Alan Peacock and Francesco Forte, eds., *The Political Economy of Taxation* (New York: St. Martin's Press, 1981), p. 98.

11. Jonathan R. Hobbs, *Welfare Need and Welfare Spending*, Backgrounder No. 219 (Washington, D.C.: Heritage Foundation, 1982); and Charles D. Hobbs, *The Welfare Industry* (Washington, D.C.: Heritage Foundation, 1978).

12. The redistributive state is examined from a public choice perspective in Gordon Tullock, *Economics of Income Redistribution* (Boston: Kluwer-Nijhoff, 1983). For a study of the historical development of the transfer state, see Terry L. Anderson and Peter J. Hill, *The Birth of a Transfer Society* (Stanford, Calif.: Hoover Institution Press, 1980).

Although those programs are generally available to everyone, their terms typically become more favorable as income falls. Unemployment insurance provides a greater share of the lost income the lower that income. Although the OASI component of social security substitutes to some extent for a market purchase of retirement annuities, the payments people receive during retirement are more favorable, in relation to the payments they made during their working years, the lower their incomes. Indeed, an important ingredient in the rationalizations advanced in support of such programs as OASDHI is that they are important for enhancing the standard of living of people who would otherwise be poor—that is, that they are to an important extent transfer and not insurance programs.

Until the mid-1960s the programs of the welfare state generally refrained from making payments to working people. Since then, those programs have come to make significant payments to such people and have come increasingly to be seen as a means of enhancing the standards of living of people who are thought by program supporters to be unjustifiably poor. And since the mid-1960s, expenditures on the welfare state have grown about 150 percent as fast as the gross national product (GNP). In the process, spending on those programs has more than doubled as a share of aggregate output (see Table 1–1). When the welfare state is construed broadly to include social insurance programs, spending has gone from less than 5 percent to more than 10 percent of net national product (NNP). And even when the welfare state is construed narrowly to cover only public assistance programs, spending has gone from less than 1 percent to more than 2 percent of NNP.

JUSTIFICATION, COMPETENCE, AND THE WELFARE STATE

The welfare state is commonly justified by arguments that it is needed to correct various failings of a market economy. It is generally acknowledged that a market economy is successful in harnessing people's self-seeking activities in directions that promote the general welfare, for in a market economy one becomes wealthier by serving the interests of others. However, it is also argued that a market economy tends to be deficient in the distribution of income that results. This line of argument leads to support for antipoverty activities, as well

Table 1–1. Expenditures on Major Income Transfer Programs (In Billions of Dollars).

Program	*Expenditures*		
	1965	*1975*	*1985*
Social insurance			
Social security (OASDHI)	$16.5	$63.6	$177.6
Medicare	0.0	14.8	65.8
Unemployment insurance	2.5	13.5	17.5
Veterans' benefits	4.1	16.6	26.3
Railroad retirement	1.1	3.1	3.9
Subtotal	24.2	111.6	291.1
Percent of NNP	4.0%	7.7%	8.6%
Public assistance			
Medicaid	$0.5	$6.8	$27.0
Food stamps	0.0	4.6	12.5
Housing assistance	0.3	2.1	10.0
Supplemental Security Income (SSI)	2.7	4.8	9.4
Aid to Families with Dependent Children			
(AFDC)	1.7	5.8	9.2
Energy and emergency assistance	0.0	0.2	2.1
Earned-income tax credit	0.0	1.2	1.1
Subtotal	5.2	25.5	71.3
Percent of NNP	0.9%	1.7%	2.2%
Total transfer expenditures	$29.4	$137.2	$362.4
Percent of NNP	4.9%	9.4%	10.7%

Sources: Office of Management and Budget, *The Budget of the United States Government and Appendix* (Washington, D.C.: Government Printing Office, 1977); Office of Management and Budget, *The Budget of the United States Government and Appendix* (Washington, D.C.: Government Printing Office, 1987); 1965 data from Robert D. Plotnick and Felicity Skidmore, *Progress against Poverty* (New York: Academic Press, 1975).

as for some types of social insurance. Chapter 2 explores the various approaches used to justify some form of welfare state.

For the most part, the welfare state has been justified by the same market failure argument that has been used to justify an enormous variety of other regulatory policies. Such approaches to justification seek to explain why some of the programs of the welfare state are necessary to enable the participants in the economic process to exploit more fully the gains-from-trade among them. It is typically argued that people would generally be worse off without the transfer programs of the welfare state than with those programs, so a welfare state is necessary for the promotion of the general welfare.

However, the accumulated evidence from numerous studies over the past two decades has revealed myriad and systematic disparities between the common rationalizations for regulatory policies and the subsequent record of their actual accomplishments.[13] It is well documented that minimum wage legislation reduces employment and does not, on the whole, raise the incomes of the poor. It is well documented that rent controls reduce housing quality and do not lower real, as distinct from nominal, rents. It is well documented that government control over money has been an important reason for its debasement. And the list of such examples of divergence between the common rationalization for a policy measure and its subsequent reality is lengthy and growing.

Wishing something were so does not make it so: we all know the truth of this statement, but is easy to forget it in dealing with public policy. To wish that government would redistribute income to soften the distributional results of market processes is not to ensure that government will actually do so. A government may not have the ability, even if it has a single-minded interest in doing so. And a government that has the ability may be driven by other interests that propel policies in contradictory directions. In short, government may lack the competence to act as the common rationalizations or justifications would have it act. Because government has limited ability to control market processes, government policies may be negated through market processes as people react to those policies. Also, the dominant outcomes that emerge as people participate in political processes, at least within our prevailing institutional-constitutional order, may be contrary to those required by the justifications. This general problem of state competence is examined in Chapter 3.

TRANSFERS, MARKET PROCESSES, AND INCOME REDISTRIBUTION

The state can try to redistribute income through its budgetary and regulatory policies. For the most part, studies of income redistribution have examined the effects of taxation and public expenditure, but government regulation can also serve as an instrument of income re-

---

13. See, for one instance among many, George J. Stigler, *The Citizen and the State: Essays on Regulation* (Chicago: University of Chicago Press, 1975).

distribution.[14] An effort to assess the redistributive impact of the welfare state must consider all three instruments. Furthermore, any such effort must be informed by a presumption that people are rational in their actions within market processes. What this means, though, is that the redistributive impact of government actions cannot be gauged by simple before-and-after comparisons. It is illegitimate to assume that everything is the same before and after some redistributive measure, save for the measure itself. Those measures will typically change what constitutes rational conduct within market processes, and the consequence of these changes will often be a reversal of the redistributive measures—sometimes completely and sometimes only partially, but a reversal nonetheless. Indeed, government may have very little ability to modify the distribution of income, at least so long as production is largely self-organized through market processes.

For instance, despite the explosion in spending by the welfare state, or possibly even because of it, the number of people whose money income would place them below the poverty line has generally increased since the War on Poverty began (see Table 1–2). Although 1965 represents the start of the War on Poverty, with its extension of public assistance to the "working poor," the program matured in 1968. Throughout the postwar period, poverty was declining due to general economic growth. While the poverty rate for all families was 18.5 percent in 1959, it was 32.0 percent in 1947. A similar comparison holds for the different age categories listed in Table 1–2. After 1968 the overall rate of poverty stopped falling, remaining roughly constant through the 1970s and rising during the 1980s.[15]

The average for all families conceals a sharp difference among age categories. For families with a head of household of age 65 and over, the poverty rate fell from 17.0 percent in 1968 to 8.8 percent in 1985, a nearly 50 percent decline. But the results were just the opposite for all categories of people of working age, and the younger the age of the head of household, the greater the poverty. For families with a

---

14. The essential equivalence of taxation and regulation is explored in Richard A. Posner, "Taxation by Regulation," *Bell Journal of Economics* 2 (Spring 1971): 22–50.

15. Technical reasons involving measurement of the housing cost component of the Consumer Price Index explain why the poverty rate has been exaggerated the past decade or so by 1 or 2 percentage points. See John C. Weicher, "Mismeasuring Poverty and Progress," *Cato Journal* 6 (Winter 1987): 715–30.

Table 1–2.   Poverty Rate of U.S. Families, 1947–1985, by Age of Head of Household.

	1947	*1959*	*1965*	*1968*	*1970*	*1975*	*1980*	*1982*	*1985*
Under 25	45.0	26.9	19.4	13.2	15.5	21.0	21.8	26.1	28.0
25–44	27.0	16.5	12.8	9.3	9.5	10.3	11.8	14.2	12.3
45–64	27.0	15.0	9.6	7.0	6.6	6.6	7.6	8.9	9.7
65 and over	57.0	30.0	22.8	17.0	16.5	8.9	9.1	9.3	8.8
All families	32.0	18.5	13.9	10.0	10.1	9.7	10.3	12.2	13.6

SOURCES: Bureau of the Census, *Money Income and Poverty Status of Families and Persons in the United States: 1984* (Washington, D.C.: Government Printing Office, 1984), Table 15; and Bureau of the Census, *Receipt of Selected Non-Cash Benefits: 1985* (Washington, D.C.: Government Printing Office, 1985), Table 3. This table is an updated version of that presented in James Gwartney and Thomas S. McCaleb, "Have Antipoverty Programs Increased Poverty?" *Cato Journal* 15 (Spring 1985): 2.

head of household in the 45–64 age range, poverty increased from 7.0 to 9.7 percent, an increase of nearly 40 percent. For families with a head of household in the 25–44 age range, poverty increased from 9.3 percent in 1968 to 12.3 percent in 1985, an increase of about one-third. Most bleak were the fortunes of families in which the head of household was less than 25 years old: for them the poverty rate more than doubled, going from 13.2 percent in 1968 to 28.0 percent in 1985.

Inspired to some extent by such observations as these, people in growing numbers have come to question whether there might be a conflict between the welfare state's rationalizations and goals and its actual accomplishments. The common rationalizations for the welfare state presume that a natural outcome of a market economy is substantial poverty and that the welfare state is a means of softening those harsh features while still retaining the central characteristics of an enterprise economy. However, both economic reasoning and evidence about the distributive impact of budgetary and regulatory policies cast doubt on the explanatory power of those justifications, as Chapters 4 through 6 explore.

PUBLIC CHOICE, CONSTITUTIONAL ORDER, AND THE GENERAL WELFARE

The point of departure for the literature on public choice is that policy outcomes result from people's pursuing their interests within a particular institutional or constitutional setting that constrains and shapes the specific expression of those interests. Scholars have with increasing intensity begun to look beyond the standard presumptions about policy outcomes in democratic regimes. Many of the earlier presumptions about democracy and public policy, such as those reflected in the justifications for the welfare state, were based on notions of market failure and on the use of public policy to correct those failures. The scholarship in public choice, however, has developed a portrait of "government failure" to describe contemporary policy outcomes.

The divergences between the justifications for the programs of the welfare state and the actual consequences of those programs—divergences that have by now been documented for a large variety of regulatory programs—are an understandable and predictable outcome of an institutional order that can be characterized as a *majoritarian democracy*, or an *unlimited democracy*. A regime of majoritarian democracy stands in contrast to one of constitutional or contractarian democracy. The central idea of a *constitutional democracy* is that government itself is limited and bound by the same rules as all other participants in the economic life of a society. Government is not a source of rights but rather is a reflection of people's use of their rights. People and their rights of person and property are normatively prior to government, as represented, for instance, in John Locke's axiom of individual self-ownership.[16] Government, then, represents a compact created out of and constrained by those rights of person and property. Government may be involved in policing violations of those rights, but it is not the source of those rights; it may be the guarantor, but it is not the creator. Rather, government is as much limited by those rights of person and property as is every other person and corporate body in the society. Government as custodian of the sphere of *gubernaculum* is subject to the limits of *jurisdictio*, to the same extent as all other participants in the society.[17]

This was clearly the idea of government that informed the founding of the American republic. The essays in the *Federalist* were written to rebut the argument of the Anti-Federalists that the constitution being

16. Various implications of this perspective are developed in Robert Nozick, *Anarchy, State, and Utopia* (New York: Basic Books, 1974); as well as in Epstein, *Takings*, and Buchanan, *Limits of Liberty*.

17. For a historical review of the concepts of *jurisdictio* and *gubernaculum* in constitutional theory, see Charles H. McIlwain, *Constitutionalism: Ancient and Modern*, rev. ed. (Ithaca, N.Y.: Cornell University Press, 1947).

proposed in place of the Articles of Confederation would create a system of government in which *gubernaculum* would invade *jurisdictio*. It is certainly arguable these days that the Anti-Federalists were correct: government has to a significant extent become a maker of rules for others and in the process has become an arena for the dispensing of favors and the imposition of penalties among the citizenry.[18] The idea of majoritarian democracy, in contrast with that of constitutionally limited democracy, portrays a regime in which there is little if anything that cannot be done through majority votes in legislative assemblies.[19]

The contemporary scholarship on public choice has reaffirmed the veracity of the insights of a host of past scholars, in which group the authors of the *Federalist* and their opponents, the Anti-Federalists, stand relatively late in the line of succession. According to these insights, policy "failures" are not so much the result of poor information or bad intentions as inappropriate institutions that nonetheless lend strong survival value to those outcomes. The failings of the welfare state, as well as those in other areas of public policy, are to a significant extent an understandable and predictable consequence of a regime of relatively unlimited, majoritarian democracy.

Chapter 7 sets forth the theory of majoritarian democracy as developed in the literature on public choice and contrasts this form of democracy with a constitutionally limited, contractarian state in which individual rights are secured through appropriate constitutional rules.[20] Chapter 8 examines the welfare state from the perspective of the theory of majoritarian democracy, explaining why the consequences of the welfare state documented in recent scholarship are an understand-

18. On the Anti-Federalists, see Herbert J. Storing, *What the Anti-Federalists Were For* (Chicago: University of Chicago Press, 1981). For a cogent presentation of the federalist position by one of the seminal contributors to the theory of public choice, see Vincent Ostrom, *The Political Theory of a Compound Republic: Designing the American Experiment*, 2d ed. (Lincoln, Neb.: University of Nebraska Press, 1987). For an illuminating essay on this topic, though from a different perspective than Ostrom's, see Martin Diamond, *"The Federalist's* View of Federalism," *Essays in Federalism* (Claremont, Calif.: Institute for Studies in Federalism, Claremont Men's College, 1961), pp. 21–64.

19. For an examination of the erosion of constitutional limitations on legislative majorities as these relate to the welfare state, see Charles Warren, *Congress as Santa Claus: National Donations and the General Welfare Clause of the Constitution* (Charlottesville, Va.: Michie, 1932). See also Anderson and Hill, *The Birth of a Transfer Society*, and Epstein, *Takings*.

20. On the conjunction of natural rights morality and constitutional constraints in regard to transfers, see Terry L. Anderson and Peter J. Hill, "Constraining the Transfer Society: Constitutional and Moral Dimensions," *Cato Journal* 6 (Spring 1986): 317–39.

able outcome of a regime of majoritarian democracy. For instance, there is a strong basis for suggesting that a significant aspect of the welfare state is its promotion of the expansionary interests of the "welfare industry." To some degree these interests may be promoted not so much by a reduction or elimination of poverty as by an expansion of welfare spending through the liberalization of benefits, the development of new programs, and the centralization of programs.

In trying to understand the actual conduct of the welfare state and of public policy generally, the public choice perspective begins with the idea that the creation and operation of public programs is guided less by wishes and high motives than by interests and strong motives. When we examine the conflict between the rationalizations for the welfare state and its actual conduct in light of public choice theory, we must deemphasize the degree to which better public policy can be achieved by developing better scholarship about the consequences of particular policies. More emphasis must be given to the need for securing political reformation that would transform government from an infringer upon the rights of person and property to a participant within the framework of those rights. This reformation in turn calls for a constitutional perspective, in contrast to the familiar policy perspective. Central to the constitutional perspective is the presumption that political outcomes are largely governed by constitutional rules, so "better" outcomes result more from developing alternative constitutional rules than from giving alternative information and advice to politicians and other public officials.[21]

Therefore, this book examines democratic institutions themselves instead of the particular policy outcomes that constitute the present-day welfare state. A constitutional perspective shows that the outcomes of the welfare state are produced by the same forces that generate all of the other policy outcomes of our government. There is nothing fundamentally different about the creation of a rule that people cannot offer their labor services for less than $3.35 per hour, a network of welfare payments that can make it more attractive to be out of the labor force than to be in it, and the purchase by the military of a toilet seat for $400. Charity does not dominate one set of policies and greed another. People are the same in all endeavors. The price of military

---

21. The distinction between a constitutional perspective and a policy perspective is developed in Dwight R. Lee and Richard B. McKenzie, *Regulating Government* (Lexington, Mass.: D. C. Heath, 1987), pp. 1–16.

toilet seats, the attractiveness of living on welfare, the level of the minimum wage, and all other public policies reflect the working out of people's pursuit of their interests within a particular institutional environment.

There would seem, then, to be little point in seeking reform in the subset of policies that is called the welfare state without addressing the systematic causes of all forms of public policy. Wasteful policies concerning government-owned lands arise from the same forces that produce wasteful agricultural policies. Wasteful policies on military expenditure arise from the same forces that produce wasteful programs of safety regulation. And these policies, and many more, arise from the same forces that produce the programs of the welfare state. All of these outcomes result from the pursuit of personal interest in an institutional regime. In this regime government is a maker of rules for others (a circumstance that leads to a market for legislation), rather than simply being one participant among many, all governed by the same rules.

Accordingly, the problems of the welfare state are unlikely to be overcome within the framework of a constitutional order of majoritarian democracy. This prediction follows from the theory of public choice. Conversely, should such reform systematically occur in the programs of the welfare state but not elsewhere, this would be negative evidence about the theory of public choice. Chapter 9 describes ways the provision of personal economic security might be harmonized with the general welfare, with regard to both public assistance and social insurance. Chapter 10 sets forth the general political-constitutional considerations that would be necessary to generate a clientele for the production and maintenance of more sensible policies.

While the analysis in the first eight chapters is largely positive, as is much of that in the final two chapters, normative considerations must necessarily become more prominent in any discussion of reform. The normative theme of this book rests upon an affirmation of the broadly liberal heritage of the American experiment with constitutionally limited government. It takes seriously the presumption of the Declaration of Independence that government derives its just powers from the consent of the governed, so its outcomes should reflect that consent. To take this presumption seriously is not to adopt the tautological version so commonly expressed, in which the mere presence of what are called democratic institutions is taken to mean that those institutions necessarily reflect the consent of the governed. Legislative actions may reflect the consent of the governed, and hence be legitimate, but they also might not, and hence be illegitimate. The victim who gives up her purse to the knife-wielding intruder "consents" to do so in light of the alternative, just as citizens "consent" to be taxed, regulated, and otherwise governed in light of the alternative. But it is possible to move beyond the tautology only by recognizing that contractarian principles are the only principles appropriate for a society of free people. Such a free or liberal society requires in turn a political and constitutional order consistent with its own promotion.[22]

22. For elaboration, see Richard E. Wagner, "Morals, Interests, and Constitutional Order: A Public Choice Perspective," *Oregon Law Review* 67 (No. 1, 1988): 73–92; and Richard E. Wagner and James D. Gwartney, "Public Choice and Constitutional Order," in James D. Gwartney and Richard E. Wagner, eds., *Public Choice and Constitutional Economics* (Greenwich, Conn.: JAI Press, 1988).

2

THE WELFARE STATE: APPROACHES TO JUSTIFICATION

Numerous arguments have been advanced to rationalize the programs of the welfare state. The common theme that unites these varied efforts is the proposition that the "natural" outcome of a contractarian state—whose economic reflection is the enterprise or market economy—entails "excessive" inequality. Although welfare state proponents might agree that an enterprise economy generally promotes the wealth of a nation, they would also argue that the distribution of that wealth or income tends to be excessively unequal.

The basic facts concerning inequality in the distribution of income are quite simple and have changed relatively little over the postwar period (see Table 2–1). The lowest 20 percent of families ranked by their income earn about 5 percent of the total income earned by all families. The second-lowest 20 percent of families earn about 12 percent. On the other end of the scale, the highest 20 percent of families earn a little more than 40 percent, and the second-highest 20 percent of families earn close to 25 percent. The middle 20 percent of families, then, earn a little less than 20 percent.

If we set aside the lowest 40 percent and the highest 20 percent of families, the remaining 40 percent of families earn just over 40 percent of the income, meaning their incomes are about average. The highest 20 percent have an average income a little more than twice the overall average, while the lowest 40 percent have an average in-

Table 2–1.   Percentage Income Shares for Families, Various Years.

Year	Lowest	Second	Third	Fourth	Highest	Top 5 Percent
			Income Quintile			
1952	4.9	12.2	17.8	24.0	41.3	15.9
1965	5.2	12.2	17.8	23.9	40.9	15.5
1970	5.4	12.2	17.6	23.8	40.9	15.6
1975	5.4	11.8	17.6	24.1	41.1	15.5
1979	5.3	11.6	17.5	24.1	41.6	15.7
1983	4.7	11.1	17.1	24.4	42.7	15.8

SOURCES: *Statistical Abstract of the United States* (Washington, D.C.: Government Printing Office, 1981), p. 438; *Statistical Abstract of the United States* (Washington, D.C.: Government Printing Office, 1985, p. 448.

come a little less than half the overall average. Much of the effort to justify the income transfer activities of the welfare state revolves around arguments that this degree of inequality is unwarranted. This argument is advanced to rationalize the public assistance programs, which are explicitly designed to make payments to people only in the lower income ranges. But it is also used in support of the social insurance programs, for these offer more favorable terms of payment the lower one's income.

This chapter will describe the various approaches developed to justify the welfare state as a remedy for what some regard as the excessive inequality thought to be the natural product of a market economy and contractarian state. First, some consideration must be given to income distribution within a contractarian state. The remainder of the chapter will then explore justifications for the redistributive activities of the welfare state.

INCOME DISTRIBUTION IN A CONTRACTARIAN STATE

Much of the rationalization for the welfare state presumes that the distributions of income and wealth that would result from the operation of a contractarian state would reflect excessive inequality. It is, to be sure, somewhat problematical to determine exactly what is being criticized when the object of criticism is the distributive outcome of a contractarian state or market economy. After all, the market economy is not a person who makes a conscious choice to distribute "his" or "her" output. A market economy is an abstraction representing the interactions of people within a set of rules described by the principles of property and contract. Accordingly, the distribution of income in a market economy is simply the unintended by-product of the personal choices of the participants in the economic process.[1] Hence, criticism of that distribution represents, to a large extent, criticism of those personal choices. For instance, people who possess skills in short supply but in high demand will fare particularly well in a market economy. Singers and athletes are among the more obvious of these cases. Criticism of such distributional outcomes is ultimately a criticism of people for liking to watch singers and athletes perform, as well as possibly a criticism of God for restricting the supply of such talents.

In a free-market economy, income differentials among occupations tend to cause the net subjective advantages of various occupations to move toward equality at the *margins* of choice. Indeed, given the genetic distribution of capacities, along with the distribution of attitudes, talents, and values that arise out of the family and environment, such equalization is a necessary condition for labor-market equilibrium in a market economy. As a result, the pattern of differences in income arising in a market economy will produce an underlying equality of real income at the margin, with the observed differences in measured income being necessary to offset at the margin other differences.

For instance, if occupations differ in their nonmonetary advantages and in the monetary expenses of entering and pursuing them, they will need to differ in their monetary returns as well, if the labor market is to equilibrate. Occupations that require long and expensive training before their practitioners can earn a livelihood will require higher monetary returns to compensate for the greater cost of preparation. Occupations with agreeable working conditions will require lower monetary returns than occupations with less pleasant working environments to attract the same quality of labor. Where people are free to choose among occupations, there will result an inequality in measured income that is necessary to offset at the relevant margins opposing inequalities in other relevant characteristics.

---

1. This point is developed clearly in Milton Friedman, "Choice, Chance, and the Personal Distribution of Income," *Journal of Political Economy* 61 (August 1953): 277–90.

A fundamental condition of equilibrium in the labor market is a margin of choice where some people are neutral in choosing among occupations. Suppose, for instance, the alternative occupations are working on highway construction or on fishing boats. Further suppose the two occupations are alike in all relevant mental and physical respects, save that people generally have a greater fear about working on the sea than on land. If both occupations were initially to offer $30,000 per year, everyone would prefer to work on highway construction. A wage premium must be paid to induce people to work on fishing boats. The size of the premium varies directly with the intensity of people's fear about working on the sea. Some people, of course, may be positively attracted to the sea and would work on the sea even if annual earnings were less than $30,000. Some might have only a slight fear of the sea and might choose to work on fishing boats for only $31,000. Others with a stronger fear might require a larger premium. In any event, a labor-market equilibrium will result where the premium paid leaves the marginal worker indifferent between the two occupations. If this condition did not hold, one occupation would be in the process of contracting relative to the other.

The relation between age and income shows how easy it is to exaggerate the degree of inequality by looking only at measured income. Suppose all people have identical income profiles over their lifetime. If the incomes of people of different ages are merged to produce a distribution of current income, inequality will appear despite the perfectly equal distribution of lifetime income. Morton Paglin estimates that failure to consider the relation between age and income exaggerates the actual extent of inequality by about 50 percent.[2] Similarly, James Davies, France St.-Hilaire, and John Whalley find considerably greater equality in the distribution of lifetime income than in the distribution of annual income (see Table 2–2).[3]

For example, consider a set of people who are identical in their preferences and abilities and who must choose between two occupations. To ease the burden of computation, assume that a person's

2. Morton Paglin, "The Measurement and Trend of Inequality: A Basic Revision," *American Economic Review* 65 (September 1975): 598–609. For an extensive discussion of this point by Eric R. Nelson; William R. Johnson; Sheldon Danziger, Robert Haveman, and Eugene Smolensky; Joseph J. Minarik; and C. John Kurien, along with a reply by Paglin, see *American Economic Review* 67 (June 1977): 497–531.

3. James Davies, France St.-Hilaire, and John Whalley, "Some Calculations of Lifetime Tax Incidence," *American Economic Review* 74 (September 1984): 633–49.

Table 2–2.   Lifetime and Annual Income Distribution in Canada.

	Income	
Income Quintile	*Lifetime*	*Annual*
Lowest	10.4	4.1
Second	15.6	11.2
Third	18.8	16.7
Fourth	22.7	22.5
Highest	32.4	45.5

SOURCE: Adapted from data in James Davies, France St.-Hilaire, and John Whalley, "Some Calculations of Lifetime Tax Incidence," *American Economic Review* 74 (September 1984): 640.

working life lasts only five years and the rate of interest is zero. Occupation A yields an income of $15,000 per year for each of the five years. Occupation B requires a two-year period of training that involves no personal expense. With a zero rate of interest, labor-market equilibrium requires that the annual income in occupation B be $25,000. When the distribution of income is examined for any single year, considerable inequality would seem to exist, for practitioners of occupation B would be earning 67 percent more than those in occupation A. Yet it would be a mistake to interpret the disparity as evidence of inequality, for the two occupations and their associated earnings profiles are viewed as equivalent by the people who make the choice between A and B. For if such equivalence of assessment did not exist, there would be a shift in relative labor supplies away from the occupation viewed as less favorable, and this shift would change the earnings differential between the occupations and would continue to do so until an equilibrium was established.

Furthermore, recognition that interest rates are positive increases still further the amount of inequality that would be necessary for market equilibrium. With a 20 percent rate of interest, for instance, the present value of the income profile offered by occupation A is $44,859. To achieve an equivalent present value, occupation B must offer an annual income of $30,666. Even though practitioners of occupation B would now be receiving twice the income of practitioners of occupation A, the participants would judge the two occupations as equivalent.

Much of the difference in incomes reflects differences in choices regarding income and leisure. People in the upper income categories typically work more hours and so have less leisure than people in the lower income categories. Indeed, when income distributions are stated in terms of hours of work, so as to incorporate the effects of choices on the amounts of labor to supply and leisure to take, the inequality falls substantially. For instance, Cotton M. Lindsay has shown that a great deal of the higher earnings of physicians is due simply to the much longer than average hours they work per week.[4] More generally, when figures on the distribution of annual incomes are converted into a distribution of hourly earnings, there is little variation over the first four quintiles, and the highest quintile earns only about twice as much on an hourly basis as people in the other quintiles. In other words, much of the variation in annual earnings is due to differences in the number of hours people choose to work per year.[5]

Much of the inequality in the distribution of money income is also necessary to offset an opposing inequality in the distribution of non-monetary forms of income and monetary expenses of earning income. Other things being equal, if people prefer to live in less populous rather than more populous areas at equal incomes, they will choose to live in more populous areas only if they are compensated by higher incomes. Generally, the higher the educational requirements for entering an occupation, the higher the annual income in that occupation. But part of this higher annual income is necessary merely to offset the higher costs of entering that occupation—both the monetary costs of education and the income that could have been earned during the years of schooling. Many additional illustrations could be given of inequalities in annual incomes that are compatible with an underlying equality at the margins of choice in the conditions associated with the earning of those incomes. Moreover, what holds for the choice among

4. Cotton M. Lindsay, "Real Returns to Medical Education," *Journal of Human Resources* 8 (Summer 1973): 331–48.

5. To be sure, it may be inapt to speak of "choice" in this regard in some cases, because there can surely be cases where people willing to work cannot find work. However, too rapid an embracement of this notion of involuntary unemployment should also be avoided. Some of the reasons for this caution will be examined in later chapters but should perhaps be noted here in passing. In short, a considerable amount of what appears to be involuntary unemployment may reflect *not* the qualities of a contractarian state and market economy, but rather the consequences of restrictions on the market economy and of activities of the welfare state. The former might be illustrated by minimum wage legislation that reduces opportunities for employment; the latter might be illustrated by welfare payments that reduce people's incentive to seek employment.

occupations applies equally to the earnings of people in any particular employment. Those differences reflect such things as different ages and differences in the amount of labor supplied. In any event, statistics on the inequality of incomes exaggerate substantially the actual amount of inequality.

Statistics on the distribution of wealth are perhaps subject to greater exaggeration than those on the distribution of income. It is widely claimed that wealth is even more unequally distributed than income. Whereas the top 20 percent of families earn just over 40 percent of the income, they own over 70 percent of the wealth. And whereas the bottom 20 percent of families earn about 5 percent of the income, they own hardly any wealth at all. However, such references to the distribution of wealth refer to the ownership of physical capital. They exclude the value of human capital, as well as the wealth that is implicit in pension programs such as social security. Yet social security, through its claims upon the earnings of others, is the most important source of "wealth" for most Americans and amounts to about two-thirds the amount of physical capital upon which statements about the distribution of wealth are commonly based.[6] Under social security people have claims to future benefit payments, and these claims are as much a source of wealth, from a personal if not from a social point of view, as are, for example, endowment insurance policies that might be expected to yield the same payments during retirement. Indeed, in the absence of social security, people would accumulate greater amounts of such alternative sources of wealth. Since social security wealth is distributed with considerably more equality than physical capital, the inclusion of this form of wealth would reduce the degree of measured inequality, as would the elimination of social security and its replacement with an expanded use of individual retirement accounts (IRAs).

It is common, though erroneous, to think of production and distribution as separate processes. This tendency was articulated by John Stuart Mill in his proposition that while the principles of production are on the order of natural laws, the distribution of that production is purely an environmental matter open to human choice. Although it is generally recognized that efforts to redistribute income may diminish

6. Martin S. Feldstein, "Social Security, Induced Retirement, and Aggregate Capital Accumulation," *Journal of Political Economy* 82 (October 1974): 905–26. See also Martin S. Feldstein, "Social Security and Saving: The Extended Life Cycle Theory," *American Economic Review*, Proceedings, 66 (May 1976): 77–86.

incentives to produce, even this conceptualization envisions production and distribution as distinct though connected processes. Actually, there is only one process, *exchange,* in a market economy. What are referred to as *production* and *distribution* are simply alternative manifestations of the same exchange process.

Economists recognize that the outcome of an exchange process will be influenced by the initial endowments of the participants. What is open to question, though, is the extent to which those endowments themselves are open to human choice. The position associated with John Stuart Mill would seem to suggest that there is relatively wide, if not unlimited, scope for choosing among different initial endowments. To the extent that this is so, a wide variety of distributional outcomes would seem to be attainable, depending upon the initial endowments chosen as a point of departure. In the continuing nature-nurture controversy, this would represent an emphasis on nurture— on man-made, environmental influences overwhelming biological, genetic influences. Indeed, research programs in the social sciences in the twentieth century have been overwhelmingly, if not exclusively, environmental in their orientation. But increasingly biology and psychology—as represented by fields such as sociobiology and behavioral genetics—are emphasizing genetic differences and considering the importance of nature as contrasted with nurture in human action and social life.

One can reasonably posit that genetic differences are important sources of differences in initial endowments. To the extent that this is so, there would seem to be some more or less natural distribution of talents that will be immune to human choice, at least at the present time. What will be subject to human choice will be the institutional environment within which those talents can express themselves.[7] The same talents imported into a rigid, caste-like society with a planned economy might, accordingly, generate a less progressive economy than would result if those talents were imported into a fluid, open society with a market economy. If so, we may well find roughly the

7. See, for instance, Lowell Gallaway, "The Folklore of Unemployment and Poverty," in Svetozar Pejovich, ed., *Government Controls and the Free Market* (College Station, Texas: Texas A & M University Press, 1976), pp. 41–69; and Richard Vedder, Lowell Gallaway, and David Sollars, "The Tullock-Bastiat Hypothesis, Inequality-Transfer Curve and the Natural Distribution of Income," *Public Choice* 56 (March 1988): 285–94.

same distributional rankings or patterns for the same set of people, only with different levels of overall well-being.

APPROACHES TO REDISTRIBUTIONAL ARGUMENT

Several types of argument have been advanced to support the use of government as an instrument for transferring income among citizens, thereby transforming a contractarian state into a welfare or transfer state. A redistributional argument can be advanced merely as a matter of preference, by invoking some assertion that equality of income is desirable and should be promoted by government. This approach is exemplified by Henry C. Simons's noted declaration that he found inequality beyond a certain degree to be "distinctly evil or unlovely."[8] Such a normative assertion can also be treated in a positive or explanatory vein. For instance, William Breit argues that people can be treated as having preferences for particular degrees of equality, with the median preference then winning out in collective choice processes.[9]

When equality is regarded as merely a matter of preference, it is often taken for granted that a tax policy change that reduces inequality is good and one that increases inequality is bad. Often no argument is advanced to explain why a movement toward income equality should be treated as superior to a movement away from it. A number of scholars, however, have sought to move the discussion of equality out of the sphere of personal preferences by developing analytical foundations for notions of optimal or desirable inequality. Most of these efforts rest upon a utilitarian framework that assumes diminishing marginal utility of income. The older utilitarian literature on sacrifice theories of taxation asked how to distribute the tax burden so as to raise the required amount of revenue with the least sacrifice of utility.[10] If it is assumed that the marginal utility of income declines

---

8. Henry C. Simons, *Personal Income Taxation* (Chicago: University of Chicago Press, 1938), p. 19.

9. William Breit, "Income Redistribution and Efficiency Norms," Harold M. Hochman and George E. Peterson, eds., *Redistribution through Public Choice* (New York: Columbia University Press, 1974), pp. 3–21.

10. The classic reference on this topic is F. Y. Edgeworth, "The Pure Theory of Taxation," [1897] reprinted in F. Y. Edgeworth, *Papers Relating to Political Economy*, Vol. II (London: Macmillan, 1925), pp. 63–125.

as income increases, the amount of utility sacrificed from a dollar taken as tax is less the higher the income of the taxpayer. The total amount of utility sacrificed to support the government's budget is thus minimized when taxes are imposed so as to pare down incomes from the top until the required amount of revenue is raised.

The more recent utilitarian literature on optimal taxation and income distribution accepts the older assumption of diminishing marginal utility of income. But rather than envisioning the government's budget as determined exogenously, the newer literature sees the budget as part of an effort to transfer income among people so as to maximize aggregate utility. If the amount of income available for redistribution is independent of the amount of redistributive taxes and subsidies, this literature finds the optimal amount of inequality to be zero.[11] The total size of the government's budget is that which is necessary to achieve the required transfers.

But once it is recognized that the effort to redistribute income will reduce the incentive to produce income in the first place, the optimal amount of inequality increases. This optimal level can even be comparatively high if the production of income decreases relatively rapidly as taxes are increased. In any event, the central analytical perspective is one of how equally to slice the pieces of a pie. If the pie is of a fixed size, the answer is equal slices. But if the size of the pie declines as the slices become more equal, the optimal degree of inequality in this literature is positive and increases with the rate at which the pie shrinks in response to greater equality in the slicing of the pie.[12]

The literature on optimal taxation and distribution operates within what might be called a transcendent normative perspective, in that the authority of the norm is presumed to be independent of the consent of the participants. Public outcomes are assessed against some transcendent norm, in this case the maximization of aggregate utility, regardless of whether the people who populate the society agree to be assessed in terms of that norm. Such arguments do not start from

11. One now classic approach to this line of argument is Abba P. Lerner, *The Economics of Control* (New York: Macmillan, 1944), chap. 3. For a restatement of Lerner's argument, see William Breit and William P. Culbertson, Jr., "Distributional Equality and Aggregate Utility: Comment," *American Economic Review* 60 (June 1970): 435–41.

12. For a general exposition of the literature on optimal taxation and equality, see Anthony B. Atkinson and Joseph E. Stiglitz, *Lectures on Public Economics* (New York: McGraw-Hill, 1980), pp. 394–423.

individuals and their rights and then explain how the redistributive arrangements being discussed or advocated might emerge out of people's use of their rights. To do this would be to adopt an immanent normative standard, one that focuses on processes of personal interaction and not on end states.

It is, to be sure, possible to use utilitarian argument, not as an argument compelling in its own right independently of individual consent, but simply as a formal statement of reasons why people should adopt a particular approach to equality. This latter use would be consistent with the Lockean norm of individual self-ownership that is central to the construct of the contractarian state.[13] In this construct, government reflects the use of people's preexisting rights of person and property, and so the ultimate normative standard is the immanent one of consent. Accordingly, justification for a welfare state would in one way or another have to be grounded in some concept of market failure, and justificatory argument would take the form of explaining why people would choose to expand the powers of government beyond those needed for maintaining order and providing public goods to include those for organizing income transfers under the rubric of the welfare state.

INCOME REDISTRIBUTION AS COLLECTIVE CHARITY

Although a contractarian state will not actively promote income transfers, the market economy that accompanies the contractarian state will nonetheless entail a substantial volume of income redistribution. Charity, after all, is a transfer of income that is organized voluntarily through a market economy. Arguments for a welfare or transfer state must explain why the transfers that result within a market economy are insufficient, as judged by the evaluations of the participants themselves. To this end, some scholars have argued that market failure will characterize privately organized charitable activity—for essentially the same reason that market failure is thought likely to plague efforts to supply services such as flood control.

One prominent formulation of this conceptualization of private charity as subject to market failure is that of Harold M. Hochman and James

---

13. For an argument that rights-based normative arguments ultimately rest upon utilitarian presumptions, see Leland B. Yeager, "Rights, Contract, and Utility in Policy Espousal," *Cato Journal* 5 (Spring 1985): 259–94.

D. Rodgers.[14] Their formulation sees income redistribution as result-ing from voluntary transfers from donors to donees; redistribution is essentially an act of charity, in which people react to what they regard as excessive inequality by trying to mitigate it. What is used to ra-tionalize state participation in the redistribution of income, in place of an exclusive reliance upon private charity, is the presumption that free-rider problems will plague private efforts at redistribution. Al-though each person might like to see inequality reduced, no one person acting alone can make a significant contribution toward the reduction of inequality, so without some guarantee that everyone will contrib-ute, few or none will do so. The use of government to redistribute income is rationalized as a vehicle for overcoming the free-rider di-lemma, thereby promoting a more efficient allocation of resources. In other words, income redistribution through the state is seen as agreeable to the donors or taxpayers, as representing a use of re-sources they would evaluate more highly than the uses that would otherwise result.

The argument that sees market failure in private charity rests on the presumption that what matters to donors is not the act of giving or the fact of donation, but the total amount of transfers that recipients receive. In such a formulation any person's contribution would be a small share of the total; free riding would seem probable because a failure to donate would have an insignificant impact on the total amount of donations. By contrast, if the value to donors inheres in the act of giving, there would be no market failure. In this case the utility from charity inheres in the fact that donations were made and not in the total amount of transfers that recipients receive.

In either case, the literature on optimal redistribution makes no effort to specify some optimal distribution of income independently of the choices people make regarding their uses of their rights of per-son and property. What might be called an optimal distribution of income emerges as a result of the essentially voluntary transfer ac-tivities of the participants. A welfare state in this case supplements

---

14. Harold M. Hochman and James D. Rodgers, "Pareto Optimal Redistribution," *American Economic Review* 59 (September 1969): 542–57. For a thorough survey of some literature that subsequently developed, see Geoffrey Brennan, "Pareto-Optimal Redistribution: A Per-spective," *Finanzarchiv* 33 (No. 2, 1975): 237–71. For a critical treatment of this perspective, see E. C. Pasour, Jr., "Pareto Optimality as a Guide to Income Redistribution," *Public Choice* 36 (No. 1, 1981): 75–87.

the contractarian state, thereby overcoming the market failures that would otherwise result. Many of the people who would value the making of charitable contributions would otherwise tend to free ride, and hence end up confronting a worse situation than if contributions could be elicited from everyone. This kind of income redistribution is fully consistent with the functioning of the productive state.

THE DIFFERENCE PRINCIPLE

One of the most thoroughgoing efforts to set forth principles of distributive justice, which might be thought of as providing justification for a welfare state, has been advanced by John Rawls.[15] Rawls conceptualized people as making basic institutional choices before they had a good idea of their comparative income prospects. This conceptualization was reflected by his hypothetical construct of the *veil of ignorance*. It seems plausible to suppose that people might prefer different social arrangements relating to income distribution if they knew only the structure of that distribution, and not their particular location within that structure, than if they knew their actual or probable location.

In addition to the construct of a veil of ignorance, Rawls advanced what he called the *difference principle,* which states that increases in the degree of inequality are to be supported only to the extent that they result in higher incomes for the least well-off members of the society. The difference principle is sometimes referred to as the *maximin principle,* to indicate that in choosing among alternative social arrangements relating to income distribution, the one to be chosen is the one that maximizes the minimum income. For instance, consider a model in which there are two people, or two sets of people, and compare two regimes governing the production and distribution of income. Under one regime—call it an egalitarian regime—total income is $100, with the richer and the poorer members of the society receiving $60 and $40 respectively. Under the other regime—call it a liberal regime—total income is $120, with the richer and the poorer members of the society receiving $90 and $30 respectively. The maximin principle would select the egalitarian over the liberal regime, be-

15. John Rawls, *A Theory of Justice* (Cambridge, Mass.: Harvard University Press, 1975).

cause the poorer member of the society has a larger income under the egalitarian regime.

Alternatively, John Harsanyi uses the construct of moral preferences, which describes the hypothetical preferences of a person placed in the position of acting impartially and impersonally, as when faced with an equally likely chance of occupying each possible place in the distribution of income. Harsanyi argues in support of that income distribution that maximizes aggregate income.[16] Hence, Harsanyi's utilitarian formulation would choose the liberal regime, because total income was higher, an outcome that would maximize the expected income of the participants if they had an equally likely chance of occupying any position in the income distribution.

This utilitarian formulation reflects an assumption of risk neutrality. A choice among different regimes regarding the production and distribution of income is made on the basis of which one generates the largest average or expected income. The $90–$30 liberal regime has a higher expected income, $60, than the $60–$40 egalitarian regime, $50. However, if people are risk averse, they will be willing to accept some reduction in expected return in exchange for having some floor placed under the lowest possible return. This, of course, is precisely the rationale for buying insurance. The purchase of insurance lowers the buyer's expected wealth, but it also puts a floor under the minimum outcome, a floor that would not exist without insurance. For instance, a person without insurance might have $100 in the absence of a calamity and $0 in its presence. If that calamity has a probability of 0.1 and if the price of full-coverage insurance is $15, the purchase of insurance guarantees an income of $85, with or without the calamity. Without insurance, the expected value is $90. With respect to income distribution, it is conceivable that a person would choose to participate in a lottery offering prizes of $60 and $40 in preference to participating in one offering prizes of $90 and $30.

But it seems hardly compelling to assert this type of choice as a normative principle. The maximin criterion entails infinite risk aversion, in that there is no possible increase in expected return that will be sufficient to offset even the slightest reduction in the size of the smallest return. A person who is risk averse might well prefer to par-

16. John C. Harsanyi, "Cardinal Welfare, Individualistic Ethics, and Interpersonal Comparisons of Utility," *Journal of Political Economy* 63 (August 1955): 309–21.

ticipate in a $60–$40 lottery over participating in a $90–$30 lottery. However, some increase in the expected return would be sufficient to induce that person to switch to the lottery with the smaller lowest return. Although that person might choose the $60–$40 lottery over the $90–$30 lottery, this $60–$40 choice is less likely to dominate a $120–$30 lottery and even less likely to dominate a $220–$30 lottery.

Under the maximin criterion, however, it does not matter how high the higher return is in the option with the higher expected value. The option with the lower expected value will always be selected so long as its smallest return is higher than the smallest return of the option with the higher expected value. To put the point somewhat differently, the maximin criterion will select a certain return of $100 over a 90 percent chance of $1,000 and a 10 percent chance of $99. This property of infinite risk aversion has perhaps been the main source of objection to the maximin principle as a criterion for assessing the distribution of income and the place of the welfare state. In principle, of course, some intermediate position between risk neutrality and infinite risk aversion could be advocated.

A somewhat different, more positive, and less normative interpretation of the difference principle has been articulated by James M. Buchanan.[17] Consider again the comparison between the liberal order with its $90–$30 distribution and the egalitarian order with its $60–$40 distribution. Suppose both participants would prefer to participate on equal terms in the $90–$30 lottery. If so, they would both prefer the liberal order from an ex ante perspective, and in this sense the liberal order can be judged normatively superior to the egalitarian order. But is the liberal order sustainable in subsequent periods, after the lottery has taken place and the participants know their general positions in the income distribution? Not if one person's income is less than it could have been under Hobbesian anarchy, Buchanan argues.

Suppose that under Hobbesian anarchy each person would be able to secure an income of $35. Even though both participants might prefer to take a chance in the liberal order at 50–50 odds, the one who ends up with $30 will have an incentive to undermine that order by forcing the system back to Hobbesian anarchy. A minimal condition

17. James M. Buchanan, "A Hobbesian Interpretation of the Rawlsian Difference Principle," *Kyklos* 29 (No. 1, 1976): 5–25.

of social stability is surely a requirement that people receive higher returns by adhering to the rules of a particular social order than they would receive by violating those rules and living instead under Hobbesian anarchy. If the analytical point of departure is Hobbesian anarchy and if the topic of interest is the sustainability of a particular social order, sustainability would surely require at the least that all participants recognize that they are better off under the set of rules they are asked to live under than they would be under Hobbesian anarchy. Rather than being interpreted within a quasi-utilitarian framework as implying infinite risk aversion, the difference principle can be interpreted within a contractarian framework as stating one necessary condition for the stability of a particular institutional order.

UNCERTAINTY AND SOCIAL INSURANCE

Whereas the rationales for a welfare state that have been considered to this point deal mainly with what might broadly be referred to as public assistance, in that they deal with the low end of the income scale, rationalizations have also been advanced for the general provision of social insurance. These rationalizations deal with people's interest in acquiring protection against unforeseeable contingencies. People can never be certain of their future incomes; even without the Rawlsian veil of ignorance, people will face uncertainty about their future, and that uncertainty increases the further they try to look into the future.

One formulation of how people might try to insure against such uncertainty was advanced by James M. Buchanan and Gordon Tullock.[18] While Buchanan and Tullock developed a rationalization for progressive over proportional taxation, their line of reasoning is applicable generally to the social insurance of personal incomes. In the face of uncertainty about the future, people may, among other things, prefer progressive over proportional income taxation. A progressive income tax allows people to concentrate their tax payments in years when their incomes are relatively high. If people are aptly characterized as having diminishing marginal utility of income, the ability to concentrate their tax payments in years when their income is relatively

18. James M. Buchanan and Gordon Tullock, *The Calculus of Consent* (Ann Arbor, Mich.: University of Michigan Press, 1962), pp. 189–99. See also James M. Buchanan, *Public Finance in Democratic Process* (Chapel Hill: University of North Carolina Press, 1967), pp. 225–40.

high will reduce the utility sacrificed through taxation, compared to what it would be if the same amount of taxes were extracted under a proportional income tax.

Moreover, this uncertainty about future income surely looms larger when future prospects are projected forward from youth than when they are seen from the perspective of middle age, let alone when seen from the hindsight of old age. Therefore, the younger people are, the greater would seem to be the scope for their reaching some agreement about the type of tax system they would prefer to live under, and the more likely it is that their choices would approximate those made from behind a veil of ignorance. Much of the observed variation in distributional outcomes reflects the operation of uncertainties that people might wish to insure themselves against. Many of the activities of the welfare state can surely be rationalized in this light.

One of the sources of uncertainty against which people might plausibly seek some protection is the generally progressive character of a market economy. G. L. S. Shackle advanced the notion of a *kaleidic* society, one that is confronted continually with disruptions and new opportunities that result from inventions, the introduction of new products, and changes in personal wants.[19] Compared to a protection-choked economy, a free economy allows people to achieve a higher average level of wealth. But a free economy also entails greater uncertainty about the future value of present investments in human and physical capital because of the quickened pace of change in such an economy. The more open the economy is to competition, the quicker will be the flow of disruptions and new opportunities. The realized value of any investment in physical or human capital will be more fully open to future challenge the freer the economy. Skills acquired in youth will be less likely to be serviceable throughout a lifetime the quicker the pace of change. Enterprises may be left behind by new technologies, changing consumer preferences, or population relocations. For example, someone who invests in equipment for washing cars may subsequently find that equipment rendered obsolete by the development of a car finish that repels dirt.

This line of reasoning suggests that some of the apparent transfers that constitute the welfare state might be seen more appropriately as

19. G. L. S. Shackle, *Epistemics and Economics* (Cambridge: Cambridge University Press, 1972).

methods by which the members of a society seek to protect themselves against the uncertainty inherent in a progressive market economy. That progressiveness raises the average level of income above that in a static economy. Some type of insurance against being in the losing subset in a progressive economy might potentially be agreeable to all participants from an ex ante perspective and would thereby serve as a rationale for an income-sharing program that would constitute an element of a welfare state.

Indeed, such an approach could be used to justify a variety of restrictions on market processes—for instance, aid to declining industries. Although a number of industries might be equally robust initially, some would be negatively affected by future developments in technology or consumer desires, while others would be positively affected. It is arguable that people might like to purchase some insurance on their investments in specific forms of human and physical capital. A tax on what turn out to be especially profitable industries, with the proceeds used to subsidize declining industries, could be rationalized as an embodiment of such an approach to social insurance—though the reasonableness or the explanatory power of such a rationalization is another matter, as will be explained in subsequent chapters.

Many of the things that people might desire protection against are commonly referred to as "accidents of birth." A person who contracts multiple sclerosis will face a more constrained set of options than someone who does not. A transfer program from those who do not have multiple sclerosis to those who do might be conceptualized as not truly a transfer program, but as the outcome of a type of insurance contract that everyone would agree to, if they had to participate in some genetic lottery. This would represent social insurance applied to individual rather than industrial situations.

But once accidents of birth are raised as a justification for a welfare state, a wider territory is opened for examination, for the inheritance of a particular genetic deficiency is but one aspect of the accident of birth that affects everyone: the family situation into which they are born. Both genetics and family environment constrain and guide the course of people's lives. Family income and wealth is obviously important, for wealthier parents can provide their children with more opportunities for acquiring material goods than can less wealthy parents. These opportunities can range from intangibles, such as a higher quality of education, to material things, such as shares in a business. But more factors than wealth or income are important. Being born to parents who place little emphasis on achievement and who offer little discipline or guidance will likewise tend to foreclose future opportunities. The course of people's lives will to a significant extent necessarily be a product of accidents of birth. Just how severe those accidents of birth might be with respect to the material conditions of life will be considered in the next section.

OUTCOMES VERSUS OPPORTUNITIES

Discussions about the distributive characteristics of the market economy and the accompanying justifications for a welfare state focus almost exclusively on the static distributions of wealth and, in particular, income. As noted earlier in this chapter, there are many reasons measures of the degree of inequality exaggerate considerably the actual amount of inequality. But suppose there were a correctly compiled set of statistics that, everyone agreed, managed to portray accurately the degree of inequality in the distribution of income. There would, of course, still be room for people to disagree about the significance of that degree of inequality. Doubtless, some people would think there was still too much inequality, and some of those might continue to think so as long as anything less than total equality was achieved. Others might think the existing degree of inequality was about right. There might even be a few who thought there was too little inequality.

In discussions of tax reform, for instance, even in the discussions of flat-rate taxation during the mid-1980s, most participants concur that the degree of tax progressivity should not be lowered. While many support the present degree of progressivity, most of the remainder take it as axiomatic that increased progressivity is desirable. But some members of the latter group note with sadness that the increased use of the tax system for redistributive purposes will entail too high a cost in sacrificed production. It is hard to find people who think there is too much progressivity and who would prefer to see the tax burden on upper income groups reduced relative to that on lower income groups.

But the object of interest in this discussion is the distribution of income. People may disagree about how to measure or describe that distribution, but there is little dissent from the presupposition that the distribution of income is overwhelmingly the appropriate summary statistic for examining issues of fairness and justice. Yet this near consensus has problematical features, some of which relate to the earlier discussion of the difference principle. Consider a model in which there are two people, one of whom has a higher income than the other. Call the person with the higher income *H* and the other *L*. Compare two distributions of income, an egalitarian distribution in which *H* has 60 percent of the income and a liberal distribution in which *H* has 70 percent. In assessing distributions per se, most people would undoubtedly say the egalitarian distribution is fairer than the liberal. But distributional measures are just that, and the shares necessarily add up to 100 percent.

However, what if the liberal society contains stronger incentives to produce, so that total income is higher in the first place? Suppose total income in the egalitarian society is $100, with $60 being received by *H* and $40 by *L*. Suppose that in the liberal society, with its 70–30 distribution, total income is $150, so *H* receives $105 and *L* receives $45. In this case the liberal society would be judged superior to the egalitarian society by the difference principle, even though that principle is commonly thought to be an egalitarian principle.[20] The point of this illustration, of course, is that evidence about distribution is not by itself significant evidence. To provide significance it would be necessary to join such distributive evidence to evidence about the levels of real income that would accompany those different distributions.

And even if this step were taken, there are still problematical features involved in using static distributional measures to describe and assess social arrangements. Suppose the total income is $100 in both the egalitarian and the liberal societies. In this case both the difference principle and common egalitarian intuition would support the egalitarian society over the liberal society. Indeed, if total income were truly invariant to its distribution, the egalitarian society would be inferior to the supra-egalitarian society, in which income was distributed equally. Perhaps the most damaging argument against the supra-egalitarian society is that few people would want to live in it.

---

20. It should be kept in mind that Rawls regarded the principle of equal liberty for all as prior to the difference principle. See *A Theory of Justice*, especially pp. 60–65.

Much economic activity has the character of sport and play, for which the standard dichotomy between production and consumption gives inadequate treatment. People differ in the intensity of their desire to win, but few people play for ties. And one cannot win without facing the risk of losing. The supra-egalitarian society would be one in which all games ended in ties. Yet the concept of success is meaningless without a concept of failure; the concept of dignity implies a concept of shame. The elimination of failure and shame, which is part of the egalitarian economic program, would at the same time be the elimination of success and dignity.

While few people want tie games, most want fair games. But the fairness of a game has little if anything to do with the size of the rewards offered at the end of play. One game, the egalitarian game, may offer $60 to winners and $40 to losers. Another, the liberal game, may offer $70 to winners and $30 to losers. It is possible, perhaps likely, that people will differ in the type of reward structure they would prefer. And to a large extent a market economy allows people the liberty to choose their preferred reward structure. For instance, people who prefer a game that offers massive rewards for winning and only a pittance for losing can go into business for themselves. People who prefer a game that offers a more equal distribution of rewards can work for other people, particularly large corporations.[21]

Either of these two types of games can be fair or unfair, but the distribution of prizes is not itself evidence in either respect. What is perhaps most relevant are the reasons for or circumstances surrounding success or failure, particularly the extent to which success or failure is a product of personal choices rather than the result of an absence of choices. To build that proverbial better mousetrap and to have quotas placed on the importation of other people's mousetraps are both recipes for economic success. The former type of success largely stems from personal choices and illustrates personal qualities. But the latter type of success largely stems from the restriction of other people's choices and illustrates systemic more than personal

---

21. In an interesting experimental study, Elizabeth Hoffman and Matthew Spitzer found that their subjects showed no interest in redistribution when the initial entitlements were the result of effort. Only when those entitlements were random did some degree of egalitarian sentiment arise. See Elizabeth Hoffman and Matthew L. Spitzer, "Entitlements, Rights, and Fairness: An Experimental Examination of Subjects' Concepts of Distributive Justice," *Journal of Legal Studies* 14 (June 1985): 259–97.

qualities. Conversely, the quest for that better mousetrap could fail because someone else developed a rodent bait that people generally preferred or because zoning ordinances or other legislation prevented some people from working at home, thereby conferring an advantage on the owners of mousetrap factories.

There may be little relation between end-state measures of income distribution and process-oriented considerations of fair opportunities. What might be of central importance to process-oriented considerations is the relation, or lack thereof, between outcomes in different periods. In place of the two-person model of H and L, consider now a four-person model of H_p, H_c, L_p, and L_c, where the subscripts p and c refer to parent and child respectively. At one extreme, the outcome in one period fully determines the outcome in the next period: the parent's position in life is fully inherited by the child. Such a situation might be characterized as a status or caste society. At the other extreme, there is no relation between the parent's position and the child's. An infinity of intermediate positions are possible, two of which are illustrated in Table 2–3. The table shows four possible relationships between the positions of parents and children. Each entry refers to a set of probabilities: the horizontal rows show the probability that a child of H_p or L_p will occupy a high- or low-income position; the vertical columns show the probability that a particular child came from either high- or low-income parents.

The first entry illustrates a caste system. The child inherits the par-

Table 2–3.   Probabilities of Intergenerational Income Mobility.

Entries		H_c	L_c
1.	H_p	1.0	0.0
	L_p	0.0	1.0
2.	H_p	0.5	0.0
	L_p	0.5	0.5
3.	H_p	0.6	0.4
	L_p	0.4	0.6
4.	H_p	0.8	0.2
	L_p	0.2	0.8

ent's income position. The second entry illustrates the opposite situation, in which there is no relation between the economic positions of parents and their children. The remaining two entries illustrate intermediate positions. In the third entry, a child has a 60 percent chance of occupying a high-income position if the parent occupied one and a 40 percent chance if the parent occupied a low-income position. Similarly, a child has a 60 percent chance of occupying a low-income position if the parent occupied such a position, and thus only a 40 percent chance of occupying a high-income position. In the fourth entry, a child from high-income parents has an 80 percent chance of occupying a high-income position and only a 20 percent chance of occupying a low-income position. Likewise, a child from low-income parents has only a 20 percent chance of occupying a high income and an 80 percent chance of occupying a low-income position.

The extent to which economic status is inherited and the way income is distributed are two conceptually unrelated measures. For any measure regarding the inheritability of economic status, there are an infinite number of possible distributions of income. Conversely, for any possible distribution of income, there are an infinite number of possible characterizations of the degree to which economic status is inherited. To the extent that unfairness means being locked into positions through a lack of choice rather than acquiring positions through the exercise of choice, considerations of income mobility would seem to be more relevant than considerations of the distribution of income. And substantial fluidity seems to characterize economic positions across generations.[22] For instance, in his study of income mobility over time, Lowell Gallaway found that 77 percent of the difference among the average incomes in the United States in 1960 was eradicated within one generation.[23] Individual incomes across generations clearly have a strong tendency to regress toward the mean.

Moreover, some positive correlation between the economic positions of parents and children may be both inescapable and of questionable normative significance. One aspect of parenthood is the

22. On this topic across generations, see, for example, Alan S. Blinder, "Inequality and Mobility in the Distribution of Wealth," *Kyklos* 29 (No. 4, 1976): 607–38. Similarly, for a consideration of year-to-year mobility, see Bradley R. Schiller, "Relative Earnings Mobility in the United States," *American Economic Review* 67 (December 1977): 926–41.

23. Lowell E. Gallaway, "On the Importance of 'Picking One's Parents,'" *Quarterly Review of Economics and Business* 6 (Summer 1966): 7–15.

passing on of values and interests. There will be some tendency for families with plumbers to beget plumbers, for families with musicians to beget musicians, for families with physicians to beget physicians, and so on. Some inheritance of economic position would surely characterize a free, well-ordered society with just institutions.[24] Indeed, it would be possible to construct a model of an evenly rotating economy that perfectly reproduced itself, with carpenters begetting carpenters and only carpenters and so on. In practice, of course, there would always be some divergence between the experiences of parents and the choices of children, even assuming that parents were pleased with their choices and transmitted that sentiment to their children. Moreover, the ever-changing nature of societies ensures that they will not exactly duplicate themselves.

The importance of the family in personal development and value formation works toward some positive correlation between the economic positions of parents and children. What is perhaps of more concern for questions of justice is neither the distribution of income nor even the correlation between the economic positions of parents and children, but the extent to which people feel stifled by their backgrounds and locked into modes of life they do not truly choose. The widespread growth of such a sense could well undermine the basis for social order, as elucidated by Buchanan's Hobbesian formulation of the difference principle. If so, the legitimacy and stability of a social order would seem to require conditions that prevent the growth of such sentiments. However, objective measures of the results of economic activity may have little ability to describe the extent of this stifling of personal development.

24. This theme is examined in David N. Laband and Bernard F. Lentz, *The Roots of Success: Why Children Follow in Their Parents' Footsteps* (New York: Praeger, 1985).

3

POLICY NORMS AND THE QUESTION OF STATE COMPETENCE

It is easy to call upon government to inject greater equality into the distributive outcomes of a market economy. But government may have little ability actually to accomplish the equalization envisioned by the rationalizations for the welfare state. Wishing something would happen does not bring the event about, for it is always possible to wish for the impossible. Fantasies and daydreams may also occur in the form of public policies. One may wish for the state to equalize incomes, but the state might not have the ability to do so. Whether it does or not raises the question of the state's competence.

KNOWLEDGE, INCENTIVE, AND THE PROBLEM OF COMPETENCE

George Stigler once described the competence problem by the aphorism: "We can get on a bus labelled Economic Reform, but we don't know where it will take us."[1] A bus loading passengers in Washington announces it is going to New York, but it arrives in Chicago instead. Two categories of reasons can explain how this might happen, reasons that relate to the problem of competence.

One type of reason would be ignorance, a lack of knowledge about

1. George J. Stigler, *The Citizen and the State* (Chicago: University of Chicago Press, 1975), p. 24.

how to get to New York. This situation might represent a story of good intentions gone astray, or possibly of good intentions mugged by reality. The driver wanted to take the bus to New York, but took a wrong turn, perhaps inadvertently or because of an inability to read English. In any event, the driver acted with a single-minded dedication to taking the bus to New York.

Extending Stigler's metaphor to the programs of the welfare state, this explanation of a divergence between the justifications for the welfare state and its actual accomplishments would take for granted that the welfare state programs are driven by a single-minded dedication to promoting equalization as envisioned by the various rationales. The state's failures would thus have to be explained by incomplete knowledge, unpredictable events, and outside forces. The welfare state might fail because it cannot control all the conditions necessary to promote equalization. Or it might fail because no one knows everything that is necessary to promote equalization successfully. But the presumption that the state is a single-minded and benevolent entity whose desires are aptly characterized by the justifications for the welfare state does not by itself imply that the state will be able to carry out what is on its mind.

Alternatively, the bus driver might well have known how to go to New York but desired to go to Chicago instead, regardless of the announced destination. He may have wanted to go to Chicago because someone offered him a bonus sufficient to induce him to drive the bus to Chicago. Or it could be that he took the bus to Chicago under duress, possibly because his wife and children had been kidnapped and would be murdered if the bus did not arrive in Chicago by some stipulated time. Perhaps the driver had paternalistic motives for driving the bus to Chicago: he believed, thought, or "knew" that going to New York would be harmful for the passengers; recognized that he could not convince them to avoid New York; and took them to Chicago anyway.

Regardless of the reason for the divergence between the announced destination and the actual destination, the divergence resides in the driver's incentives and not in his lack of knowledge. Scholars who have been working on the theory of public choice have developed a variety of explanations for why incentives within the state may lead its actions to differ from its official pronouncements. Public choice theory is a proposition about inferring intentions from outcomes; it looks to what people do rather than what they say they are doing. There may be little or no incentive to promote equalization. The force of incentive may operate strongly in other directions.

It is, after all, unreasonable to speak of the state in a personal way as having a single-minded desire to do anything. The *state* is simply an abstraction used to represent various institutions and processes through which people relate to one another.[2] The programmatic outcomes that constitute the state's activities are an admixture of many minds tugging in many directions; it would be truly astonishing if those outcomes represented any sort of single-mindedness. What gets done by the state, accordingly, depends on the incentives that many people face, and those incentives may well produce policies that contradict simple notions of equalization.

Considering the impact of the welfare state on the distribution of income requires asking questions about knowledge and incentive as these relate to state activity, realizing that the state is not some unified soul but simply a set of processes or relationships. The state may not have the knowledge needed to promote equalization, even if it were to have a single-minded interest in doing so. After all, it is by now well established that even if a state were to have a single-minded interest in planning economic activity, it could not accumulate the knowledge necessary to do so.[3] To achieve distributional objectives requires essentially the same type of knowledge as that required to plan an economy, as will be discussed more fully later. There are many ways that individuals may undo efforts of the state to promote equalization. Furthermore, there is little reason to believe that equalization weighs heavily in the conduct of state programs, although there is every reason to believe that transfers weigh quite heavily. This question of competence will be central to the examination of the welfare state in the remainder of this book.

---

2. In this regard the *state* is no different from the *market economy*, which was discussed in Chapter 2. While personification can be a great linguistic convenience, it can also lead thinking astray if those abstract nouns are reified.

3. For lucid surveys of this subject see Don Lavoie, *Rivalry and Central Planning: The Socialist Calculation Debate Reconsidered* (New York: Cambridge University Press, 1985); and Karen I. Vaughn, "Economic Calculation under Socialism: The Austrian Contribution," *Economic Inquiry* 18 (October 1980): 535–54.

DISSONANCE BETWEEN RATIONALE AND REALITY?

It is one thing to develop a rationalization for the activities of the welfare state; it is quite a different thing to develop an explanation of those activities. The redistributive activities of the welfare state may well be rationalized by an argument based on utility interdependence, but such an act of rationalization cannot be equated automatically and necessarily with an act of explanation. There may be other, more satisfactory explanations of why such transfers are actually made. The literature on utility interdependence treats redistribution as an agreement among donors that allows them to escape the free-rider dilemma of charity as a purely private activity. Since in the utilitarian framework the size of the transfer is chosen by the donors, the extent to which actual transfers are congruent with this framework can be gauged only if the amount of transfer is voted upon only by those who make the transfers. But if recipients are also able to vote on the amount of transfers, transfers could be chosen beyond what donors would have agreed to. The presence of transfers, therefore, cannot be used to validate the presumptions of utility interdependence as an explanation for transfers. This is not to say that notions of utility interdependence play no part in explaining transfers of income, but only to note that they can at most provide only a partial explanation.[4]

For instance, consider a five-person polity, in which two of the members are recipients of transfers. Suppose initially that the recipients do not vote on the amount of transfers. Further suppose that the three members of the polity who will provide the transfers differ in the amount of transfer spending they most prefer, with these preferred amounts being $100, $200, and $300. One simple model of collective choice is that majority rule produces the median preference as the outcome. In this case, the three donors would, acting under majority rule, choose a transfer budget of $200, which would give a transfer of $100 per recipient.

Now suppose the two recipients can vote also and would each pre-

---

4. For an examination of how government transfers have crowded out private charity, as well as becoming excessive in comparison with the requirements of utility interdependence, because of the political power of recipients, see Russell D. Roberts, "A Positive Model of Private Charity and Public Transfers," *Journal of Political Economy* 92 (February 1984): 136–48.

fer the $300 transfer budget to the two lower budgets. In this case the budget preferred by the median voter is $300. Hence, the transfer budget rises from $200 to $300 when recipients can participate in the choice of how much they are to receive. Although this illustrates a case where the transfer budget becomes too large and where explanation clashes with rationalization, it should also be kept in mind that while this illustration has the transfer budget as too large by $100, it is not an argument for the rejection of all transfers. Rather it argues that the rationalization for transfers that arises out of the literature of utility interdependence is more likely to reflect or explain actual outcomes the more fully the franchise is restricted to those who finance the transfers.

Arguments about income insurance would similarly seem to have some value in explaining the development and support of welfare state programs. However, those arguments would also seem to be at most only partial explanations, because actual programs are not chosen in the absence of knowledge of particular circumstances, as behind some veil of ignorance, but are chosen in light of a good deal of knowledge about relevant circumstances. The approach based on the construct of a veil of ignorance attempts to envision the choices people would make if they had equally likely chances of occupying any particular place in the resulting distribution of income. However, choices regarding the activities of the welfare state are made by people who know their present positions and have good information about their future prospects. The effect of this knowledge about one's position could be avoided or mitigated only if other collective choices—or at least some general rules pertaining to the making of those choices— were made in advance, as when one generation chooses rules that are to apply for a subsequent generation. This possibility has been explored in different ways but in the same spirit by James M. Buchanan and F. A. Hayek.[5]

When people know their present positions in the distribution of income, it is possible for excessive transfers to emerge from democratic processes, so long as the median income is below the mean income. The veil-of-ignorance construct envisions people's assessing

5. James M. Buchanan, *Public Finance in Democratic Process* (Chapel Hill: University of North Carolina Press, 1967), pp. 280–300; and F. A. Hayek, *The Political Order of a Free People*, Law, Legislation and Liberty, vol. 3 (Chicago: University of Chicago Press, 1979).

distributions of income while assuming they are equally likely to occupy each position in that distribution. But once people know their
distributional positions, their evaluation of those distributions will
change. The majority of people who have below-average incomes will
tend to value more equal distributions more highly than before, because that evaluation will be less tempered by the possibility of having
an above-average income. Therefore, people are likely to choose more
equalization than is consistent with the veil-of-ignorance framework,
even though that framework may well explain some aspects of the
support for the redistributive activities of the welfare state.

Gordon Tullock has argued that the main explanation for transfers
is neither utility interdependence nor income insurance, but rather the
interest of recipients in receiving transfers.[6] But even if redistribution
is explained to an important extent by the recipients' desire for transfers, a question remains as to why there is such a demand in the first
place. The demand for transfers could be interpreted as a sign of the
poverty-spreading character of an enterprise economy. Suppose those
critics of enterprise economies who argue that the affluent rise at the
expense of the poor are correct. If so, the demand for the transfers
of the welfare state might represent a cry for justice. This demand
might even be interpreted as consistent with a veil-of-ignorance
framework, in a context in which the affluent dominate political outcomes and are reluctant to support the degree of equality they would
have agreed to from behind the veil. In this case, the very presence
of a significant demand for transfers might itself be construed as an
indictment of an enterprise economy.

Alternatively, the demand for transfers might represent a desire by
recipients for transfers, and the supply of transfers might represent a
desire for market restrictions by nonrecipients. The poor, rather than
being the victims of a poverty-spreading enterprise system, might be
rationally pursuing their interests in response to opportunities offered
by a democratic polity and might well have different incomes under
some alternative institutional regime. In other words, transfers might
substitute for income that would otherwise have been earned, rather
than providing income that could not have been earned.

Questions of knowledge and incentive must be addressed in any

---

6. Gordon Tullock, "The Rhetoric and Reality of Redistribution," *Southern Economic
Journal* 47 (April 1981): 895–907.

effort to distinguish between rationale and reality. The question of knowledge concerns the sources of poverty or of wealth. The rationales for the welfare state see it as acting to overcome "natural" and inescapable defects of an enterprise economy. That form of economy, it is argued, may well promote the general wealth of a nation, but it also leaves behind many people in the wake of progress. Alternatively, poverty might result not so much through the operation of a genuine market economy as because of innumerable restrictions on the very operation of such an economy. Such restrictions may tend, on the one hand, to insulate people in established wealth positions from competition from outsiders and, on the other, to enfeeble the ability of others to cultivate and employ their talents. As will be discussed in Chapter 6, a considerable amount of inequality is itself a product of legislation. For reasons to be examined in Chapters 7 and 8, legislation tends to produce adverse distributional outcomes, and legislatures tend to enact further legislation purportedly to promote contrary distributional outcomes.

The question of incentive concerns the properties of different political or institutional regimes. Economists have begun to recognize that the production of public policy can itself be usefully conceptualized as a type of economic activity.[7] The types of policies that are produced, however, may reflect outcomes that differ greatly from the common rationalizations or justifications. For instance, the interests of the people who are decisive in policy outcomes may lead them to promote measures that create rather than avoid poverty, as illustrated in Chapter 6, for instance, by minimum wage legislation and prohibitions on working at home. These considerations of how knowledge and incentive operate within a system of majoritarian democracy are crucial to the question of the state's competence to perform as the common rationalizations examined in Chapter 2 would have it perform.

KNOWLEDGE, INCENTIVE, AND POLICY FAILURE

It is one thing to develop a rationalization that the welfare state is necessary to correct defects that plague a market economy; it is quite different to develop an explanation for the actual conduct of welfare

---

7. For a lucid treatment of this theme, see Robert E. McCormick and Robert D. Tollison, *Politicians, Legislation, and the Economy* (Boston: Martinus Nijhoff, 1981).

state programs. To successfully correct "market failure," government must posssess knowledge both of the existence of failure and of ways to correct it. Government must also have an incentive to act upon that knowledge. But scholarship in public choice has begun to explore various ways in which government may lack the knowledge or the incentive to correct market failure. As a result, public policies such as those that constitute the welfare state may themselves become sources of policy or "government failure," rather than means of correcting market failure.

Knowledge and Public Policy

Any effort to create and implement public policy must confront the issue of knowledge concerning both the causes of the problem under consideration and the ability of different policy options to treat that problem. Constructing a bridge between a conceptual analysis of market failure and concrete policy recommendations is no simple effort; it involves confronting questions about the extent to which that conceptual framework is applicable to the case at hand. This point can be illustrated by a hypothetical program for flood control. Suppose a floodplain containing a number of residents and businesses is subject to intermittent flooding—typically not severe, but on occasion quite severe. Is there a problem to be dealt with by public policy here? If so, what concrete policy measures are required to shift resources from less valued to more valued uses?

Obviously the residents would prefer to be free from flooding rather than subject to flooding. But this preference does not imply that the construction of a flood control project would convert resources from less valuable uses to a more valuable use. The damage done by flooding may be less than the value of alternative wants that the resources used in the flood control project could have fulfilled. If the value of those resources in other uses is $5 million per year and if the value to residents of the reduction in flooding is only $3 million, the flooding, though regrettable, is not worth doing anything about. People would value the reduction in flooding less than they would value the things they would have to sacrifice to construct the flood control project.

In principle, the problem of knowledge is one of assessing the anticipated benefits and costs of various policy measures. Benefit-cost analysis and related approaches to economic calculation represent efforts to develop techniques for bridging the gap between the analytical principles of welfare economics and the actual formation and implementation of public policies. The estimation of benefits and costs is not a simple exercise; it is essentially the same type of exercise that businesses confront in deciding whether to open a new plant or introduce a new product. Even if flood control could be provided through market transactions, an entrepreneur would still have to engage in some form of benefit-cost calculation in deciding whether or not to produce flood control protection. All acts of production take place in advance of consumption, so producers must form expectations about benefits and costs, and subsequent experience may show those expectations to have been erroneous. It may, for instance, be more costly or less costly to provide the service than the producer thought, or consumers may value the service more or less strongly than the producer expected.

The problem of knowledge is the same in questions of public policy as in questions of business investment. In both cases, someone must reach a judgment about whether a potential use of resources will be more or less valuable than the alternative use of resources that would have to be sacrificed for the project in question to be undertaken. Whenever a business introduces a new product, opens a new plant, acquires a subsidiary, or undertakes any other activity for which the result does not live up to its initial expectation, that action can be thought of as a policy failure. The absence of omniscience means that policy failures will always be present. Businesses, after all, are continually confronted with the need to rescind choices they made earlier in the expectation of more desirable consequences than proved to be the case.

Incentive and Public Policy

Although people in the private and public sectors may face similar problems of knowledge, they may face different incentives to exercise caution in estimating benefits and costs and to act quickly in incorporating and reacting to new information. The care that people will take in trying to attain success and avoid failure will depend on the costs and rewards that result from the choices they make among policy options. In business enterprises the profit motive creates a strong incentive, because the rewards of success and the costs of failure are concentrated upon those who are responsible for the choice. For example, that infamous case of the Ford Motor Company's choosing to produce the Edsel was surely undertaken in the expectation that it would be a success, but it turned out to be a definite failure. Production of the Edsel was halted quickly once it was determined to be a failure, because to continue with its production would only have made the losses worse. Moreover, the determination that it was a failure was reached from within a realistic rather than a roseate perspective, because of the concentration of costs that would have resulted from failing to be realistic.

But the regimen of profit and loss that firms face in a market economy is not faced directly by governments in a democratic polity. And the weakening of such a regimen weakens the incentive that policy entrepreneurs have to seek policy successes and avoid policy failures. For instance, what if the Edsel had been a government product, say the outcome of a public policy similar to the federal government's creation of Amtrak? Would production have been halted as quickly? Or would there have been efforts to continue the program, such as requiring government contractors to use Edsels? Any such measure would make the Edsel look more successful, at the expense of an increased burden on taxpayers. Government regulation would have been used to cover up an added tax burden that was used to subsidize the government's Edsel.

A significant portion of the contemporary scholarship on public choice has examined how incentives influence the character of collective choices. It is an open question just how strongly (or weakly) the incentives within political institutions lead to policies that shift resources from less valued to more valued uses, as against shifting resources from more valued to less valued uses. John Semmens, for instance, estimates that the economic impact of the policy failure that Amtrak represents has been to destroy about $12.5 billion of capital through the diversion of resources from more efficient employment to Amtrak.[8] This outcome could be attributed to ignorance, but it

---

8. John Semmens, *End of the Line for Amtrak*, Backgrounder No. 226 (Washington, D.C.: Heritage Foundation, 1982). While the Amtrak case might be characterized as a policy failure when compared with the principles of welfare economics, it may well have been a success from the perspective of those responsible for the measure.

could also be attributed to intent and could be understandable in terms of existing political incentives.

The standard approach to the economic analysis of public policy has assumed—tacitly if not explicitly—that, while the formation of public policy may confront problems of knowledge, it does not confront problems of incentive. Consequently, better public policy requires only an improved analysis of the various consequences of the measures under consideration. Within this context, the agenda of policy analysis is understandably dominated by efforts to develop better information about the consequences of different policy options. But once it is recognized that the formation of public policy also depends on what incentives policy makers have and how their incentives may differ under different institutional regimes, the character of those incentives becomes an important part of the agenda of public policy analysis. Developing the best possible knowledge about policy measures is always a concern, but analyzing the strength of the incentives to create and utilize that knowledge is also of major consequence.

For the most part, economists have presumed that democratic processes of public policy formation work as well as can be expected to promote value-enhancing over value-diminishing policies. It is taken for granted that the tools of public policy are put to the best use possible, limited only by such things as irreducible ignorance, unavoidable error, or unforeseeable events. This common presumption was well portrayed by Herschel I. Grossman in a review article on James Tobin's contributions to macroeconomics. Although Grossman's particular references were to Tobin, he was speaking of economists in general when he noted:

> Tobin presumes that the historical record of monetary and fiscal policy involves a series of avoidable mistakes, rather than the predictable consequences of personal preferences and capabilities working through the existing constitutional process by which policy is formulated. Specifically, Tobin shows no interest in analysis of either the economically motivated behavior of private individuals in the political process or the behavior of the government agents who make and administer policy.[9]

But with the development of public choice analysis, the incentive

9. Herschel I. Grossman, "Tobin on Macroeconomics: A Review Article," *Journal of Political Economy* 83 (August 1975): 845–46.

aspect of public policy has also begun to command attention. The effect has been that policy failures are seen to result not just from ignorance, but also from rational political conduct in light of the incentives within an institutional order. Indeed, one prominent scholar has suggested, at least as a first approximation, that all policy failures should be attributed not to error at all, but to intent: "The announced goals of a policy are sometimes unrelated or perversely related to its actual effects, and the *truly intended effects should be deduced from the actual effects.*"[10]

Ultimately, the incentive and knowledge components of public policy have a reciprocal connection. The incentive to acquire knowledge and the judgment to identify something as knowledge in the first place depend upon the institutional setting within which people act. The incentive aspect of public policy and the reciprocal relation between incentive and knowledge have been largely neglected in studies of public policy. Whereas instances of policy failure are commonly attributed to ignorance or unforeseeable events, those failures may often be an understandable and predictable outcome of prevailing institutions—either as the intention of policy or as the by-product of a separate intention. Policy failure has often been attributed to mistakes and ignorance, but it might rather be the result of the rational pursuit of interest and not really a failure from the perspective of those whose interests are controlling the choice at hand.

For instance, what if the main effect of the flood control project hypothesized above were to make a parcel of land that was subject to the most severe flooding now suitable for a housing development? Suppose that parcel of land, furthermore, is owned by a legislator who chairs the committee that oversees flood control projects or perhaps by a significant political supporter of that legislator. How disinterested is the legislator likely to be in assessing the benefits and costs of the proposed project? The project might cost $6 million, and the benefits might be worth only $2 million, but the legislator might nonetheless judge the project profitable. While the project might impose losses in general, it would offer gains to particular people who were able to influence the choice. Although wealth may be destroyed in the aggregate or on average, some people who are influential in making the choice become wealthier as a by-product of this value-

---

10. Stigler, *Citizen and the State*, p. 140 (Stigler's emphasis).

diminishing use of resources. Although a standard of social or aggregate profitability might show costs in excess of benefits, the project may be profitable to the people who control the choice. These people, in turn, would capture most of the benefits and avoid most of the costs, because those costs would be borne by others who have no influence over the choice. In such cases as these, policy failure may be not so much the unavoidable consequence of ignorance as an understandable product of self-interest operating within an institutional framework that allows the enactment of such wealth-eroding activities.

MARKET FORCES AS CONSTRAINTS ON STATE ACTION

Although the state has instruments of compulsion at its disposal that people acting in their private capacities do not, the ability of the state to implement policy measures is nonetheless limited within a market economy. State policy may encroach in various ways on the principles of property and contract that underpin a market economy, but the participants in the economy will typically have wide latitude for negating those policy measures. After a brief consideration here, more illustrations of this point will be explored in later chapters.

Several policy measures for giving more favorable credit terms to people with relatively low incomes have been advocated. One example is usury legislation, which places a ceiling on the maximum allowable rate of interest.[11] It is often argued that without usury legislation people with low incomes have to pay excessively high interest rates, so a ceiling on interest rates is a way of shifting the terms of trade in favor of those people. But we are not yet a police state, so lenders cannot be forced to enter into contracts against their will. Therefore, usury legislation will not induce a lender to extend credit under the expectation of taking a loss.

An important factor in variations in interest rates charged on contracts is the perceived likelihood that the borrower will repay the loan. The lower the perceived likelihood of repayment, the higher will be the interest rate on credit sales. Suppose for a category of potential borrowers the risk of default would yield an interest rate of 24 per-

---

11. See Steven M. Crafton, "An Empirical Test of the Effect of Usury Laws," *Journal of Law and Economics* 23 (April 1980): 135–45.

cent. A usury ceiling of 18 percent would lower the cost of credit to those buyers, *if they could get credit*. But lenders will not lend to them at 18 percent, because to do so would be charity rather than business.

Such usury legislation will be repealed or avoided by the participants through market processes. Fewer loans will be made as the high-risk buyers disappear from the credit market. Other market adjustments will also take place—adjustments that further illustrate the ability of market forces to constrain state action. For example, people for whom 24 percent is necessary to compensate lenders for the risk of default and who cannot borrow at 18 percent, may turn to extralegal or underground sources of finance, thus borrowing at, say, 30 or 40 percent. The premium above 24 percent is necessary in part because default cannot be handled by use of the state's police powers; it must be handled extralegally through self-remedy by the lender, an action that increases the cost to the lender—including the cost of being subject to a police action by the state in the event of detection.

Alternatively, such borrowers may be allowed to borrow at 18 percent, but only after making larger down payments, agreeing to shorter periods of amortization, or possibly accepting more stringent collateral provisions. This latter option is illustrated by *Williams v. Walker-Thomas Furniture Co.*[12] A woman who received substantial support through welfare had over a period of years made a number of installment purchases. The collateral provision operated so that the furniture company could repossess everything that had been purchased in the past, so long as a subsequent purchase was made before the previous balance was brought to zero.

It was subsequently argued that such a collateral provision was unconscionable. Whether or not it was is irrelevant here.[13] What is relevant is the way market processes would work to negate what might otherwise be the effect of legislation or judicial rulings that would generalize that particular case. One type of generalization would be to restrict the types and terms of enforceable collateral provisions. This would increase the risk to lenders and reduce their willingness to make credit available to borrowers—so long as interest rates could

---

12. *Williams v. Walker-Thomas Furniture Co.* 350 F.2d 445 (1965). Also see *Toker v. Westerman* 274 A.2d 78 (1970).

13. For a careful treatment of unconscionability, see Richard A. Epstein, "Unconscionability: A Critical Reappraisal," *Journal of Law and Economics* 18 (October 1975): 293–315.

not be increased because of usury ceilings. An alternative general-ization would be to disallow repossession once the amount paid on installment contracts had exceeded, say, 80 percent of the amount of the contract. This too would increase the cost of installment sales, and lenders would respond by increasing down payments and raising prices, as well as raising interest rates if usury ceilings allowed. Re-gardless of the particular course of market reaction, the state will not be able to enact measures on interest rates that result in lenders' mak-ing charitable contributions to installment buyers.

Throughout this book cases will be examined in which market pro-cesses operate in various ways to offset what would otherwise be the consequences of policy measures. For such market-generated offsets not to emerge, one of the parties to the contract would have to agree to economic self-mutilation. For instance, vendors would have to re-frain from increasing prices or down payments in response to a re-striction on collateral provisions—thereby engaging in charity instead of in commerce. The general disinclination to self-mutilation will cur-tail, if not eliminate, the effectiveness of many policy measures.

RECIPIENT COMPETITION AND THE DISSIPATION OF STATE TRANSFERS

Just as market processes will often operate to erode the effectiveness of state policies that on the surface would appear to transfer income to people with low incomes, so too will competition among potential recipients often operate to erode the effectiveness of programs. Such competition can make it difficult, if not impossible, for the state to act charitably. Consider further the preceding illustration on the avail-ability of credit to relatively low-income borrowers. Suppose that the state, perhaps realizing the futility of relying on self-mutilation for its measures to work, decides to institute its own program that would make 18 percent loans available to high-risk buyers. By substituting state compulsion through taxation for the voluntary contractual pro-cesses of the market economy, such a program might seem capable of transferring income to low-income borrowers.

However, it is unlikely—indeed, even impossible—for the state to make any such transfer, even if it wanted to. So long as the amount of credit the state makes available is less than the amount of credit that potential borrowers desire, those borrowers will engage in var-ious processes of competition to secure those loans, and that very competitive process can consume much if not all of the gain the program offers. Suppose that $10 billion is made available under the state program, with loans restricted to people whose incomes are below the official poverty line or who are being supported under the AFDC program. Further suppose that the demand for loans at 18 percent by those eligible at the time the program is instituted is $20 billion. With the demand for loans exceeding the supply by $10 billion, some process of credit rationing must be employed, and the potential borrowers will compete among themselves for credit, eroding the value of the subsidy in the process.

Precisely how the value of the state transfers will be eroded will depend on the particular processes of credit rationing that are used and the recipient competition that results. Suppose there are 10 million eligible applicants. The average loan that can be made is $1,000, whereas the average desired loan at 18 percent is $2,000. Suppose that 5 million loans are made available in $2,000 blocks. With a market rate of interest of 24 percent, the annual value of the subsidy is $120 (6 percent of $2,000), and there will be 10 million people competing for the 5 million loans. If loan applications must be submitted in person and if they will be accepted starting at 9 A.M. the first Monday in April, people will start queuing in front of loan offices well before 9 A.M. that first Monday in April. The greater the value of the subsidy, the earlier they will queue; the longer they queue, the higher the price they will pay in time for the subsidized loan. One plausible outcome is that 5 million people will end up waiting in line, because it would be irrational for additional people to join the queue, unless they do not know exactly how many people are already in line.[14] If the average time spent waiting is 30 hours per recipient, for a total of 150 million hours, and if those who wait value their time at $4 per hour, the value of the subsidy will have been dissipated by recipients in their effort to compete for it. Those who do not join the queue and who fail in the competition do not get the $120 subsidy, but they save the 30 hours. Those who get the subsidy also spend 30 hours waiting, and the value of this time is equivalent to the subsidy. Little, if anything, has actually been given away in this case, because the state is unable to prevent people from competing for what is scarce.

---

14. If more than 5 million people join the queue because of such ignorance, the cost to recipients of the subsidy program will be even higher than that illustrated in the test.

Perhaps this competition among potential borrowers could be prevented by restricting the loans to $1,000, thus making a loan available for each eligible borrower. If there were no scarcity there would be no competition among borrowers. Of course the value of the subsidy has been reduced by half, to $60 annual value, through cutting the size of the loans in half. But even in this case the presence of the subsidy increases the value of acquiring the characteristics to which the subsidy adheres. There are margins everywhere. There will be people on the margin of belonging to the poverty population or being covered by AFDC. Because the subsidized loan program increases the returns of belonging to those populations, some people who were formerly on the margin but outside those populations will now choose to reduce their incomes (or at least their declared incomes) sufficiently to become eligible for the subsidies. The state will still be unable to prevent erosion of the subsidy through competition among potential recipients. And the larger the value of the subsidy, the stronger will be the incentive for potential recipients to acquire the characteristics that will make them eligible.

Alternatively, the loans could be rationed by basing the amount of credit on how far below the official poverty line reported income falls. In this case people would be eligible for larger loans and subsidies the lower their incomes. This program would encourage people to compete for credit by reducing their reported income. To be sure, the extent to which the subsidy is dissipated will depend on the rationing method used, for this in turn governs the nature of the competitive process that will arise. The more fully potential recipients are able to influence their chances of success in acquiring a subsidy, as through queuing, the more fully the subsidy will be dissipated through competition among recipients. In these and in the myriad other ways that borrowers compete for credit, even the gains from what appears to be governmental charity will be eroded—partially for certain and wholly under some circumstances—as will be explored in later chapters.

PERSONIFIED STATES AND REAL GOVERNMENTS

To give a justification or rationalization for a state action is not automatically to ensure that the state performs as the rationalization requires. The state is not a person; it is not a benevolent despot who acts to right the wrongs of the world, as those wrongs are articulated in economic models such as those in Chapter 2. The *state* is simply an abstraction representing a subset of social relationships, and the content of actual state action depends on the character of those relationships.

It is, of course, common to use such language as "the market works this way" or "the market fails under these circumstances"; however, it is important to recognize that there is no such entity as "a market" or "the market." There are only people who relate to one another in various ways and with regularities such as rules, conventions, and laws. One can comprehend "market outcomes" only by coming to understand the principles that guide personal relationships and actions as these are shaped and constrained by rules and conventions.

Personification can be useful in simplifying language, so long as the act of personification is grounded in an understanding of the underlying processes and relationships the personification represents. But once government action is understood as an outcome of various actions and interactions, it is clear that government is not a single entity or mind that can be exhorted to action or blamed or praised. Collective outcomes will depend primarily on the incentives of the various participants and on the rules and conventions governing their relationships. Changes in knowledge may lead to changes in collective outcomes, but only to the extent that people revise their evaluation of policy measures in light of this new knowledge. Knowledge is important in understanding state action, but the rules governing personal action and interrelationships are also important. These rules may produce a network of incentives that induce policy outcomes sharply divergent from those of the proverbial benevolent despot.

NORM, REALITY, AND THE TRANSFER STATE

As will be explained in later chapters, there can be many reasons why the actual content of state action will vary sharply from the rationalizations for a welfare state. Even if the state could be aptly described as having a single-minded devotion to transferring income in an equalizing fashion, it may not be able to do so because of the competition that will arise among potential recipients. Additionally, it is questionable whether government policy measures could reasonably be characterized by a devotion to transferring income. While market process may impinge severely on the ability of government to equalize the distribution of income, political processes also may limit severely the sustainability of such measures. These considerations of the importance of incentives within political processes can be illustrated briefly as they relate to the three rationalizations for a welfare state described in Chapter 2.

Income Transfers as Collective Charity

Within the analytical framework described in Chapter 2, the amount of income to be transferred is chosen by the donors. Recipients are not allowed to vote on the size of the transfers. But in a world in which the recipients *are* able to vote on this question, the size of the transfers is likely to expand beyond the amount consistent with the case for collective charity that is grounded in arguments about market failure. This dissonance between rationale and reality was discussed earlier in this chapter. For actual transfer programs to be consistent with the market failure justification, the choice about how much to transfer must be limited to those who make the transfers. Even though income redistribution can be rationalized on market failure grounds, those grounds may be inadequate for explaining the actual course of income redistribution; the reality of a transfer program may differ from its rationalization.[15]

Guaranteed Income for Social Order

The contractarian interpretation of the difference principle can serve as a rationalization for some form of guaranteed income, though perhaps a relatively low one: a particular institutional order will not be sustainable unless it offers people at least as much as they think they could get under Hobbesian anarchy. But such a rationalization for the principle of a guaranteed income may be far removed from the actual operation of a guaranteed income. For one thing, there is the problem of what might be called the spoiled-child syndrome. This problem concerns the ability to distinguish legitimate grievances from tactics designed to cajole someone into giving up something. If donors au-

---

15. For empirical examinations relating to this point, see Werner W. Pommerehne, "Public Choice Approaches to Explaining Fiscal Redistribution," in Karl W. Roskamp, ed., *Public Choice and Public Finance* (Paris: Cujas, 1980), pp. 169–90; and Russell D. Roberts, "Recipient Preferences and the Design of Government Transfer Programs," *Journal of Law and Economics* 28 (April 1985): 27–54.

tomatically treat complaints as legitimate and award some form of compensation, the supply of complaints by potential recipients will increase because complaining pays. Similarly, if complaints about an existing social order are automatically treated as legitimate and interpreted as evidence of unjust treatment, as compared with Hobbesian anarchy, and if compensating payments are thereby made, the volume of such complaints will increase. Complaining becomes a profitable activity.

The problem of distinguishing between rationale and reality arises once again. It seems reasonable that the sustainability of a particular social order depends on its participants' believing they are better off living under that order's rules than they would be under an alternative order, such as Hobbesian anarchy. An arrangement that provides such a guarantee can thus be rationalized or justified. However, it is necessary to find out how the existing order is determined to be unjust to some people, because complaining can also be an alternative to working or saving.

The determination process would operate through complaints and various forms of disruptive activity. But once such activity comes to be rewarded, the amount of that activity will increase and will continue to do so until its marginal return equals the marginal return from ordinary economic activities. Parents who reward complaining children will be run by their children. Sometimes, of course, children have legitimate grievances. And wise (and lucky) parents will be able to distinguish between the legitimate complaints and tactics for changing the distribution of wealth within the family. There is necessarily a tension between the two types of judgment, and it is easy to go too far in either direction. But, for reasons to be considered in Chapters 7 and 8, public officials in democratic governments may be less able than parents to deal properly with this tension and may be more prone to reward complaints, mainly because their personal share in the resulting cost is minuscule, whereas for parents it is large.

Income Transfers as Income Insurance

Although various types of inherent uncertainty in life can be used to rationalize transferlike programs, to provide rationale for a program is not to explain either the causes for or the reality of that program. The insurance analogy can be carried too far. Insurance is purchased before an accident, not afterward. If insurance purchases were made after the outcome was known, those without accidents would not want insurance and those with accidents would want more comprehensive coverage. Because there would be no room for agreement between the two groups, insurance would be impossible. Agreement is possible only when choices are made before outcomes are known, because the identities of accident victims are unknown.

Tax institutions and public spending programs, on the other hand, are chosen, at least to a substantial degree, after the outcomes are known—or at least when their general outlines are fairly clear. Those who have high incomes will be in the position of those who have had no accidents; they will desire little coverage. Those with low incomes, by contrast, will be in a position analogous to those who have had accidents, and they will tend to opt for more extensive coverage through the transfers of the welfare state than they would otherwise have chosen. Furthermore, as will be explained in Chapter 7, there is a basis for thinking that democratic processes will bring about an excessive supply of whatever programs might be consistent with this insurance justification.

4

TAXATION AND INCOME REDISTRIBUTION

Whatever the merits of the justificatory arguments for a welfare or transfer state over a contractarian state, it does not follow that government will accomplish what those justifications envision. As noted in Chapter 3, this may be either because people acting through market processes will undo the transfers of the welfare state or because people acting through democratic processes are more strongly motivated to act otherwise than the justifications would require.

This chapter and the next examine the impact of government's budgetary operations on the distribution of income. Many government spending programs are, of course, explicitly redistributive. But redistributive concerns also animate discussions of taxation, particularly in the arguments for progressive over proportional income taxation. Most of the complexities of tax administration and compliance would vanish if the progressive rate structure were replaced by a proportional or flat-rate tax. As Robert E. Hall and Alvin Rabushka demonstrate, with a flat tax a taxpayer's return could be written on a postcard and the instructions on one page.[1] Much of the opposition to the simplicity of flat-rate taxation is grounded in the use of progressive taxation for income redistribution. This chapter will first consider briefly the ef-

1. Robert E. Hall and Alvin Rabushka, *Low Tax, Simple Tax, Flat Tax* (New York: McGraw-Hill, 1983).

fect of government on the distribution of income, then it will examine
the redistributive impact of progressive income taxation. Chapter 5
will look at the redistributive impact of government spending.

GOVERNMENT AND THE REDISTRIBUTION
OF INCOME

Discussions about the welfare state almost universally presume that
the distributive outcomes of a contractarian state would violate reasonable canons of distributive justice. For this reason the welfare state
is considered necessary to soften the distributive harshness of a market economy. Most participants in these discussions accept this presumption and differ only in degree, with some advocating a more
extensive welfare state than others, perhaps because they think the
distributive outcomes of the market economy are significantly more
harsh than do their colleagues.

But exactly how much equalization does the welfare state actually
bring about? Several scholars have sought to assess the government's
impact on the distribution of income. Some of these studies have focused on the redistributive impact of taxation, comparing the distribution of tax payments by income category under the prevailing tax
system with what it would be under a proportional and presumably
nonredistributive tax system. Others have focused on the redistributive impact of government spending. The point of such efforts is to
enable people to make an informed judgment about how much income
redistribution government's budgetary activities actually produce.

Although it is typically taken for granted that redistribution entails
programs that reduce the degree of inequality, *redistribution* simply
refers to transfers among people. The actual impact of those transfers
can be to increase the extent of inequality. State-sponsored income
redistribution may increase or decrease the actual degree of income
inequality or may have no significant impact on it. This latter possibility may occur because the effects of redistributive measures are
repealed through market processes; it may also occur because the redistributive impact of state programs has less to do with transfers among
broad income categories than with transfers from weak to strong interest groups. This chapter and the next examine both the extent of
income redistribution and its direction, as part of the effort to consider

the actual conduct of the welfare state in light of the rationales advanced for it.

The programs of the welfare state—including social insurance programs such as social security, unemployment insurance, and Medicare, but particularly public assistance programs such as Aid to Families with Dependent Children (AFDC), Supplemental Security Income (SSI), and food stamps—are generally seen as governmental efforts to reduce inequality in the distribution of income. There are many ways the distribution of income can be described and government's impact upon that distribution assessed. The most commonly used indicators are Lorenz curves and Gini coefficients. Table 2–1 showed data on the distribution of income resulting from putative market transactions for various postwar years. That distribution showed both a significant and a persistent inequality throughout the period.

Figure 4–1 uses a Lorenz curve to describe data like that displayed in Table 2–1. A Lorenz curve that coincided with the diagonal line would describe a perfectly equal distribution of income. The more a Lorenz curve is bowed toward the southeast, the greater the extent of inequality. A simple measure of this inequality is the ratio of the area between the Lorenz curve and the diagonal line to the total area lying beneath the diagonal. This ratio is called a *Gini coefficient* and is equal to $X/(X + Y)$ in Figure 4–1.

A common way of assessing the impact of present taxing and spending programs on the distribution of income is to compare Lorenz curves and Gini coefficients as they exist with estimates of what they would be in the absence of those programs. For instance, a Gini coefficient in the presence of a progressive income tax could be compared with one constructed under the assumption that income were taxed at a flat rate. As will be described shortly, several scholars have constructed estimates of the impact of taxing and spending policies on the distribution of income.

The central idea behind such approaches is straightforward. There will be some Lorenz curve that describes the distribution of income that exists in the presence of a policy. This represents the postpolicy distribution of income. An effort is then made to estimate what the distribution would have been in the absence of that policy. For instance, a progressive income tax might be replaced by a proportional income tax. Alternatively, public spending on education might be

Figure 4–1.   Lorenz Curve and Gini Coefficient to Describe Income Inequality.

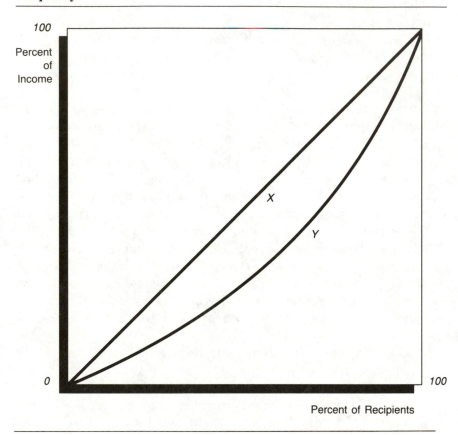

eliminated, to be replaced by purely private provision. In any case, the distribution estimated to result in the absence of the state policy would represent the prepolicy distribution. The difference between these two distributions would represent the estimated impact of the program upon the distribution of income.

Suppose Lorenz curve *B* in Figure 4–2 describes the existing post-policy distribution of income. If the estimated prepolicy distribution would be characterized by Lorenz curve *A*, the program being examined would be credited with reducing the degree of inequality in the distribution of income. Alternatively, if the estimated prepolicy

Figure 4–2. Assessing Government's Impact on the Distribution of Income.

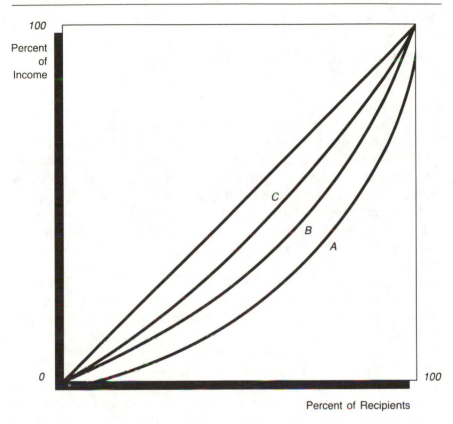

100

Percent
of
Income

C

B

A

0   *100*

Percent of Recipients

distribution would be characterized by the Lorenz curve *C*, the program would be credited with increasing the degree of inequality. To be sure, there are a number of well-recognized difficulties in using Gini coefficients to make judgments about the effect of government on the distribution of income. Lorenz curves can intersect, with both curves having the same Gini coefficient. A Gini coefficient can fall, indicating less inequality, and yet the share of income received by members of the lowest income category could actually have declined, with the measured equalization coming about because income was transferred from upper- to middle-income categories. Although for these and other reasons Lorenz curves and Gini coefficients are far from perfect indicators of the degree of inequality in a distribution, they are nonetheless a convenient and simple means of describing the impact of taxes and expenditures on that distribution.

ASSESSING THE REDISTRIBUTIVE EFFECT OF TAXATION

Considerations of tax progressivity are ubiquitous in discussions of tax reform. Even the interest in flat-rate taxation, which to some extent reflects a stronger awareness of the economic disincentives that result from high marginal rates of tax, has exhibited much concern that such a tax reform not reduce unduly the progressivity of the tax system. There are several ways that *progressivity* can be reduced, each of which may entail different consequences for income *redistribution*. Although progressivity, as typically used by economists, refers to *marginal* rates of tax, redistribution is commonly assessed in terms of *average* rates of tax. It is possible to design a reduction in progressivity that does not lower the share of taxes paid by people in the upper income categories and raise the share paid by people in the lower categories. For instance, the reduction in marginal tax rate in the upper income categories could be offset by eliminating from the tax base exclusions and deductions that give particularly heavy benefits to people in those categories. And the increase in tax rates in the lower income categories could be offset by an increase in the personal exemption. Nonetheless, as a practical matter a reduction in progressivity is commonly associated with some shift in the distribution of tax payments away from people with relatively high incomes onto people with relatively low incomes.

The assessment of how progressive our tax system really is has proven to be a controversial endeavor, but the central idea behind the scholarly efforts to this end is straightforward. Table 4–1 uses hypothetical data designed to describe the common method of approach and to explain some of its problematical features. The polity comprises three people who are named in column 1; their taxable incomes are listed in column 2. Taxes are collected through a progressive income tax, under which the first $20,000 of taxable income is taxed at 10 percent, the next $10,000 at 20 percent, and all income over $30,000 at 50 percent. The resulting distribution of tax liabilities is

Table 4–1.   Income Redistribution through Progressive Taxation.

	Real, Observed Amounts			Hypothetical Amounts		
	Taxable Income	Progressive Tax	Net Income	Proportional Tax	Net Income	Redistribution 4 − 6
1	*2*	*3*	*4*	*5*	*6*	*7*
Poorman	$20,000	$ 2,000	$18,000	$ 4,000	$16,000	$2,000
Midman	30,000	4,000	26,000	6,000	24,000	2,000
Richman	50,000	14,000	36,000	10,000	40,000	−4,000
Total	$100,000	$20,000	$80,000	$20,000	$80,000	

shown in column 3, the payment of which leaves the distribution of posttax income shown in column 4.

The effect of this tax structure upon the distribution of income can be gauged by comparing the posttax distribution of income in column 4 with what would result under some alternative method of assigning tax liabilities. Studies of redistribution through taxation assume that alternative method to be a proportional income tax, in which everyone pays the same rate of tax on their taxable income. Column 5 shows the distribution of tax liabilities that would result under a 20 percent proportional rate of tax, which would yield the same revenue as the progressive tax, assuming taxable income to be invariant to the form of tax used. The resulting distribution of net income in column 6 is then compared with the actual distribution of net income in column 4, and the result of this comparison appears in column 7. Column 7 shows that the use of the progressive tax in place of the proportional tax has redistributed $4,000 away from Richman, with Poorman and Midman each gaining $2,000.

The pivotal assumption in this common approach to analyzing the impact of tax policies on income distribution is, as shall be explored more fully in the next section, that neither the amount of taxable income nor its distribution are affected by shifts in the progressivity of the tax system. Not only is this assumption unlikely but it is also inconsistent with the axiom that people seek to replace lower yielding assets with higher yielding assets. Nonetheless, this approach has been predominant in efforts to examine the redistributive impact of taxation. The central structure and findings of two of these efforts, one by Joseph A. Pechman and Benjamin A. Okner and the other by Edgar K. Browning and William R. Johnson, will be examined here.[2] Although these studies differ substantially in their conclusions, they have the same approach: they compare a market distribution with a posttax distribution, much as Table 4–1 illustrates.

Although these two studies provide not one, unique conclusion about the redistributive impact of the American tax system but rather a range of possible estimates, each does exhibit a central tendency that differs substantially from that of the other. Table 4–2 shows the main conclusions about the redistributive impact of taxation in the United States reached by Pechman and Okner and by Browning and Johnson. Pechman and Okner argue that tax policies have little effect in equalizing the distribution of income, because the average rate of tax paid by people in different income categories is approximately constant at all income levels. In only two income deciles did the estimated rate of tax differ by more than 1 percentage point from the overall average rate of tax: the second lowest decile was 1.1 percentage points below the national average, and the lowest decile was 1.6 percentage points above the national average.

In sharp contrast, Browning and Johnson argue that taxation in the United States has had a substantial effect in reducing inequality in the distribution of net income. They estimate that average rates of tax rose continuously and rather sharply throughout the income scale, rising from 11.7 percent imposed on the lowest decile to 38.3 percent imposed on the highest decile. Moreover, Browning and Johnson also estimate that progressivity increased to the very end of the income distribution, for they estimate that the top 1 percent paid an average tax rate of 47.9 percent (data not shown in Table 4–2). According to Pechman and Okner, the only deciles to pay more than the average rate of 25.9 percent that pertained to the 1966 data they studied were the lowest and third lowest deciles. But according to Browning and Johnson, the only deciles that exceeded the average tax rate of 29.1 percent that pertained to their 1976 data were the top two deciles.

Any estimation of the effect of a tax or a tax system on the distribution of income requires a comparative analysis of the distribution of tax liability under different taxes or tax systems. Both Pechman and Okner and Browning and Johnson compare the entire array of

2. Joseph A. Pechman and Benjamin A. Okner, *Who Bears the Tax Burden?* (Washington, D.C.: Brookings Institution, 1974); and Edgar K. Browning and William R. Johnson, *The Distribution of the Tax Burden* (Washington, D.C.: American Enterprise Institute, 1979).

Table 4–2.   Average Rates of Tax by Income Decile.

Income Decile	Pechman and Okner	Browning and Johnson
First	27.5	11.7
Second	24.8	12.5
Third	26.0	16.3
Fourth	25.9	20.2
Fifth	25.8	23.2
Sixth	25.6	25.5
Seventh	25.5	26.7
Eighth	25.5	28.1
Ninth	25.1	30.0
Tenth	25.9	38.3
Average	25.9	29.1

SOURCES: Joseph A. Pechman and Benjamin A. Okner, *Who Bears the Tax Burden?* (Washington, D.C.: Brookings Institution, 1974), p. 64; and Edgar K. Browning and William R. Johnson, *The Distribution of the Tax Burden* (Washington, D.C.: American Enterprise Institute, 1979), p. 51.

federal, state, and local taxes, as they now exist with a proportional tax on income. The difference between actual tax rates and the proportional rate that would raise the same revenue is thus seen as showing the amount of redistribution accomplished through the tax system, just as Table 4–1 illustrates.

The reason for the substantially different conclusions about the amount of income redistribution achieved through taxation that the two studies reach lies in differences in assumptions the two pairs of authors make about the burdens of the different taxes in the tax system. For the personal income tax, both pairs of authors assume that the tax was paid by the designated taxpayer, an assumption that is actually questionable, as explained later. The main source of difference on subsequent implications for tax progressivity is in assumptions about sales and excise taxes. Pechman and Okner assume that sales and excise taxes led to higher prices paid by consumers, whereas Browning and Johnson assume that they led to lower prices received by producers. The distributional implication of this assumption differs substantially. The assumption of Pechman and Okner resulted in a threefold decline in average rate of tax from the lowest to the highest decile: with an average rate of 5.1 percent, the lowest decile paid only 3.2 percent.[3] But under Browning and Johnson's alternative as-

3. Pechman and Okner, p. 61.

sumption, the average rate of tax paid through sales and excise taxes rose from 2.3 percent for the lowest decile to 5.5 percent for the highest, with the overall average rate being 4.9 percent.[4]

The authors also make different assumptions about the burdens of the other taxes. Although these differences do not individually make as great a difference as that for sales and excise taxes, they nonetheless add to the different interpretations about the progressivity of taxation in the United States. Pechman and Okner assume that at least part of the property tax and corporation income tax were paid by consumers through higher prices for housing and for the output of corporations. In contrast, Browning and Johnson assume those taxes were paid for by the suppliers of capital for housing and to corporations.

That differences in assumptions about the incidence of taxes could make such differences in conclusions about the redistributive impact of the present tax system is not surprising. Pechman and Okner and Browning and Johnson, as well as others who have explored the topic, are, however, united in their central approach.[5] In that approach some market-produced distribution of income is compared with some alternative distribution in which the market outcome has been modified through taxation and government spending. Figure 4–2 can illustrate this approach and the differences between Pechman and Okner and Browning and Johnson. In Figure 4–2, the Lorenz curve labeled *A* describes the distribution of income that is observed to result from market activity, and the Lorenz curves *B* (postpolicy) and *C* (prepolicy) describe alternative distributions that take into account the redistributive impact of various government programs—taxation, in this case. The stronger the equalizing effect of governmental programs, the more the postfisc Lorenz curve *B* will move away from the prefisc curve *A* toward the diagonal line of full equality. For instance, the postfisc Lorenz curve *B* describes a government that has reduced inequality by less than a government represented by the postfisc Lorenz curve *C*. Pechman and Okner would say that the postfisc Lorenz curve

4. Browning and Johnson, p. 51.

5. For a sample of these other studies, see Tibor Barna, *Redistribution of Incomes through Public Finance in 1937* (Oxford: Oxford University Press, 1945); Alfred H. Conrad, "Redistribution through Government Budgets in the United States," in Alan T. Peacock, ed., *Income Redistribution and Social Policy* (London: Jonathan Cape, 1954), pp. 178–268; G. A. Bishop, "The Tax Burden by Income Class, 1958," *National Tax Journal* 14 (March 1961): 41–59; and Richard A. Musgrave, Karl E. Case, and Herman Leonard, "The Distribution of Fiscal Burdens and Benefits," *Public Finance Quarterly* 2 (July 1974): 259–311.

lies relatively close to *A,* whereas Browning and Johnson would say that it has moved some substantial distance away from *A* toward the diagonal line of full equality.

Both pairs of authors, however, as well as most others who have studied the effect of taxing and spending on the distribution of income, would concur in the essential method: comparing a prefisc distribution of income, as indicative of the properties of a market economy, with a postfisc distribution identifies the extent to which governmental activities represented by the welfare state modify that initial free-market distribution. As Chapter 6 will explain, this entire approach is biased toward finding that the welfare state softens the distributive outcome of a market economy. This bias is due mainly to the initial income distribution's being incorrectly ascribed to the operation of a market economy or contractarian state. Actually, that distribution has already been severely contaminated by the operation of myriad governmental policies and regulations. Furthermore, even if this common framework is accepted for purposes of discussion, it is subject to substantial deficiencies that also tend to overestimate the degree to which government decreases—or is even capable of decreasing—the extent of inequality in the distribution of income. And this is to say nothing of the failure to recognize that governmental programs affect the amount of income and not just its distribution. To say that some of the tax burden has been transferred from one to another does not imply that the former is better off; a larger share of a smaller pie, along with a reduction in social or income mobility, is not necessarily an improvement.

LABOR-MARKET OFFSETS TO PROGRESSIVE TAXATION

Efforts to assess the redistributive impact of the present tax system reflect two main types of assumptions; one might be called external and the other internal, and both are questionable. The external assumption, which will be examined in Chapter 6, is that the pretax or prebudget distribution of income, such as that indicated by column 2 in Table 4–1, truly represents what would be the distribution of income in a contractarian state or market economy. The existing distribution is strongly contaminated in many ways by the various transfer programs of the welfare state. The internal assumption is that the welfare state's redistributive programs, represented in column 7 in Table 4–1, do not affect the initial distribution of income, represented by column 2. But the programs of the welfare state will generally affect that initial distribution of income, as well as affecting the amount of total income generated within a society. This is true for both the taxing and spending sides of the budget; this section will examine why this is true for taxation, and Chapter 5 will do the same for public expenditure.

Consider what is involved in the assumption that the shift from a progressive to a proportional income tax, or vice versa, will have no effect on either the distribution of income or the amount of income generated. In a competitive labor market, there will be a tendency for the net advantages of different occupations offering different incomes to be equalized at the relevant margins of choice. This proposition is simply a corollary of the presumption that in a competitive market profit opportunities will not remain unexploited. With respect to the supply of labor, for instance, if people require $5,000 more per year to be induced to practice occupation A instead of occupation B, an annual income differential of $10,000 in favor of occupation A will be eroded through competition. This will happen through an increase in the supply of labor in A relative to that in B. Through such changes in the willingness of people to supply labor to different occupations, competition will tend to cause a differential in earnings that at the relevant margins reflects and offsets the advantages and disadvantages associated with different occupations.

Progressive Taxation and Absolute Labor Supply

It is commonly claimed that a personal income tax is paid by the nominal taxpayer, in which event the distributional estimates in such works as those by Browning and Johnson and by Pechman and Okner are valid. The validity of this claim depends in turn on a presumption that an income tax elicits no change in personal conduct. If this is so, if labor supplies have zero elasticity, a change in tax rate will not affect pretax earnings, so any change in tax will be accompanied by an equivalent change in posttax earnings. The reasonableness of such a presumption about labor supply is an empirical matter, of course, but the presumption also depends on the way labor supply choices are conceptualized.

Labor supply choices are usually conceptualized within a simple model of people's choosing between supplying labor and taking leisure.[6] An income tax or an increase in the rate of tax reduces the net returns per unit of labor supplied, which will induce people to substitute leisure for labor because leisure now involves a lesser sacrifice of posttax earnings. However, the tax also reduces real income. Under the presumption that people take more leisure as their incomes rise, the effect of the tax in lowering income will induce people to take less leisure and, thus, to supply more labor. In this standard conceptualization, the effect of an income tax on the amount of labor supplied is an empirical result that depends on the relative strengths of two opposing tendencies: a substitution effect that tends to reduce labor supply and an income effect that tends to increase it. Some empirical studies have claimed to find little systematic effect, a finding that is certainly consistent with the underlying conceptual framework of a choice between labor and leisure.[7]

A proportional income tax is characterized by a constant marginal rate of tax, but a progressive tax has a rising marginal rate of tax. The income effect of the tax depends on the average rate people have to pay, but the incentive to substitute leisure for labor depends on the marginal rate of tax. In his estimation of a model that allowed him to distinguish between income and substitution effects, Jerry A. Hausman estimated that a progressive tax would have a substantially more negative impact on labor supply than would a proportional tax.[8] In particular, Hausman estimated that the amount of labor supplied by

6. For a sample of a voluminous literature see Richard Goode, "The Income Tax and the Supply of Labor," *Journal of Political Economy* 57 (October 1949): 428–37; Richard A. Musgrave, *The Theory of Public Finance* (New York: McGraw-Hill, 1959), pp. 232–46, Marvin Kosters, "Effects of an Income Tax on Family Labor Supply," in Arnold C. Harberger and Martin J. Bailey, eds., *The Taxation of Income from Capital* (Washington, D.C.: Brookings Institution, 1969), pp. 301–21; Harvey S. Rosen, "What Is Labor Supply and Do Taxes Affect It?" *American Economic Review* 70 (May 1980): 171–76; and Anthony B. Atkinson and Joseph E. Stiglitz, *Lectures on Public Economics* (New York: McGraw-Hill, 1980), pp. 23–61.

7. See, for instance, George F. Break, "Income Taxes and Incentives to Work: An Empirical Study," *American Economic Review* 47 (September 1957): 529–49; and Donald B. Fields and W. T. Stanbury, "Incentives, Disincentives, and the Income Tax," *Public Finance* 25 (No. 3, 1970): 381–415.

8. Jerry A. Hausman, "Labor Supply," in Henry J. Aaron and Joseph A. Pechman, eds., *How Taxes Affect Economic Behavior* (Washington, D.C.: Brookings Institution, 1981), pp. 27–72. See also Charles E. Stuart, "Swedish Tax Rates, Labor Supply and Tax Revenues," *Journal of Political Economy* 89 (October 1981): 1020–38.

husbands was reduced by 8 percent under the progressive income tax, whereas it would have been reduced by only 1 percent under a proportional income tax. And Hausman estimated that progressive taxation reduces the amount of labor supplied by wives by 30 percent.

To the extent that people substitute leisure for labor, total income will be reduced. It could also be argued that the reduction in aggregate labor supply would lead to some increase in wages relative to returns to capital, which could have a slightly equalizing effect on the distribution of income, to the extent that the recipients of capital income have higher incomes than the recipients of labor incomes. But regardless of these outcomes, an examination of income tax progressivity within the framework of a choice between labor and leisure may fail to account for the primary impact of progressive income taxation on market processes. To illustrate this possibility, assume for a moment that neither a proportional income tax nor its replacement with a progressive income tax of equal yield affects the aggregate supply of labor. Even so, it does not follow that a shift from a proportional to a progressive income tax will result in a straightforward transfer of income from people who earn relatively high incomes to those who earn relatively low incomes, because the shift in taxation may also alter the occupational structure within the economy, altering the pre-tax distribution of income in the process.

Progressive Taxation and Relative Labor Supplies

As noted in Chapter 2, differences in earnings among occupations are necessary to offset differences in their relative agreeableness, the regularity and certainty of their returns, and the cost of acquiring and maintaining requisite skills. An occupation that requires $5,000 more per year to practice than does another occupation will tend to generate an offsettingly higher annual income. If this differential does not exist—if the two occupations yield the same income—people will alter their choices of labor supply. As people switch their choice from the occupation that is more costly to practice to the one that is less costly, either through outright shifts by existing practitioners or through changes in the rate of entry by new workers, relative wages will rise in the more costly occupation because of the shift in relative labor supplies. This shift in supply will continue until the necessary differential is established.

Income taxation can alter the relative returns among occupations, and to the extent that it does, the composition of the labor force will change in response. Changes in taxation, then, can alter the distribution of income even if the aggregate supply of labor is completely inelastic. Suppose that two occupations, H and L, are equivalent in all relevant respects, except that H is relatively hazardous and L is quite safe. Occupation H might involve painting bridges while riding on wind-buffeted scaffolding 300 feet above the water, while occupation L involves painting single-family houses. In the absence of income taxation, assume that the average annual returns to people working at H and L are $30,000 and $25,000 respectively. Assuming that no other sources of equalizing differences exist, this difference of $5,000 reflects the negative evaluation people place on the hazards involved in occupation H.

What would be the impact of a proportional income tax of 20 percent on the division of the labor force between H and L? After enactment of the tax, the posttax return falls to $24,000 in H and $20,000 in L. The tax favors occupation L because a nonmonetary aspect of the occupation—its greater safety—is not included in the tax base. When the posttax differential in net income falls to $4,000, the labor market will no longer be in equilibrium. There will now be an excess supply of labor in H. Labor will shift from H to L, either directly as people leave the one to practice the other or indirectly through changes in the rates of new entry, and as this happens pretax incomes will rise in H and fall in L. This shift in the composition of the labor force will continue until the net differential of $5,000 is restored. In the new equilibrium, pretax income in H might be $30,800, while pretax income in L is $24,550. In this event, posttax returns in H and L will be $24,640 and $19,640 respectively, which maintains the $5,000 differential.[9] In general, a proportional income tax increases the sup-

---

9. People may differ in their assessments of the hazards encountered in occupation A, and as labor supplies shift, the marginal person may come to evaluate the necessary compensation for the hazards as somewhat less than $5,000. Bringing in such complicating considerations, however, does not modify the essential point being made. Also, the compensating differentials people attach to various occupations may be in the form of a percentage difference in wages rather than an absolute amount. Instead of costing an additional $5,000 to get people to paint bridges, it may require a 20 percent premium over what they can get for painting houses. In either case the central point is the same. For a study of the extent to which occupational hazards are reflected in wage differentials, see Richard Thaler and Sherwin Rosen, "The Value of Saving a Life: Evidence from the Labor Market," in Nestor E. Terleckyj, ed., *Household Production and Consumption* (New York: Columbia University Press, 1975), pp. 265–98.

ply of labor in occupations in which nonmonetary advantages are more significant because those advantages are free of tax.

Whatever impact a proportional income tax has on relative labor supplies, a progressive income tax has an even stronger impact because it discriminates among occupations on the basis of their monetary returns. In terms of the preceding illustration, the replacement of a proportional income tax by a progressive income tax increases the tax paid by people in occupation H and lowers the tax paid by people in occupation L. Such a shift in taxation would appear on the surface to be redistributive. However, the shift will narrow the differential between the two occupations to something less than $5,000, which means there will be an excess supply of labor in H. Restoration of equilibrium in the labor market requires a shift in the composition of the labor force away from H toward L. As people alter their occupational choices, pretax income in H will increase relative to that in L. As a result of this adjustment in pretax income in response to the progressive tax, part of the tax burden that appears to be paid by those with higher incomes is actually paid by those with lower incomes. The pretax income received by people in the lower paying but less hazardous occupation L will decline relative to the pretax income received by those in occupation H. Consequently, the impact of the progressive tax on the redistribution of income will be softened compared with what it would have been in the absence of any tax-induced adjustments in the composition of the labor force.

Indeed, conditions are imaginable, though not probable, under which a progressive income tax would have no impact on the distribution of posttax income compared with what would result under a proportional income tax. This lack of impact is possible even if the aggregate supply of labor, as measured by total hours worked, is unaffected by the tax. Even though the supply of labor may be of zero elasticity in the aggregate, it can be quite, even perfectly, elastic to any particular occupation.

To be sure, perfect elasticity would imply that everyone had the same preferences and abilities for different occupations, so everyone would have to be at the margin of indifference for the labor market to be in equilibrium. When people differ in their preferences and talents, relative labor supplies will be less than perfectly elastic. But labor supplies will be elastic, which means that changes in taxation will affect the margins of indifference, will lead to changes in occupational choices, and hence will modify the pretax distribution of income.

It is useful, when comparing a progressive tax with a proportional tax, to think of the progressive tax as constituting two conceptually separable components: (1) a proportional tax on everyone and (2) a set of tax surcharges on high-earning activities that are used to finance a set of tax rebates on low-earning activities. This system of surcharges and rebates will modify the composition of the labor force, inducing transfers of labor from H, where the surcharge is levied, to L, where the rebates are offered. The progressive income tax alters the net returns to the different types of labor, which in turn alters the composition of the labor force in favor of the occupation that becomes more attractive, L. People will reduce their investments in those kinds of human capital on which a surtax is imposed and increase their investments in those for which a tax rebate is offered. And equilibrium in the labor market will require that pretax earnings adjust sufficiently to create indifference in posttax earnings at the relevant margins of choice.

The extent to which labor will shift from H to L depends, of course, on the elasticities of the supplies of labor to the two occupations. If the labor supply to each occupation is perfectly responsive to the wage differential that reflects the higher cost of preparing for and practicing in H, the only effect of the progressive tax will be to induce a transfer of labor from H to L of sufficient magnitude to restore the necessary posttax differential. After the tax is imposed, pretax incomes will be higher in H and lower in L by an amount that leaves the posttax differential unchanged from what it would be under proportional taxation. In this case, the replacement of a proportional income tax with a progressive income tax has no effect upon the distribution of posttax income. The change in the form of the tax leads to an increase in the inequality in the distribution of pretax income—an increase that is sufficient to negate the change in the distribution of tax payments required by the change in the form of the tax.

This proposition is illustrated in Figure 4–3. The subscript *0* pertains to the proportional tax and the subscript *1* pertains to the progressive tax. The initial equilibrium with the proportional tax is characterized by wages of W_0^h in H^l and W_0^l in occupation L, and with the quantities of labor of H_0 and L_0 respectively. The introduction of the progressive tax reduces the net return to the practice of oc-

Figure 4–3. Impact of Progressive Taxation on Relative Labor Supplies.

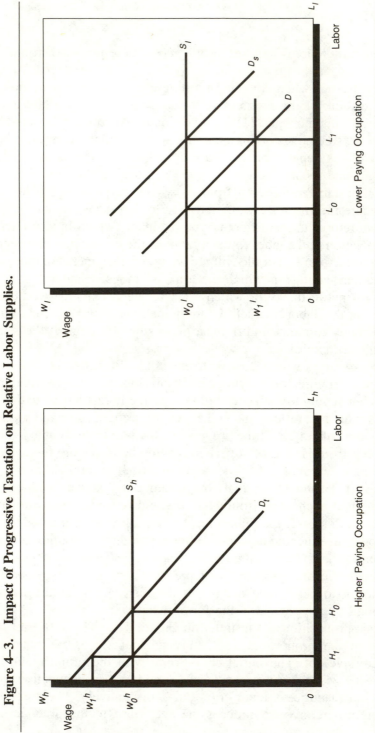

cupation H, as indicated by the lower curve of net demand, D_t, and increases the net return to the practice of L, as shown by the higher curve of net demand, D_s. In response, labor shifts from H to L, as shown by H_1 and L_1 respectively. As a result, pretax wages rise in H to W_1^h and fall in L to W_1^l. The pretax distribution of income has become more unequal, and at this widened differential the posttax differential under progressive taxation is the same as under proportional taxation.

To assume that the progressivity of the tax system has no impact on the initial distribution of income is to assume that the distribution of labor among occupations is invariant to the net returns offered by those different occupations. Once it is recognized that relative labor supplies do respond to the pattern of net returns, it must be acknowledged that changes in the tax system influence the distribution of labor among occupations because taxation alters the pattern of net returns to different occupations. Taxation influences wage differentials, thus modifying relative labor supplies, which in turn modify the initial distribution of income. Moreover, redistributive taxation works in a particular direction: it increases the attractiveness of lower paying occupations relative to higher paying occupations, and the resulting shift in relative labor supplies will increase the degree of inequality in the initial distribution of income. In other words, the replacement of progressive with proportional taxation will reduce the degree of inequality in the initial distribution of income. Referring to Table 4–1 and ignoring the likelihood that total income would increase because of stronger incentives to be productive, we can see that the entries in columns 5 and 6 would be wrong because the distribution of income described in column 2 would no longer hold. Instead, under proportional income taxation the initial incomes of Poorman and Midman would be more than $20,000 and $30,000 respectively, and the initial income of Richman would be less than $50,000.

The case where labor supplies are perfectly elastic among occupations is, of course, a polar one. If labor supplies are less than perfectly elastic, the transfer of labor will cease before pretax income has risen in H and fallen in L sufficiently to restore the original posttax differential. Nonetheless, the tax will still increase the pretax differential in the distribution of income, thereby shifting part of that tax from those with high incomes onto those with low incomes. It seems clear that the redistributive impact of progressive taxation is overestimated in the various studies that have been made to date. The very ability of government to redistribute income is limited not by the elasticity of the aggregate supply of labor but by the much more elastic supply of labor to specific occupations.

SOCIAL COSTS OF REDISTRIBUTIVE TAXATION

Progressive taxation clearly accomplishes less redistribution of the tax burden than would be indicated by simple arithmetic comparisons of distributions of the tax burden under the assumption that labor supplies are invariant to changes in tax rates. As noted above, it is even possible as a limiting case for progressive taxation to have no effect on the distribution of income, but to exert its effects wholly through changes in the composition of economic activity. In this case people would shift away from the higher taxed activities into the lower taxed activities until the previous posttax differential had been attained once again. While the progressive tax accomplishes no equalization in this case, it does impose what economists call an *excess burden* on the economy. This excess burden represents a waste that results because the tax induces people to shift away from employments in which people place a relatively high value on the output into employments in which they place a relatively low value on the output. In this limiting model where relative labor supplies are perfectly elastic, there is no trade-off between equality and efficiency; any initial equalizing impact of progressive taxation will be undone through changes in relative labor supplies as people respond to the tax-induced changes in the net returns to different forms of human capital.

With less than perfect elasticity in relative labor supplies, progressive taxation will achieve some equalization, along with imposing an excess burden through changes in the composition of labor. In this setting there can be a trade-off between equalization and efficiency (output). Even if we ignore the effect of progressive taxation on relative labor supplies and consider only its effect on the absolute amount of labor people supply, progressive taxation can entail a quite steep trade-off between equalization and output. For instance, Browning estimates that the welfare cost or waste associated with progressive taxation can range from 15 to 50 percent of revenues collected, even under the assumption that the elasticity of labor supply is a relatively low 0.2 or 0.3.[10]

---

10. Edgar K. Browning, "On the Marginal Welfare Cost of Taxation," *American Economic Review* 77 (March 1987): 11–23. See also Charles Stuart, "Welfare Costs per Dollar

This estimated loss in efficiency is due merely to the use of progressive taxation in place of proportional taxation. The magnitudes of estimated inefficiency would increase greatly if the redistributive impact of progressive taxation were accomplished by increasing taxes across the board and transferring the revenues to people with relatively low incomes. In this regard, Browning and Johnson estimate that with a labor supply elasticity of 0.2, for each $1 transferred to people in the two lowest income quintiles, more than $9 is lost by people in the upper three quintiles.[11] One simple way of modeling an increase in tax progressivity, or a shift from a proportional tax to a particular progressive tax, is to assume the imposition of a flat-rate tax that is used to finance a program of equal grants per capita. As a result of such a program, those with high incomes will be losers because their grants will be lower than their taxes, and those with low incomes will be winners because they will be in the opposite position.

Suppose, following Browning and Johnson, that the increased progressivity is pursued by increasing taxes by 1 percentage point to finance the "demogrants." At prevailing tax rates of about 40 percent, this will lower net wages from $0.60 to $0.59 per dollar of earnings. This is a 1.66 percent reduction in net wages, which if the elasticity of labor supply were 0.2 would bring a 0.35 percent reduction in total earnings. The implications for the trade-off between equalization and production are illustrated in Table 4–3. The data in the table describes

Table 4–3.   Illustrative Trade-off between Equalization and Output.

Household	Earnings	Taxes	Grants	Lost Earnings	Income Change
A (2 people)	$ 5,000.00	$ 50.00	$ 90.00	$ 17.50	+ $ 22.50
B (4 people)	15,000.00	150.00	180.00	52.50	− 22.50
C (4 people)	25,000.00	250.00	180.00	87.50	− 157.50
Aggregate	45,000.00	450.00	450.00	157.50	− 157.50

SOURCE: Adapted from data in Edgar K. Browning and William R. Johnson, "The Trade-Off between Equality and Efficiency," *Journal of Political Economy* 92 (April 1984): 175–203.

---

of Additional Tax Revenue in the United States," *American Economic Review* 74 (June 1984): 352–62.

11. Edgar K. Browning and William R. Johnson, "The Trade-Off between Equality and Efficiency," *Journal of Political Economy* 92 (April 1984): 175–203.

a society containing three households and roughly approximates the prevailing distribution of income. A proportional tax is used to finance a program of demogrants, the end result of which is the same as a progressive income tax. It is assumed that the program reduces each household's earnings by 0.35 percent, giving a total reduction of $157.50 from the $45,000.00 that would otherwise have been earned. Taxes equal to 1 percent of initial earnings are to be levied, giving $450.00 to be distributed at $45.00 per capita. The impact of the tax-and-transfer program, by itself, is equivalent to a redistribution of the tax burden that would lower household A's tax bill by $40.00 and B's by $30.00, while raising C's tax bill by $70.00. But when the impact of the program in reducing the amount of labor supplied is also taken into account, the end result of the program is to increase A's disposable income by $22.50. By contrast, B's disposable income is lowered by $22.50 and C's is lowered by $157.50. In other words, the $22.50 gain to A requires the imposition of a loss of $180 on B and C. The cost of achieving a $1 transfer is nearly $9.00 in this illustration.[12]

Even if labor-market adjustments to progressive taxation are limited to changes in the absolute amount of labor supplied, the equalization that is accomplished can entail a quite high sacrifice in output. When allowance is made for the effect of progressive income taxation on relative labor supplies, less redistribution will be accomplished and the social cost of progressive taxation will rise even higher. This is not to deny that some income redistribution may be accomplished, nor is it to assert that the social cost of such redistribution exceeds its value. Rather, this conclusion points out that the operation of market processes will place limits both on government's ability to redistribute income and on its ability to avoid injecting costs into the economy as a by-product of such efforts at redistribution.

---

12. And should the impact of the redistributive taxation on relative labor supplies be taken into account, the social cost of redistributive taxation would rise even higher.

5

PUBLIC SPENDING AND INCOME REDISTRIBUTION

The impact of government on the distribution of income depends on the distribution of the benefits from public spending, as well as on the distribution of tax liabilities. A finding that a tax system is regressive does not warrant the conclusion that government is responsible for increasing the degree of inequality in the income distribution. A regressive tax system can be combined with a distribution of expenditure benefits that more than offsets that regressivity, thereby producing a budget that is progressive even if the tax component of that budget is regressive.

For instance, a head tax, which extracts the same absolute tax payment from everyone, is strongly regressive when translated into an income base. Consider the data illustrated in Table 4–1, only now assume that government is going to raise $30,000 by using a head tax that requires each person to pay $10,000. For Poorman the tax burden is 50 percent of income, for Midman 33 percent, and for Richman 20 percent. The use of the head tax in place of a proportional or a progressive income tax clearly transfers the tax burden away from people with relatively high incomes to those with relatively low incomes.

However, the regressive nature of this tax burden does not mean that government is acting to increase the degree of inequality in the distribution of income. Whether it actually does so depends also on the distribution of the benefits from government's expenditure of its tax revenues. Should the $30,000 budget be used in such a way that Poorman and Midman each receive $15,000 of value while Richman receives nothing, government will have reduced the degree of income inequality, despite its use of a regressive tax to finance its activities.

The impact of government on the distribution of income can be assessed only after comparing the distribution of expenditure benefits with that of tax burdens. But at the same time, as with taxation, it is not adequate to gauge the impact of government spending by examining only the initial apportionment of that spending. Spending programs will in turn elicit various forms of personal response, the effects of which must be attributed to the programs being examined. Just as it is easy to exaggerate the impact of progressive taxation in equalizing the distribution of income, it is easy to exaggerate that of government spending. The very effort to use a spending program to redistribute income will induce reactions by recipients or beneficiaries that will at least partially, and perhaps even wholly, dissipate the ultimate redistributive impact of the program. As with the case of progressive taxation discussed in Chapter 4, the more fully market processes operate to offset the equalizing effect of transfer programs, the more the effects of those programs will be excess burdens and related forms of social waste.

REDISTRIBUTION THROUGH PUBLIC EXPENDITURE

As Chapter 4 noted, there is substantial disagreement among economists as to how progressive, or redistributive, the American tax system is. But regardless of the conclusion reached about the progressivity of the tax system, the distribution of the benefits from public expenditure must also be considered in any assessment of government's impact on the distribution of income. In this respect, a few studies have attempted to bring the distribution of the benefits from public spending into consideration. Studies by Irwin Gillespie and by Morgan Reynolds and Eugene Smolensky assumed that the tax structure was not particularly progressive.[1] This assumption about the incidence of various taxes is generally the same as that used by Joseph A.

1. Irwin Gillespie, "Effect of Public Expenditures on the Distribution of Income," in Richard A. Musgrave, ed., *Essays in Fiscal Federalism* (Washington, D.C.: Brookings Institution, 1965), pp. 122–86; and Morgan Reynolds and Eugene Smolensky, *Public Expenditures, Taxes, and the Distribution of Income* (New York: Academic Press, 1977).

Pechman and Benjamin A. Okner, rather than that used by Edgar K. Browning and William R. Johnson (as discussed in Chapter 4). Column 2 of Table 5–1 shows the average rates of tax by income class, based on the assumptions about tax incidence that Reynolds and Smolensky used. Reynolds and Smolensky estimated the tax structure to be quite regressive in 1970, for the average rate of tax fell from a high of 58.8 percent for the lowest income class to a low of 29.2 percent for the second highest income class. The tax structure then turned progressive, with the average rate of tax rising to 39.7 percent for the highest income class.

Despite the regressive nature of the distribution of the tax burden, the benefits of public expenditures were distributed in a progressive manner that more than offset the regressive tax burden, as column 3 shows. For people within the three lowest income categories, the benefits from government spending programs were greater than their incomes.[2] People in the lowest income category paid nearly 60 percent of their income in taxes, but they also received more than $3 in government benefits for each $1 they earned. When taxes and expenditures were combined, it was estimated that people in the lowest income category received a net gain from all governmental budgetary operations of more than 250 percent of their income, as shown in column 4.

By contrast, people in the highest income category paid just under 40 percent of their income in taxes, slightly more than two-thirds the average tax rate paid by people in the lowest income category. But people in the highest income category received benefits from government programs equal to an estimated 17.2 percent of their income. When the combined effects of all budgetary operations were taken into account, as shown by column 4, people in the highest income category suffered a loss estimated at 22.5 percent of their income, and people in the three highest income categories were net losers from the combination of taxing and spending. By contrast, people with incomes below $10,000 were net gainers. Moreover, the rate of gain becomes larger the lower the income. Even if the tax system is assumed to be regressive, a notion that Browning and Johnson dispute,

---

2. On the distinction between income measures based only on money income and those that include the in-kind benefits of government programs, and the substantially different interpretations of recent trends that result, see Edgar K. Browning, "The Trend toward Equality in the Distribution of Net Income," *Southern Economic Journal* 43 (July 1976): 912–23.

Table 5–1.   Distribution of Taxes and Expenditures by
Income Class, 1970.

Income Category 1	Tax Rate 2	Benefit Rate 3	Redistribution (3 − 2) 4
$ 0–2,000	58.8%	315.7%	256.9%
2,000–3,000	45.9	173.7	127.8
3,000–4,000	44.7	118.4	73.7
4,000–5,000	41.4	85.5	44.1
5,000–6,000	38.5	60.9	22.4
6,000–7,000	36.2	48.4	12.2
7,000–8,000	34.4	41.0	6.6
8,000–10,000	34.0	35.8	1.8
10,000–15,000	31.2	29.4	−1.8
15,000–25,000	29.2	22.7	−6.5
25,000 and over	39.7	17.2	−22.5

SOURCE: Adapted from Morgan Reynolds and Eugene Smolensky, *Public Expenditures, Taxes, and the Distribution of Income* (New York: Academic Press, 1977), p. 51.

the overall impact of government's budgetary operations would seem to be strongly progressive, based on the data presented by Reynolds and Smolensky, because of the strongly equalizing character of government spending.

THE SHIFTING AND INCIDENCE OF PUBLIC EXPENDITURE

The theory of tax incidence recognizes that the nominally or legally designated taxpayer might not be the real taxpayer. This theory explores the ways the burden of a tax might be shifted away from the nominal taxpayer. The shifting of tax burdens occurs as people change their conduct in response to the imposition of a tax. For example, a tax of $1 might be imposed on movie theater admissions, perhaps with the proceeds even being used to finance programs benefiting the film industry. If the admission price before the tax was $5, it does not follow that the price will rise to $6 after the tax. Indeed, it might not rise at all. How much the price of admissions will rise depends on various types of substitutability, both by consumers and by producers. The greater the willingness of consumers to substitute other activities for film watching as the price they must pay rises, the less of the tax burden they will bear. And the greater the willingness of people who work in the film industry to shift into other lines of employment as theater admissions fall, the less of the tax burden they will bear. The distribution of the tax burden in this case is not under the control of the legislature but of the myriad individuals who participate in various ways in the market for entertainment.

Any analysis of the redistributive impact of public spending must confront the same questions of incidence that the analysis of the redistributive impact of taxes must confront. As with taxes, different assumptions about the incidence of public spending will produce different conclusions about the progressivity or redistributive impact of public spending. The redistributive impact of public spending can be examined only by making assumptions about the incidence of the public spending programs. Whether a public spending program truly benefits the nominal beneficiary is an issue to be analyzed and demonstrated instead of validated merely by assumption. To be sure, a number of studies of the redistributive impact of government transfer programs have "concluded" that those programs have reduced income inequality, but as Sheldon Danziger, Robert Haveman, and Robert Plotnick observed in their survey article, "most studies measure redistribution as the simple difference between a household's final or post-transfer income and its income excluding transfers (pre-transfer income)."[3] In other words, they simply assume that transfer programs have no effect upon personal conduct.

The Reynolds and Smolensky study, findings from which were shown in Table 5–1, assumed that the beneficiaries of public spending were those who could readily be identified as intended beneficiaries. For instance, spending on elementary and secondary education was assumed to benefit children, so the amount of such expenditure was distributed among income classes in proportion to the number of children in each class. Spending on public assistance programs was assumed to benefit the recipients of those programs. Spending on highways was assumed to benefit the owners of automobiles. And in general the total amount spent on a particular program was apportioned among the members of what appeared to be the immediate beneficiaries of the program. Such an assumption about the benefits

---

3. Sheldon Danziger, Robert Haveman, and Robert Plotnick, "How Income Transfers Affect Work, Savings, and the Income Distribution," *Journal of Economic Literature* 19 (September 1981): 1006.

of public programs, however, may often be incorrect, just as it would often be inaccurate to assume that the effects of a tax were limited to the group taxed.

The redistributive effects of spending programs may in various ways be offset through changes in the choices of market participants. Suppose that, instead of paying a tax on theater admissions, theater owners are given a subsidy of $1 per admission. Suppose a theater has 120 admissions per performance, charges a ticket price of $4.50, and receives a $120 subsidy payment from the government.

It does not follow that this $120 expenditure benefits the nominal beneficiaries—the theater owners. If the subsidy program were re-

---

Figure 5–1.   Shifting of Benefits from Government Spending.

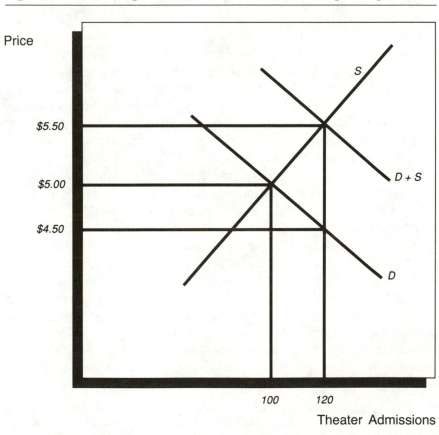

Price

$5.50

$5.00

$4.50

S

D + S

D

100   120

Theater Admissions

pealed, it would not follow that theater owners would be $120 poorer. Just as the initiation of the subsidy would induce owners to expand the supply of theater seats, the repeal of the subsidy would induce them to contract that supply. Figure 5–1 illustrates a situation in which there are 120 admissions, customers are paying $4.50 each for admission, and the government is giving a subsidy of $1 per admission. But if the subsidy were eliminated, theater owners would not supply 120 seats when they received only $4.50 per admission. And as they came to reduce the number of seats they were willing to supply, the willingness of consumers to pay for admission would rise. As shown in Figure 5–1, without the subsidy theater owners would supply 100 seats and customers would pay $5 for admission. In this case theater owners would lose only $0.50 per admission and not $1.00. The other $0.50 would come from customers, who must pay $0.50 more per admission. One-half of the benefit from the program is shifted away from theater owners onto theater customers. Even though it is the theater owners who receive the $120 payment from the government, they have in turn been forced through the competitive market process to give half that subsidy to consumers through price reductions. Numerous other illustrations could be given of ways in which the real distribution of benefits from government programs may differ from the nominal distribution.

MARKET-GENERATED OFFSETS TO REDISTRIBUTIVE SPENDING

In the preceding discussion, the subsidy to theater owners was partially dissipated through the competitive efforts of theater owners to acquire the subsidy being offered. That subsidy was, of course, an illustration of a transfer or redistributive program of government expenditure. As a general principle, all such subsidy or transfer programs will elicit competitive responses among potential recipients, and in the process will dissipate—at least partially and possibly totally—the value of the transfer.

Consider, for instance, the distribution of the benefits from public assistance programs. Suppose Poorman receives $100 from a public assistance program, paid for by a tax imposed on Midman and Richman. This spending program does not necessarily equalize the distribution of income by making Poorman $100 richer. Simply to distribute the amount of such expenditures among the recipients and to infer that equalization results is to assume that the presence or absence of the program has no impact upon people's conduct. It is, in other words, to assume that people do not respond to the incentives they face. But once we recognize that people do respond to incentives, it is no longer appropriate simply to distribute the amount of an expenditure among the recipients; it becomes necessary to take into account the economic consequences of the changes in conduct that people make in response to the program. These changes are made by both program participants and private suppliers of programs that are substitutes for the state-provided public assistance. For example, the Poormen might reduce their market earnings, and the Midmen and the Richmen might reduce their contributions to charity.

Suppose, for instance, that Poorman could earn $7.00 per hour and at this wage would choose to work 35 hours per week, thus earning $245.00. Consider the introduction of public assistance in the form of a negative income tax (NIT) that provides a weekly guarantee of $183 and reduces the amount of transfer that Poorman receives by $0.50 for each $1.00 he earns. If the introduction of the NIT induced no change in Poorman's labor supply, Poorman would receive a weekly transfer of $60.50. By earning $245.00, Poorman's NIT transfer would be reduced by $122.50 from the $183.00 it would have been had he earned nothing, giving him a transfer of $60.50.

However, it is exceedingly unlikely that Poorman would work as hard after the NIT as he did before. On the one hand, the NIT subsidy makes Poorman richer, which would lead him to take more leisure, thus supplying less labor. On the other hand, by reducing the subsidy by $0.50 for each $1.00 earned, the NIT reduces the return per unit of labor. For both reasons, then, the NIT would induce Poorman to supply less labor. On this point, in his examination of the effects of such an NIT upon labor supply, John F. Cogan found that white males reduced their work week by about 6.5 hours.[4] In the illustration at hand, Poorman's earnings would fall to $199.50, which in turn would increase the NIT transfer to $83.25. But it would be wrong to credit the NIT with transferring $83.25 to Poorman in this case, because the NIT was also responsible for reducing Poorman's earnings by

---

4. John F. Cogan, "Labor Supply and Negative Income Taxation: New Evidence from the New Jersey-Pennsylvania Experiment," *Economic Inquiry* 21 (October 1983): 465–84.

$45.50. Despite the subsidy of $83.25, Poorman's income increased by only $37.75. The remainder of the subsidy would have been shifted to other people. For instance, the decrease in labor supply by Poorman would increase the wage rate, thereby leading to increased earnings for those who were not eligible for the subsidy.[5]

Indeed, the Seattle-Denver Income Maintenance Experiment yielded some perhaps startling evidence in this regard. Transfer payments to able-bodied subjects that would have raised their incomes above what they could otherwise have obtained under AFDC and food stamps resulted in actual income gains of less than 20 percent of the value of the payments. In other words, to the extent that the experimental program was more generous to the participants than existing transfer programs, those participants transformed more than 80 percent of this potentially higher income into leisure.[6] While the precise impact of any particular program of public assistance is an empirical matter, it is fully understandable on conceptual grounds alone why the full benefit of those programs will not be confined to the nominal recipients of the program's transfers. Part of the benefit of transfer programs will be captured by other people.

There are many other ways in which public assistance can affect the choices of recipients. For instance, Victor R. Fuchs has noted that the Aid to Families with Dependent Children (AFDC) program encourages unmarried women to have children and to refrain from working. AFDC, along with food stamps, day care, subsidized housing and health care, among other programs, has clearly played a part in encouraging the growth of one-parent households since 1960.[7] Indeed, births to unmarried women have roughly tripled over the past two decades, despite the diffusion of the technological revolution in birth control that has taken place. Moreover, the substantial differences in labor-force participation rates of women with children are surely due in some measure to the incentives contained in such programs as AFDC. About 14 percent of AFDC mothers work, and this

5. This statement is subject to ceteris paribus conditions, of course, because the higher taxes to finance the subsidy may reduce the supply of labor by nonrecipients.

6. For a summary of the responses in such experiments, see Philip K. Robins, "A Comparison of the Labor Supply Findings from the Four Negative Income Tax Experiments," *Journal of Human Resources* 20 (Fall 1985): 567–82.

7. Victor R. Fuchs, *How We Live* (Cambridge, Mass.: Harvard University Press, 1983), pp. 104–6.

percentage has remained approximately constant over the past two decades. But among the population as a whole the percentage of women whose youngest child is at least six years old and who work is 62 percent. And the percentage of mothers whose youngest child is less than six and who hold a job is 45 percent.[8] It certainly seems reasonable that the guarantee offered by AFDC and related programs has something to do with the lower rates of labor-force participation by recipients. More generally, since the late 1960s, when the working poor became increasingly eligible for recipient status while working, there has been about a 50 percent increase in the number of people whose earnings lead to their being classified as poor. A reduction in the rate of labor-force participation has also occurred.

Public assistance will also generally induce the Richmen and Midmen to reduce their charitable contributions. Russell D. Roberts has shown, for instance, that government transfers have to a substantial degree crowded out private charity.[9] For the most part, public transfers and private charity are substitutes for one another. If the two are perfect substitutes from the perspective of individual donors, each dollar of public transfer will induce donors to reduce their private charity by a dollar. And even though private charity was $53.6 billion in 1981, the year to which Roberts's data pertain, it should be kept in mind that most of what is classified as charity has little to do with poverty relief these days and is dominated instead by donations for religious and educational purposes. Very little of what is called charity goes for the relief of poverty. Only $5.3 billion of the 1981 figure even fit into the category of "social services," and only a small part of this went to the poor.[10]

A full analysis of the redistributive impact of public assistance would have to include, at the very least, the reduction in private charity that resulted from the expansion in public assistance. For instance, if private charity were distributed more heavily toward people in the lower income classes than are the public assistance programs, the true redistributive impact of public assistance programs would be to increase

8. Peter G. Germanis, *Workfare: Breaking the Poverty Cycle*, Backgrounder No. 195 (Washington, D.C.: Heritage Foundation, 1982).

9. Russell D. Roberts, "A Positive Model of Private Charity and Public Transfers," *Journal of Political Economy* 92 (February 1984): 136–48. See also Jerold Schiff, "Does Government Spending Crowd Out Charitable Contributions?" *National Tax Journal* 38 (December 1985): 535–46.

10. Roberts, "Private Charity and Public Transfers," p. 141.

the degree of income inequality, even though those payments go mainly to people in the lower income categories. Simply to apportion public assistance payments among recipients is to assume that the presence or absence of that program has no effect upon such things as private charity. But such an effect clearly exists, which means that the redistributive impact of public assistance cannot be determined without incorporating into the analysis the negative impact of public assistance upon private charity. A public assistance program that transfers an average of $3,000 to the members of a particular income class actually imposes a $1,000 loss upon such people and hence is a regressive program, if it displaces private charity that would have paid $4,000. And even if the displaced charity would have paid only $2,000, that displaced payment must be subtracted. This would reduce the progressivity of the public assistance program, for that program would then have increased the amount of assistance by only $1,000 and not by $3,000.

What holds for public assistance holds for all programs of public expenditure. Social security, for instance, induces people to save less to provide for their retirement. The redistributive impact of social security cannot be examined simply by apportioning social security payments according to the income classes of the recipients. This approach would be proper only if social security had no effect upon private provision for retirement. But because social security tends to reduce private provision, that reduction must also be taken into account in assessing the effect of social security on the distribution of income. Similarly, public education cannot be apportioned among income classes according to the number of school-age children in each class, because public education reduces the amount of private provision, both because parents reduce their spending on private education and because donors reduce their contributions to the support of private education. The distributional impact of public education, then, can be examined only after such private responses are taken into account—responses that work to negate what would otherwise have been the effect of public education on the distribution of income.

The study by Reynolds and Smolensky cited earlier examined the effect of taxes and public expenditures on the distribution of income for 1950, 1961, and 1970. When any particular year was examined, the combined effect of taxes and expenditures appeared to entail a substantial equalization of income, as Table 5–1 illustrated for 1970.

However, although the relative size of government in the economy nearly doubled over the period studied, the degree of inequality was roughly the same in 1970 as in 1950. If government programs were truly having the redistributive impact that evidence such as that portrayed in Table 5–1 suggests, the growth in the relative size of government should have brought about a reduction in the degree of inequality. That the degree of inequality seems to have been unchanged despite the approximate doubling in the relative size of government—despite even a shift in the composition of public spending toward public assistance and social insurance programs—strongly suggests that some substantial market-generated offsets to redistributive spending are at work. Eugene Smolensky, Werner W. Pommerehne, and Robert E. Dalrymple compared the effect of government budgets on income distribution in the United States and West Germany and concluded that while income is distributed more equally in West Germany than in the United States, this difference has nothing to do with differences in budgetary policies.[11]

SOCIAL COSTS OF TRANSFER SPENDING

The justifications for the transfer programs of the welfare state generally rest upon simple notions of transferring income vertically from people with relatively high incomes to people with relatively low incomes. How much vertical redistribution is actually accomplished by the welfare state is an open question. Clearly, the amount of such redistribution is substantially less than is widely thought. By some accounts the size of the various welfare state programs are estimated to be four times the amount that would be required to raise everyone above the poverty line. It is quite clear that the bulk of income redistribution is *not* a simple top-to-bottom transfer. As will be explained briefly in the following section and more fully in Chapter 8, there is no reason to expect democratic political processes to produce such equalizing transfers anyway.

The studies of fiscal incidence that find the budgetary policies of the welfare state to be a force for equalizing incomes clearly exag-

11. Eugene Smolensky, Werner W. Pommerehne, and Robert E. Dalrymple, "Postfisc Income Inequality: A Comparison of the United States and West Germany," in John R. Moroney, ed., *Income Inequality: Trends and International Comparisons* (Lexington, Mass.: D. C. Heath, 1979), pp. 69–81.

gerate the amount of equalization that is accomplished. Efforts at income redistribution through public budgets will elicit reactions that will offset the effects of those taxing and spending policies. Those reactions could negate entirely the redistributive effects of those policies. Indeed, it is conceivable that a full consideration of such reactions would find that the welfare state has actually increased the amount of income inequality. And even if the market-generated offsets to redistributive taxing and spending have not worked so strongly as this, there is no doubt that the amount of equalization achieved is much less than the standard studies show, due mainly to the failure of those studies to take into account the various reactions to the incentives created by the welfare state's taxing and spending policies.

Moreover, a finding that some vertical redistribution has been accomplished—even though it is much less than would have resulted had people not reacted to those taxing and spending programs—does not imply that the welfare state has improved the lives of people in the lower income ranges. It is necessary also to consider the impact of the welfare state's programs on the creation of income and on the mobility prospects of those who are presently poor.

Although the impact of the welfare state on the creation of income, like its impact on the degree of income inequality, cannot be measured with great precision, that impact is substantial. First of all, the amount of labor supplied is lowered, both because of the disincentive effect from the taxes imposed to finance the welfare state and from the negative effect the transfer programs have on the work incentives of recipients. Perhaps particularly troubling in this respect are findings for specific groups; for instance, in periods of high employment there are more than a million adult males who, though neither disabled nor in school, do not work a single day during the course of the year. And several million others can be said to be only marginally in the labor market.[12]

The impact of the welfare state on saving and capital formation is a second factor that, over time, may have serious effects on the creation of income. Here too, especially because of the uncertain effects of social security, the precise outcome is unclear, but no one seriously believes the impact is positive. Scholars disagree only on how strongly

12. U.S. Department of Labor, Bureau of Labor Statistics, *Work Experience of the Population in 1981–82*, Bulletin 2199 (Washington, D.C.: Government Printing Office, 1984), Tables B-17, C-17.

negative the impact is. Alicia Munnell, for instance, holds that the negative effects of social security have been modest, while Martin Feldstein maintains that those effects have been severe, reducing private savings by as much as 20 to 25 percent.[13] Aside from social security, there is not only the whole panoply of other welfare state programs to consider, but also an associated tax code that until 1981 taxed savings at marginal rates often exceeding 70 percent and that still imposes heavy taxes on capital and distorts the allocation of that capital.[14]

A third factor affecting the creation of income is the effect of the welfare state on family composition. It has been reliably estimated that changes in family composition, most notably the growth of households headed by single mothers, accounted for over 2 million additional poor families in 1980. This figure accounted by itself for almost one-third of the number of poor families reported in 1980.[15] And it appears that males who separate from their children and the children's mother are no longer motivated to earn as much income as they would in an intact family; it has been estimated that married men take advantage of about twice as much of their potential earnings capacity as single men.[16]

The argument that the programs of the welfare state have created incentives for couples to separate has, of course, been most forcefully stated by Charles Murray in his book, *Losing Ground*.[17] Even a widely

13. Alicia Munnell, *The Effect of Social Security on Personal Saving* (Cambridge, Mass.: Ballinger, 1974); Martin Feldstein, "Social Security, Induced Retirement, and Aggregate Capital Accumulation," *Journal of Political Economy* 82 (October 1974): 905–26; and Martin Feldstein, "Social Security and Private Saving: Reply," *Journal of Political Economy* 90 (June 1982): 630–42. [Feldstein's "Reply" was in response to Dean R. Leimer and Selig D. Lesnoy, "Social Security and Private Saving: New Time-Series Evidence," *Journal of Political Economy* 90 (June 1982): 606–29.] See also Michael R. Darby, *The Effects of Social Security on Income and the Capital Stock* (Washington, D.C.: American Enterprise Institute, 1979), where an intermediate impact of about 10 percent is presented.

14. Edgar K. Browning, "Taxation, Capital Accumulation, and Equity," in Dwight R. Lee, ed., *Taxation and the Deficit Economy* (San Francisco: Pacific Research Institute for Public Policy, 1986), pp. 19–47.

15. See Gordon Green and Edward Welniak, *Changing Family Composition and Income Differentials*, Special Demographic Analyses CDS-80-7 (Washington, D.C.: Government Printing Office, 1982).

16. See Irwin Garfinkel and Robert Haveman, *Earnings Capacity, Poverty, and Inequality* (New York: Academic Press, 1977).

17. Charles Murray, *Losing Ground* (New York: Basic Books, 1984).

cited study by David Ellwood and Mary Jo Bane, which largely downplays these effects, finds that if AFDC benefits are increased by $100 per month, the chances of a married teenage couple's becoming divorced or separated increase by 4 percentage points if the couple is white and 10 percentage points if the couple is nonwhite.[18] And when couples are offered generous cash grants in the various experiments with so-called negative income tax programs, the rate of marital dissolution is even higher than under the current welfare system.[19] Such effects are important not only for their immediate implications for poverty levels, but also for the long-term well-being and mobility of the children who grow up in these environments.

This last consideration is a reminder of the distinction made in Chapter 2 between income distribution and income mobility. The welfare state may have produced some vertical equalization but perhaps at the cost of a stronger inheritance of economic positions from generation to generation. One reason for the latter effect is the reduced effort by low-income people to rise, because the welfare state's guarantees replace personal efforts to advance. As a result of this decreased supply of effort and entrepreneurship, there will be less competition for established wealth positions, which in turn may reduce the rate at which people with higher incomes fall in the income scale. Beyond this consideration, the overall level of income will, as argued above, be less than it would otherwise have been, due to the reduction in incentives to engage in wealth-creating activities. Thus, even according to Rawls's difference principle, which is commonly, though perhaps mistakenly, seen as an egalitarian maxim, the welfare state may be a failure, at least at the pertinent margins of choice, even if not in total or in all details.

18. David Ellwood and Mary Jo Bane, "The Impact of AFDC on Family Structure and Living Arrangements" (U.S. Department of Health and Human Services, Washington, D.C., 1984).

19. See John Bishop, "Jobs, Cash Transfers, and Marital Instability," *Journal of Human Resources* 15 (Summer 1980): 301–34. Family dissolution among whites was 36 percent higher in the Seattle-Denver experiment and 42 percent higher among blacks. In New Jersey there was no measured effect on whites; family dissolution increased 66 percent among blacks and 84 percent among Hispanics. In Gary there were no measured effects, but at the same time families there were told that "any one-person unit formed as a result of marital dissolution would not be eligible for the NIT." See Lyle P. Groenveld, Nancy Brandon Tuma, and Michael T. Hannan, "The Effects of Negative Income Tax Programs on Marital Dissolution," *Journal of Human Resources* 15 (Fall 1980): 654–74, especially p. 671.

VARIETIES OF INCOME REDISTRIBUTION

Most of the actual redistribution accomplished by the welfare state seems to be horizontal rather than vertical, as shall be explored in Chapter 8.[20] Many of the governmental programs that are rationalized or justified on the grounds that they advance the well-being of people in the lower income ranges seem more fully to advance the well-being of people in the middle-income ranges. Public education is one such program, particularly at more advanced levels where the clientele mostly have above-average incomes. Social security is another. It is questionable whether people considered poor would fare any better under a universal social security program than under a public assistance program that would have existed in the absence of social security. To the extent that transfers reflect some degree of charitable sentiment, it is unlikely that people who are poor would receive less under public assistance than under social security. But their tax burden would surely be lower under public assistance. Replacing a public assistance program that aids only the retired poor by a social insurance program that aids everyone would very likely represent a transfer of income from the poor to the nonpoor.

The varieties of horizontal income transfers are immense. And when they are taken into account, the advantage of the welfare state to the poor becomes ever more questionable. It is not legitimate to address the question of the value of the welfare state to the poor, or to anyone else for that matter, simply by looking at the immediate flow of payments from a program. The observation that public assistance payments go to poor people does not mean that those payments improve the material well-being of the recipients. Any such statement about improvement must be based on a comparison of economic positions in the presence of the program and in its absence and *must take into account the various economic adjustments and reactions that would have resulted* had the program never been created or had it been abolished.

Similarly, the observation that the present tax system taxes low-income people at lower average rates than it taxes high-income people does not mean that the tax system has improved the material well-

---

20. See, for instance, Gordon Tullock, *Economics of Income Redistribution* (Boston: Kluwer-Nijhoff, 1983), especially pp. 17–31.

being of poor people. To reach such a conclusion, it would be necessary to compare their position under the present tax system with their position as it would have been under some alternative system, perhaps a proportional income tax. While the proportional tax system would increase the average tax rate for people in the lower income ranges and lower it for people in the upper income ranges, the adjustments in labor supply that such a change in taxation would bring would, in turn, raise the pretax incomes of people in the lower income ranges. Moreover, the flattening of the marginal tax rate would strengthen the incentive to produce, which also would tend to increase pretax incomes.

Beyond this inability to assess programs simply by looking at the flow of payments ascribed to them, it is inappropriate to assess the welfare state simply by looking at a few selected programs that are commonly described as constituting the welfare state. To do so is false politics, just as looking simply at flows of payments is false economics. The welfare state does not happen in a vacuum. The welfare state does not reflect our charitable sentiments and other governmental activities such as military spending, highway construction, and safety regulation reflect our more selfish instincts. The programs of the welfare state arise out of a political system and through the operation of the incentives within that system. It is misleading to assess the welfare state without considering whatever else is produced by that political system. If the same forces that produce public assistance are those that fill caves in Missouri with cheese under the federal government's dairy program, the welfare state cannot be assessed without looking at the effects of cheese-filled Missouri caves as well as the effects of public assistance.

In other words, the whole constellation of political outcomes arises through the interplay of people in pursuit of their interests, as those interests are shaped and constrained by political and constitutional institutions. It is misleading to assess the welfare state by looking only at that subset of programs that are commonly referred to as the welfare state. Those programs are not produced in isolation but are created as part of a process that produces all the other programs as well. A state that was constituted differently so that it could not produce the welfare state or would produce a welfare state that had quite different types of programs, would produce different programs in other areas also. As Chapter 7 explains, the present-day welfare state is a product of a system of majoritarian democracy, in which there is little limit on the ability of legislative majorities to use their taxing and spending powers as they choose. Such a political order produces a wide variety of income redistributions, some of which constitute the subset of programs called the welfare state. But the programs of the welfare state *could not* be produced by themselves; they emerge only as part of a package of programs. To assess the welfare state and to consider options for reform, it is necessary to introduce questions of political incentives and constitutional orders. This proposition will become clearer in Chapter 6, and a fuller explanation of it will appear in Chapter 7.

6

REGULATION AND THE WELFARE STATE

The preceding two chapters have explained why it is easy to exaggerate the redistributive impact of government's budgetary operations. The redistributive effects of an increase in tax progressivity or an increase in spending on transfer programs cannot be gauged accurately simply by noting the change in nominal tax liabilities or expenditure benefits that result from those programs. Such an effort would be accurate only if people did not change their conduct in response to the change in budgetary policy. But such a failure to change would generally require irrational conduct: it would require that people refuse to take advantage of opportunities they face. And when people do take advantage of such opportunities, much of the nominally redistributive impact of government budgets will be negated through personal interactions within market processes. For instance, an increase in tax progressivity will alter returns to different investments in human capital, which in turn will lead, through changes in relative labor supplies, to offsetting changes in the pretax distribution of income. Similarly, transfers that increase the returns to those possessing characteristics such as being an unwed mother or a labor-force (or school) dropout will likewise lead to an increase in the possession of those characteristics, thereby reducing the pretransfer incomes of people with those characteristics.

The welfare state is, of course, commonly measured by budgetary magnitudes and assessed in terms of the equalization that is thought to result. In a setting where government has no ability to legislate and regulate, this might be reasonable because the budget would be the only means by which government could influence economic activity. But in the modern nation-state, where the legislature is a maker of law, budgets recede in relative if not in absolute importance as an indicator of government's influence over economic activity. The effect of government on the distribution of income cannot be gauged without taking into account the activities of the regulatory state. What is referred to as the prefisc distribution of income in studies of the redistributive impact of government budgets is contaminated by the effect of state regulation; the prefisc distribution does not provide evidence about income and its distribution in a contractarian state with a market economy, for the prefisc distribution is itself influenced by the welfare or transfer state. Since any regulation can be translated into an equivalent budgetary operation, and vice versa, an examination of the welfare state that is restricted to budgetary operations must be seriously incomplete. This chapter makes an effort to incorporate aspects of the regulatory state into an examination of the welfare state.

SUBSTITUTABILITY OF POLICE AND BUDGET POWERS

The approach of comparing prefisc and postfisc distributions of income as a way of determining the impact of government upon the distribution of income is grounded on the presumption that the prefisc distribution of income represents the "natural" and inescapable outcome of an enterprise economy. However, a central principle of public finance is that any statute or regulation can be translated into a budgetary equivalent. Minimum wage legislation, for instance, increases the earnings of those who remain employed in covered employments and reduces the earnings of those who either shift into uncovered employments or become unemployed. Hence, minimum wage legislation is equivalent to a program that taxes the earnings of those members of the low-wage labor force who become unemployed or who shift into uncovered employment and uses those revenues to subsidize the workers whose wages are raised. If such a program were conducted through the budget, it would surely be treated as part of the welfare state. But nothing essential is changed by having that transfer program work through the police power rather than the budget power. Government has the same impact on the distribution of income in either case.

Because any control over resources that government achieves through its taxing and spending powers can in principle also be achieved through government's use of its police power, the welfare state must be seen to include such uses of the police power. Indeed, a government could be as influential in the economy as it is presently and yet operate with very little budgetary outlay. Governments have often financed wars by requiring people to provide their bodies, food, clothing, and weapons. Although such an extensive use of conscription reduces the amount of government spending, it does not reduce government's control over the use of resources in society. The extent of that control would be essentially the same as it would be if wars were financed through the ordinary operations of taxing and spending.

Likewise, governments could eliminate their education budgets simply by requiring parents to send their children to school for a stipulated number of years. Governments provide protection against rabies by requiring owners of pets to have their pets inoculated, although it would be possible to provide inoculations through the appropriation of tax revenues to veterinary clinics. But whether government organizes the provision of education, or the protection from rabies, through a system of budgetary transactions or through a system of orders and regulations, the extent of governmental direction of the use of resources is essentially the same.

Requiring parents to send their children to approved schools would, of course, have a considerably different impact on the distribution of income than would the present system of public education. But even this distributional difference could be largely eliminated through appropriately drafted legislation; the legislation would, of course, have to be considerably more complex than merely requiring parents to send their children to school. Perhaps the main distributional differences would arise through differences in income and in the number of children. As compared with a regime of parental responsibility, the present system subsidizes people more heavily the more children they have and the lower their income.

This network of subsidies and taxes could, however, be approximated by combining legislation compelling parental responsibility with various requirements for the award of "scholarships" through some form of "extended parent" program. Under such a program, people without children or with fewer children would be compelled to treat someone else's children as partially their own responsibility. And the terms of this program could be refined so that the amount of support extracted from such people would rise directly with their income. In principle, a sufficiently complex piece of legislation and set of regulations could be developed that would duplicate the outcomes of the present system of educational finance, but the only budgetary appropriation required would be the modest amount necessary to administer the program.

Regulation is a tax, although it is relatively silent and indirect. For example, Murray L. Weidenbaum once estimated that regulation increased the price of automobiles approximately 10 percent.[1] Alternatively, government could have imposed taxes to finance the installation of the equipment it requires cars to have instead of requiring that cars be produced according to its specifications. To note the conceptual equivalence of the budget and police powers is not to say that government is indifferent to which it uses in particular cases. On the contrary, generally there are reasons why one is used and not the other, reasons that have to do with questions explored in Chapter 7.[2] The important point here is that the regulatory state must be examined as a component of the welfare state.

THE REGULATORY STATE AS WELFARE STATE

Public policy over the past half-century has restricted liberty by awarding entitlements and foreclosing options formerly open to people. And restrictions on liberty do go hand in hand with the awarding of entitlements. Protecting unionized garment workers from lower priced competition is impossible without concomitantly preventing people from making garments at home for resale and also preventing people as consumers from trying to find the best buys they can. Protecting domestic automobile manufacturers and workers is impossible without concomitantly restricting the ability of people to buy Japanese cars that they may think are better suited to their needs. Transferring wealth

1. Murray L. Weidenbaum, *Government-Mandated Price Increases* (Washington, D.C.: American Enterprise Institute, 1975).

2. See the exploration of this topic in Richard A. Posner, "Taxation by Regulation," *Bell Journal of Economics* 2 (Spring 1971): 22–50.

to tenants through rent control cannot be done without infringing on the liberty of the owners of the rental property, as well as that of other people who might want to rent in the future. One person's entitlement is necessarily someone else's encumbrance.

A duality exists between statements regarding product markets and statements regarding factor markets; what can be said in terms of product markets can be restated in terms of factor markets. One of the most prevalent statements about economics is the product market statement that people's wants are unlimited or at least that those wants vastly exceed people's ability to fulfill them. But this statement about scarcity in product markets implies the factor market statement that there is no such thing as a shortage of jobs. If the wants people have are unlimited, so must be the number of jobs they would like to have performed. Granted, the number of jobs people might like to have performed if they had to pay $10 per hour is clearly limited and is less than they would choose to have performed if they had to pay $5 per hour, which in turn is less than what they would choose at $3. But this is simply the complement to the product market proposition that the greater the price people must pay to fulfill their wants, the fewer they will choose to fulfill.

The programs of the welfare state are typically viewed from a product market perspective. The food stamp program is seen as giving people money to spend in grocery stores; other programs are similarly seen as providing people with material means of support without their having to earn them. Any act of guarantee, however, implies the imposition of a liability on someone else. The factor market side of the award of such guarantees is the imposition of an obligation to labor to fulfill the terms of that guarantee. If the state is to award guarantees, it must at the same time impose liabilities. If one person is to be awarded food or housing, someone else must be compelled to labor to provide that food or housing. When viewed from the perspective of the product market, the welfare state seems mainly to deal with the provision of income for recipients. But when viewed from the perspective of the factor market, the welfare state's provision of income entails a system of servile labor.[3]

In contrast to the product market characterization of the budgetary

3. For a perceptive treatment of servile labor, see Hilaire Belloc's 1913 work, *The Servile State* (Indianapolis, Ind.: Liberty Press, 1977).

component of the welfare state, the police or regulatory component is typically approached from the factor market, and yet it too carries a product market implication. Many of these programs, a few of which will be examined in this chapter, operate by creating protected positions or sheltered statuses.[4] For instance, American automobile manufacturers and automobile workers have been sheltered by "voluntary" quotas on automobiles imported from Japan. The reductio in the supply of Japanese cars and the concomitant increase in t price increased the demand for domestic cars. The product m: manifestation of the import quota was the imposition of a tax o tomobile buyers, particularly on potential buyers of lower priced with the revenues distributed among domestic automobile manu turers and workers. Such an act of the regulatory component of welfare state is clearly one that increases the extent of income ineq ity. And in similar fashion, any program that restricts compe tion among producers can be translated into a product market progr of taxes and subsidies—a theme that will be explored for several sp cific cases in the remainder of this chapter.

MINIMUM WAGE LEGISLATION

Minimum wage legislation has long been rationalized as a means of raising people's wages, thereby combating poverty. Someone earning the minimum wage of $3.35 per hour working 40 hours per week for 52 weeks will earn $6,968, which is just below the government's poverty line of $7,400 for a family of two in 1987, and further below the poverty lines of $9,300 and $11,200 for families of three and four respectively. On the other hand, two people receiving the minimum wage will exceed the $13,100 poverty line for a family of five.

In the first year after the imposition of minimum wage legislation, coverage was selective, but now it is almost universal.[5] In 1938 only

4. For a general examination of such sheltered status positions, see Richard E. Wagner, "The Political Economy of the Sheltered Sector," in Karl Brunner, ed., *The Sheltered Sector, the Use of Resources, and Inflation* (Rochester, N.Y.: Center for Research in Government Policy and Business, University of Rochester, 1983), pp. 7–28.

5. Minimum wage legislation and its effects are surveyed in Finis Welch, *Minimum Wages: Issues and Evidence* (Washington, D.C.: American Enterprise Institute, 1978). For examinations of effects on particular types of workers, see Yale Brozen, "Minimum Wage Rates and Household Workers," *Journal of Law and Economics* 5 (October 1962): 103–9; and Yale Brozen, "The Effect of Statutory Minimum Wage Rate Increases on Teenage Employment," *Journal of Law and Economics* 12 (April 1969): 109–22.

43 percent of nonsupervisory employment was covered by the minimum wage, and, moreover, those occupations that were covered tended generally to have relatively high wages. By 1981 coverage under the minimum wage had been extended to 84 percent of the labor force. The minimum wage has generally ranged between 40 and 50 percent of the average wage in manufacturing. Indeed, there is much political interest in indexing the minimum wage at such a level. Average manufacturing wages now stand at about $9.00 per hour, whereas the minimum wage is $3.35 per hour, though several pieces of legislation have been introduced to raise the minimum to around $5.00 per hour.

By now a vast amount of scholarship has documented that minimum wage legislation does not reduce poverty so much as it contributes to it. It also restricts liberty, for it prohibits people from agreeing to exchange services that both parties agree are worth less than $3.35 per hour. However, so long as the coverage of the minimum wage was selective, as it was during its early years, its main effects were (1) to reduce employment and increase wages to the minimum level in those covered areas that previously were paying below the minimum and (2) to increase employment and decrease wages in the uncovered areas. This latter effect resulted because the people who were displaced by the minimum wage in the covered areas were able subsequently to find employment in the uncovered areas, and the increase in the supply of labor in the uncovered employments decreased the wage rate in those employments.

But when coverage is universal, as it now nearly is, there will no longer exist any uncovered areas into which people who are disemployed can go. By raising the cost of labor, the minimum wage requirement will generally reduce the number of people that employers will hire. To be sure, there are exceptions to the proposition that an increase in the minimum wage will reduce employment, but even these exceptions do not reverse the generally negative effect on those subjected to the legislation. One exception arises because worker compensation entails more than a wage; it also entails fringe benefits and working conditions. The wage rate might be $3.35, but the total amount of compensation might be $5.35, with the extra $2 representing a combination of fringe benefits and working conditions. An increase in the minimum wage to $4.35 would have no effect on employment if employers are able to reduce nonwage costs to $1.00 per hour. The extent to which this might be done depends on the forms these nonwage costs take.[6] With respect to fringe benefits, paid vacation time might be reduced. With respect to working conditions, time allowed for breaks might be reduced. Furthermore, a portion of nonwage compensation will generally represent employer-provided training that contributes to the human capital of the employee. An increase in the minimum wage would also reduce employer outlays for such training, thereby reducing future earnings of the affected employees.[7]

Despite the clear evidence that minimum wage legislation reduces employment among the low-wage labor force, such legislation is typically supported more strongly by legislators in districts that have larger percentages of low-wage workers. This might seem irrational, as it might suggest support for a program that replaces a low wage with a zero wage. But what happens instead, as Keith B. Leffler has explained, is that welfare programs offer payments in the general vicinity of what could have been earned by working at the low wage, but without having to work.[8] Payments under the Aid to Families with Dependent Children (AFDC) program are a case in point. Since the adoption of the "unemployed parent amendment" in 1961, AFDC has increased its payments in the event of parental unemployment. What Leffler found was that an increase in the minimum wage had two simultaneous effects: one was a decrease in employment and the other was an increase in welfare payments, both under AFDC and under general relief. Over the period that Leffler examined, welfare payments generally were about 80 percent of what the recipient would have earned by working at the minimum wage.

Furthermore, the various expenses of working are commonly estimated to be about 15 percent of income. When the level of welfare payment is combined with the cost of earning income, it appears that the unemployment that results from minimum wage legislation may actually have little effect on the real income of those who become unemployed. Some people may even reach a preferred position, in

6. Walter J. Wessels, *Minimum Wages, Fringe Benefits, and Working Conditions* (Washington, D.C.: American Enterprise Institute, 1981). The cost to an employer is more than the minimum wage because such fringes as social security, unemployment insurance, and workers' compensation are a mandatory part of the employment relationship.

7. Belton M. Fleisher, *Minimum Wage Regulation in Retail Trade* (Washington, D.C.: American Enterprise Institute, 1981), examines the impact of minimum wage legislation on employer-provided training.

8. Keith B. Leffler, "Minimum Wages, Welfare, and Wealth Transfers to the Poor," *Journal of Law and Economics* 21 (October 1978): 345–58.

that they may regard the small reduction in income as worthwhile in light of the increased leisure that results. For instance, someone who works 40 hours per week at a minimum wage of $3.35 per hour earns $134.00. If various welfare benefits pay 80 percent of that amount, $107.20 per week, the unemployed person actually loses only $26.80 per week, not accounting for any possible costs of employment. Becoming employed would offer a net gain of only $26.80 for a work week of 40 hours, or $0.67 per hour, not taking into consideration any possible costs of employment. So long as such people value leisure at more than $0.67 per hour, they will prefer receiving welfare to earning a slightly higher income.

Although welfare programs may offset the loss of real income that results from the unemployment caused by minimum wage legislation, those programs may also create a type of welfare dependency. What Morley D. Glicken refers to as "learned helplessness" comes about because human capital is not accumulated in a state of unemployment and people may have little incentive.[9] Most low-wage jobs are initial and not terminal employments. And there would be many more such jobs if they were not prevented by minimum wage legislation. Such jobs are often entry points into the world of work. As people accumulate the skills and traits that are required for successful employment, they typically move on to higher paying jobs. Being an usher in a theater before that type of work was largely precluded by minimum wage legislation may have been the first step into the world of work.

If entry-level jobs are foreclosed, however, an opportunity for the creation of skills and traits is also foreclosed. Without the opportunities for personal development that are provided by such entry-level jobs as ushering in theaters, the chance or the opportunity to move into higher paying jobs is diminished. Work experiences contribute to a person's human capital and thereby increase earnings. In the absence of the experience afforded by entry-level employment that might pay less than the minimum wage, less human capital will be accumulated, which in turn will lead to lower lifetime earnings.

Minimum wage legislation, moreover, is but one example of legislation that to some extent seems to prevent people from employing

9. Morley D. Glicken, "Transgenerational Welfare Dependency," *Journal of Contemporary Studies* 4 (Summer 1981): 31–41.

their talents in ways that will lead to their fuller development. In conjunction with child labor legislation, it is surely an important factor in preventing the accumulation of human capital among those who, through aptitude or ability, are likely to end their formal education at high school graduation, if not before. For these people, the foreclosure of options to gain initial experience in the world of work can be an important factor in reducing the rate of subsequent accumulation of human capital and, hence, of future earning prospects.

The extent to which the programs of the welfare state create, as a by-product of providing a base of support, a longer term welfare dependency is a topic that deserves and doubtlessly will receive further research. Morley Glicken, for instance, estimates the rate of transgenerational welfare dependency to be about 40 percent, which means that about 40 percent of adult recipients had been recipients as children.[10] And while about half of those who receive AFDC payments are off its rolls in two years, about half of all those on the rolls are caught up in a period of eight or more years of dependence on the program.[11]

The various guarantees of the welfare state are a two-edged sword: they provide support for people, but they also weaken the ability of people to provide their own support. Furthermore, various restrictions on labor markets foreclose options by which people could support themselves, so the guarantees of the welfare state would to some degree be unnecessary were it not for such restrictions on labor markets. In conjunction with the welfare guarantees that are paid to offset the loss of income that would otherwise result, minimum wage legislation would seem actually to reduce the long-term prospects of low-wage workers. Such legislation does, however, enhance the prospects for high-wage workers and firms that thus are insulated from some sources of competition. The effects of minimum wage legislation differ greatly from the rationalizations that are commonly advanced in its support. Why this might be so will be considered more directly in Chapters 7 and 8.

10. Glicken, "Transgenerational Welfare Dependency." Also see George Gilder, *Wealth and Poverty* (New York: Basic Books, 1981).

11. Mary Jo Bane and David Ellwood, "The Dynamics of Dependence: The Route to Self-Sufficiency" (U.S. Department of Health and Human Services, June 1983).

WORKING IN HOMEMADE SWEATSHOPS

There are numerous restrictions and prohibitions on working at home. Many of these restrictions or bans originate in local zoning ordinances that allow people to work only in appropriately zoned locations. Although enforcement can be difficult and the effectiveness of the restrictions thereby weakened, bans often extend to in-house activities such as teaching piano, baking bread, sewing, and typing letters.

The prohibition on working at home that has perhaps received the most attention recently concerns a 1943 regulation forbidding people to work at home in seven types of garment manufacture: knitted outer wear, women's garments, embroidery, handkerchiefs, jewelry, buttons and buckles, and gloves and mittens.[12] This regulation was promulgated under the Fair Labor Standards Act of 1938, which authorized the establishment of minimum wages. Although, as noted above, the minimum wage originally covered less than half of the labor force, the 1943 regulation was rationalized as being necessary because the ability of people to work in their homes would undermine the minimum wage requirement.

The prohibition against working at home is often defended by claims that the ban is needed to prevent people from turning their homes into sweatshops. There are, of course, no official statistics on what must be an underground activity, but reports of earnings that are double or triple the minimum wage are common. And undoubtedly reports could be found of people earning less than the minimum wage. Such work, of course, is paid not on an hourly basis but by the amount of work accomplished, on a piece rate basis. People who are quick and hard working will earn more than people who are slow and desultory. But in any event, payments based on hours of work are rare when work is done at home, because it is difficult to monitor the amount of work actually done.

Paying by the piece or by the job avoids what would otherwise be a costly, troublesome problem of monitoring. Moreover, such a system of payment in conjunction with the opportunity to work at home

12. See the description and discussion of this prohibition against working at home in Peter Germanis, *Why Not Let Americans Work at Home?* Backgrounder No. 325 (Washington, D.C.: Heritage Foundation, 1984).

is particularly beneficial to women with young children and people with physical handicaps. The mothers can combine caring for their children at home with working; they do not have to turn their children over to day care centers if they want to work. The physically handicapped can reduce what might otherwise be the high cost of transporting themselves to and from an outside workplace. Mothers of young children and the physically handicapped are among those the welfare state is generally rationalized as seeking to help, and yet in the ban against home work the regulatory arm of the welfare state is preventing them from helping themselves.

Although Chapter 7 and later chapters will examine more directly why the welfare state might act this way, some preliminary considerations will be taken up here. A prohibition against the efforts of people to help themselves, efforts that the rhetoric of the welfare state would require it to support, must to some extent be explained by the self-serving interests of other people who would be harmed by the successful efforts of people to support themselves through working at home. At least two sets of people would be harmed and thus would gain by the imposition and enforcement of these restrictions: people employed in substitute lines of activity and people employed in the various welfare agencies.

As will be explored more fully in Chapter 8, the employees of the various welfare agencies are not generally rewarded according to their success in eliminating the conditions that elicit support. Rather, to a substantial extent the interests of the employees of the agencies are advanced as the scope of the agencies' activities expands. The greater the number of people welfare agencies can claim as their clients, the better off the staffs of the agencies are. A welfare agency that successfully promoted the independence of its clientele would be out of business, and the members of such agencies who would like to see that happen are probably rare. The opportunity to work at home operates to some extent as a substitute for being a client of one or more of the agencies of the welfare state. Among other things, working at home reduces the demand for day care facilities and for AFDC.

Secondly, and perhaps more significantly, firms and workers who are in competition with those who work at home would gain by restrictions on the ability of people to work at home. Preventing such manufacture at home reduces the supply of lower priced alternatives to garments manufactured in factories. This increases the demand for factory-produced garments, as illustrated by the shift from D_1 to D_2 in Figure 6–1 and the increase in factory production from G_1 to G_2. To the extent that the supply of labor to the manufacture of garments is less than fully elastic, as is illustrated by S, the prohibition of home work will increase the wage rate in the unionized factories from W_1 to W_2. This program is equivalent to taxing home workers and using the revenues to subsidize factory workers. Those who work at home would generally have lower incomes than those who work in the unionized factories, so the effect of this regulatory component of the

Figure 6–1.   Distributive Impact of Restrictions on Home-Produced Garments.

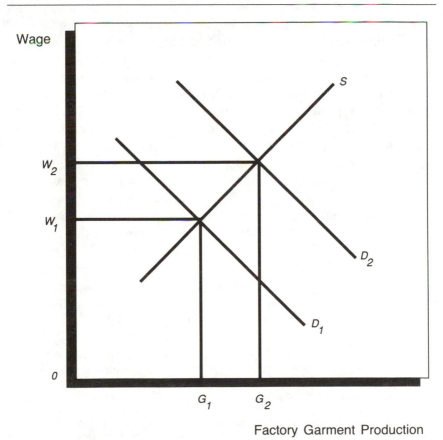

Wage

W_2

W_1

S

D_2

D_1

0

G_1 G_2

Factory Garment Production

welfare state is to increase the degree of inequality in the "market" or "prefisc" distribution of income.[13] Again, the observed distribution of income cannot be taken as indicative of what it would be under a truly contractarian state; moreover, while such legislation is clearly "redistributive," it is also clearly not "equalizing."

UNIONIZATION AND OCCUPATIONAL LICENSURE

The ability of unions and professional associations to restrict the supply of labor is one of the most fully studied illustrations of how legislation can alter what is commonly though erroneously called the "market" distribution of income. Unions presently cover about 15 percent of the labor force and occupational licensing covers over 30 percent, so together they cover nearly half the labor force.[14] Both unionization and occupational licensure operate by restricting the supply of labor to covered occupations, thereby increasing the supply of labor to uncovered occupations. One consequence is the creation of a differential in earnings between covered and uncovered occupations. Another consequence is the diminution in general economic welfare through the inefficiency that results.

The effect on relative labor supplies and wages is illustrated in Figure 6–2, where panel A refers to union labor and panel B refers to nonunion labor (the two panels could alternatively have referred to licensed labor and nonlicensed labor). Unions reduce the supply of labor in activities subject to their control from U_1 to U_2, which increases wage rates from W_1^u to W_2^u. This disemployed labor finds employment in nonunionized pursuits, as illustrated by the increased employment from N_1 to N_2, which reduces nonunionized wages from W_1^n to W_2^n. Since unionized workers generally have above-average earnings, the effect of such legislative restrictions on freedom of contract is, as compared with a contractarian state, to increase the degree of inequality in the "market" distribution of income.

---

13. Near the end of 1988, the Department of Labor announced its intention to lift the ban on home work in garment manufacture. That proposal immediately encountered stiff opposition from the International Ladies' Garment Workers Union, and regardless of whether the ban is eventually repealed, the process will be lengthy and hotly contested.

14. For broad-ranging surveys of these topics, see Morgan O. Reynolds, *Making America Poorer: The Cost of Labor Law* (Washington, D.C.: Cato Institute, 1987); and S. David Young, *The Rule of Experts: Occupational Licensing in America* (Washington, D.C.: Cato Institute, 1987).

Figure 6–2. Effect of Unionization on Relative Wages and Labor Supplies

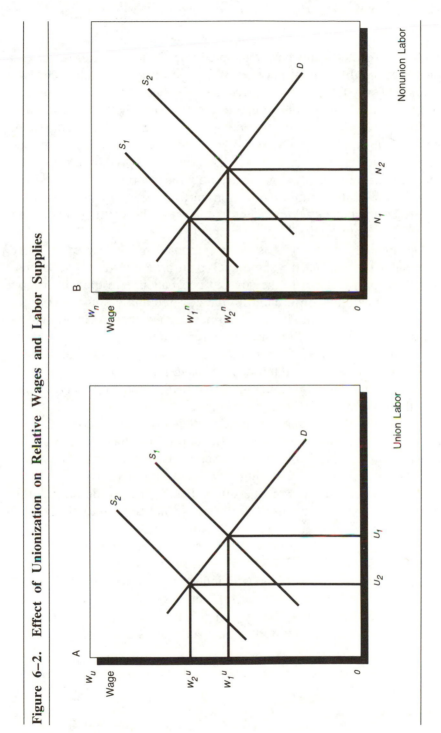

A number of scholars have attempted to estimate the effect of unions on the wage differential between union and nonunion labor. In two studies twenty-three years apart, H. G. Lewis estimated that unions in both periods were able to create a differential between union and nonunion wages of 12 to 16 percent, a differential that is consistent with that estimated by other scholars.[15] In a specific study of unions in public education, Randall W. Eberts and Joe A. Stone estimated that teacher unions, through restricting the supply of teachers, increased the cost of public education an average of 11 percent, with no effect on student achievement as measured by math scores in the fourth and tenth grades.[16]

Occupational licensing has been examined much less extensively than labor unions, but the same analytical principles apply to licensing: the supply of labor to the covered occupation is restricted, thereby causing an earnings differential in the covered and the uncovered occupations. To be sure, it is sometimes argued that occupational licensing can be justified on public interest grounds, with the licensing representing a means of economizing on the acquisition of knowledge. In this case the state through licensing provides knowledge about the quality of the service being performed, presumably knowledge that the service will be well performed.

There might be grounds in some models of welfare economics for the creation of minimum quality standards in some cases, with licensing as the vehicle for the assurance of those standards. However, it does not follow that licensing actually accomplishes what this rationalization envisions. For one thing, licensing is commonly dominated by the various licensed professions, and the interests of those professions in restricting the supply of labor will lead them to set standards that exceed those that are consistent with the rationalization, as Hayne E. Leland explains.[17] Beyond this, the higher price due to the restricted supply of labor will induce people to substitute lower cost options, including do-it-yourself activities. While electrical work done by electricians may be of higher quality when electricians are licensed, it does not follow that licensing raises the quality of elec-

15. H. G. Lewis, *Unionism and Relative Wages in the United States* (Chicago: University of Chicago Press, 1963); and H. G. Lewis, *Union Relative Wage Effects* (Chicago: University of Chicago Press, 1986).

16. Randall W. Eberts and Joe A. Stone, "Teacher Unions and the Cost of Public Education," *Economic Inquiry* 24 (October 1986): 631–43.

17. Hayne E. Leland, "Quacks, Lemons, and Licensing: A Theory of Minimum Quality Standards," *Journal of Political Economy* 87 (December 1979): 1328–46.

trical work in general. While the quality of that work done by licensed electricians may be increased, the increased volume of work done by do-it-yourselfers that would otherwise have been done by nonlicensed electricians will generally be of lower quality.

Sidney L. Carroll and Robert J. Gaston examined several cases where licensing may actually reduce the overall quality of the service subject to licensing, even though it presumably increases the quality of that share of the service provided by licensed practitioners.[18] Carroll and Gaston found that the licensing of electricians increased the number of deaths by electrocution, as a result of an increase in the amount of electrical work being done by amateurs. Using data from the U.S. Navy, they found that dental licensing led to a greater loss of teeth and generally poorer oral hygiene. In any event, the impact of licensing on the quality of some service cannot be gauged simply by looking at services provided by the licensed practitioners. It is also necessary to take into account the increase in lower quality services provided through various nonlicensed channels in response to the increased price in the licensed occupations.

By now several studies have been done on the effects of specific types of occupational licensing upon wages and earnings among covered practitioners.[19] Lee Benham and Alexandra Benham found that professional controls over the advertising of optometric services increased the prices of those services by 25 to 40 percent and reduced the amount of such services that people purchased by a similar amount.[20] Lawrence Shepard estimated that restrictions on entry into dentistry increased the prices of dental services as well as the incomes of dentists by about 12 to 15 percent.[21] Similarly, Keith Leffler estimated that physician licensure increased earnings for physicians an average of about $4,900 in 1966.[22]

18. Sidney L. Carroll and Robert J. Gaston, "Occupational Restrictions and the Quality of Service Received: Some Evidence," *Southern Economic Journal* 47 (April 1981): 959–76.

19. For a general survey of this topic, see Stanley J. Gross, *Professional Licensure and Quality: The Evidence* (Washington, D.C.: Cato Institute, 1986).

20. Lee Benham and Alexandra Benham, "Regulating through the Professions: A Perspective on Information Control," *Journal of Law and Economics* 18 (October 1975): 421–47.

21. Lawrence Shepard, "Licensing Restrictions and the Cost of Dental Care," *Journal of Law and Economics* 21 (April 1978): 187–201.

22. Keith B. Leffler, "Physician Licensure: Competition and Monopoly in American Medicine," *Journal of Law and Economics* 21 (April 1978): 165–86. See also Jeffrey M. Perloff, "The Impact of Licensing Laws on Wage Changes in the Construction Industry," *Journal of Law and Economics* 23 (October 1980): 407–28.

For more detail, consider the findings of two representative and pertinent studies, both of which treat the distributive consequences of the regulatory component of the welfare state. In one, Thomas Gale Moore estimated the effect of the regulation of entry into trucking by the Interstate Commerce Commission (ICC) and did so within a frame of reference similar to that illustrated in Figure 6–2.[23] Moore found that ICC regulation of entry allowed the Teamsters' union to raise wages sufficiently to produce an income differential of about 40 to 50 percent over that received by other truckers. Moore estimated the total amount of this income transfer to be about $1.0 to $1.3 billion in 1972. Moreover, this transfer came at the expense of those people who otherwise would have driven trucks but were precluded from doing so by the restrictions on entry. Since the incomes of such truck drivers are higher than average, the impact of ICC regulation of trucking was to increase the degree of income inequality. Moore found the same effect on the owners of trucking licenses; these people also generally have above-average incomes, and as a group they gained from $1.5 to $2 billion. The ICC seems not to have protected users from monopolistic exploitation but to have made it possible for that very exploitation to exist.

In the other study, Richard L. Smith examined the effect of governmental restrictions on the operation of the retail automobile market.[24] Both the federal and state governments have imposed restrictions on the relationship between automobile manufacturers and their retail franchisees. These restrictions curtail the ability of a manufacturer to revoke a franchise in an area or create a new one, to establish quotas for franchises, or to ship cars that a franchisee does not order. Although such policies have been rationalized as curtailing the monopolistic power of the automobile manufacturers, the actual effect is dramatically different. As Smith documented, the impact of such restrictions was to establish local monopoly positions for individual franchise holders. As a result of the restriction of competition, the

---

23. Thomas Gale Moore, "The Beneficiaries of Trucking Regulation," *Journal of Law and Economics* 21 (October 1978): 327–43. For an extension of Moore's analysis to Canada, see Moshe Kim, "The Beneficiaries of Trucking Regulation, Revisited," *Journal of Law and Economics* 27 (April 1984): 227–41.

24. Richard L. Smith II, "Franchise Regulation: An Economic Analysis of State Restrictions on Automobile Distribution," *Journal of Law and Economics* 25 (April 1982): 125–57. See also E. W. Eckard, Jr., "The Effects of State Automobile Entry Regulation on New Car Prices," *Economic Inquiry* 23 (April 1985): 223–42.

price of new automobiles rose by about 10 percent. In consequence, there was a transfer of income from consumers to dealers of about $6.7 billion in 1972. To the extent that dealers have higher incomes than consumers, this regulation increases the degree of income inequality. However, this case is clearly more an illustration of horizontal than of vertical redistribution.

But in any case, the important point is that observed prefisc distributions of income erroneously attribute those outcomes that result in the presence of state-sanctioned market restrictions to the operation of the market economy and not to government's restriction of that operation. Yet these types of measures could be treated alternatively and equivalently as tax-and-transfer programs. Moreover, a large number of similar studies could be discussed, all of which would show a wide variety of regulations that, if given a budgetary translation, would show a substantial degree of redistribution, with lower income people being taxed to subsidize higher income people.

There is, of course, no direct way to compare the distributive impact of a contractarian state with that of the existing economic order, for we have no observation of life under the former. However, by now a substantial number of studies of various types of legislation and regulation have found that in many cases governmental programs transfer wealth from people who have less to people who have more, thereby increasing the degree of inequality in what is commonly called the prefisc distribution of income. However, the observed distribution of income does not represent the distribution that would result within a contractarian state, and such an alternative distribution might well have less inequality than the prefisc distribution associated with the welfare state.

Moreover, the greater freedom of trade within such a contractarian state will surely increase total income in the first place. It is possible that within a contractarian state total income would be larger and would be distributed more equally. Morgan Reynolds estimated that, related to this possibility, unions secured transfer gains for their members of $70 billion in 1986 but at the same time were responsible for economic waste, due to inflexible work rules, absenteeism, strikes, and costs of bargaining and negotiation, of $126 billion.[25] While such figures are suggestive and not definitive, one cannot properly make

25. Reynolds, *Making America Poorer*, pp. 80–84, 189.

any inferences about the character of a contractarian state based on observation of the distributive properties of present institutions, for those institutions are vastly removed from those of a contractarian state. Moreover, the impact of that movement away from a contractarian state reduces the overall level of income and, by reducing the competition that people with established wealth positions face, reduces the degree of income mobility, as well as perhaps increasing the degree of income inequality.

JITNEYS, TAXICABS, AND URBAN TRANSIT

It is undeniably difficult to move about rapidly in urban areas, especially during the morning and evening rush hours. In response to this problem, public officials have pushed very hard for subsidies for various forms of mass transit. They have also designed schemes for automobile traffic, such as opening certain lanes only to vehicles with four or more passengers during rush hours. Efforts to cut down on the number of automobiles in downtown areas have involved zoning and other ordinances to limit severely the number of parking spaces that new buildings can contain. Ordinance after ordinance is added to regulation after regulation in attempts to reduce traffic congestion in urban areas. Moreover, bus and subway lines are heavily subsidized and yet generally reduce the volume of traffic only slightly.

The one option that is not tried in these policy meanderings is personal liberty within a regime of property and contract. Yet there is ample evidence that freedom of contract would mitigate many of the problems of urban traffic congestion and would do so considerably more cheaply than any other option. What true freedom of contract would mean, among other things, is open entry into the transit business, with any driver able to carry anyone else about for a mutually agreeable price. This is how jitney service once operated in the United States, and it was an effective way of coping with the bimodal peak demand for transit services.[26] This mode of transport was usually used for going downtown in the morning and back home again in the evening. Through a process of experimentation, some people began to haul others downtown and back again in a regular and predictable fashion. The drivers were picking up some change as part of their

26. See Ross D. Eckert and George W. Hilton, "The Jitneys," *Journal of Law and Economics* 15 (October 1972): 293–325.

own journey to work and also relieving traffic congestion, the need for land for parking, and the need for mass transit at public expense.

With jitney service there was less need to hire a special labor force to staff expensive capital equipment such as buses and subways, which were fully utilized only a few hours each day. Instead, the normal ebb and flow of traffic was used to provide effective and inexpensive transit service. With jitneys, moreover, fewer resources were invested in automobiles because fewer automobiles were in use. There was also a reduced need for investment in mass transit facilities. Jitney service could be reinstated if governments would lift restrictions on entry into the business of carrying passengers.

Yet it is clear that there are strong incentives for governments to enact such restrictions. The evidence that restrictions on freedom of contract provide more costly service rather than better service to customers is overwhelming. Ignorance does not explain the absence of freedom of contract. Such restrictions would seem more likely to be a result of the intent of legislation, with particular people thereby reaping significant gains. The case of taxicab regulation, which is related to that of urban transit, is instructive about the rational sources of ultimately harmful legislation.[27]

Jitney service differed little from taxi service except that freedom of contract does not generally exist in the taxi business. In most cities people cannot carry people for pay without procuring a taxi license, and those licenses are tightly restricted. When Walter E. Williams wrote in 1982, people had to pay about $60,000 for a license to drive a taxi in New York City, and recent reports have placed the price around $100,000.[28] And a similar situation exists in most other cities. Freedom of contract, in which one person can agree to carry another person between two places in exchange for an agreed-upon price, is rare. Instead, governments typically restrict the number of people who can offer such services. As a result, transit services become more expensive and also poorer in quality, because there is less competition. But who gains? Why might such legislation that clearly reduces the general welfare be enacted? The overwhelmingly one-sided conclusions of the studies on the topic would seem to rule out ignorance

27. See, for more detail on this and a number of related issues, Walter E. Williams, *The State Against Blacks* (New York: McGraw-Hill, 1982), especially pp. 75–88, the chapter entitled "The Taxicab Industry."

28. *The State Against Blacks*, p. 70.

as a reason.[29] Thus, the explanation would seem more likely to be found in someone's rational pursuit of self-interest, with the general welfare a casualty of that pursuit, as Chapter 7 will explore more fully.

RENT CONTROL

Rent control provides another illustration of the regulatory side of the welfare state. It is also one of numerous efforts to control the prices of various goods and services. Basic economic principles explain why rents, like prices in general, cannot be effectively controlled, even though the effort to do so can be understood in terms of those same principles. Rents will be determined by the willingness of renters to bid for properties in light of the available supply, and that supply will in turn be determined by the returns to investors of investing in rental property relative to investing in other things. If people are willing to pay $500 per month in light of the available supply, and if a rent control of $400 is imposed, basic economic principles say that the one thing that will *not* happen is that rents, in real as against nominal terms, will fall to $400. Rather, rent will tend to be $500 in real terms, despite the effort at rent control.

The imposition of a $400 ceiling when some people are willing to pay $500 means that those people will not be able to get housing, while others who pay only $400 will be able to do so but also may prefer $500 cash to the housing at $400. This situation is not sustainable, because its sustainability would require that people refuse to replace options they value less highly with options they value more highly. The rent control creates an incentive for people to "contract around" it because there are more people willing to rent housing at $400 than there is housing available. The ways that people contract around rent control will depend on a complex array of opportunities and constraints determined by, for instance, the technology of law enforcement and the imaginations of the participants. Regardless of the particular features of such contracting, there will be a divergence between appearance and reality; the appearance of compliance with

29. For a valuable compilation of essays on this topic, see Charles A. Lave, ed., *Urban Transit: The Private Challenge to Public Transportation* (San Francisco: Pacific Research Institute for Public Policy, 1985).

rent control will be maintained even though the reality is a higher rental price.[30]

The particular forms of contracting around that will be used depend on the efforts authorities make to close loopholes and the inventiveness of the people who want to reach a satisfactory agreement outside the rent control rules. The few illustrations given here cannot capture the range of responses people will undertake to conclude an exchange that both parties find agreeable but that legislation supposedly precludes. People could get around rent controls by subleasing properties at higher rentals, if subleases were not covered by the rent control. Alternatively, owners could require that something else be purchased as a condition of renting a property. Owners could require tenants to rent furniture from them at a price higher than they could rent it elsewhere to compensate for the lower rental. Owners could require tenants to belong to a pool and sauna club that might otherwise have been provided free of direct charge.

Another way to escape the rent control would be to reduce in various ways the quality of the rental unit to that of a $400 unit. Maintenance standards might be relaxed. Washer and dryer services might be higher priced or no longer made available. A swimming pool might no longer be heated for year-round use. Furthermore, owners might choose tenants differently so as to select those who would place relatively low demands on maintenance and facilities. This might include less willingness to rent to people with children and to groups of unrelated single people. Relatedly, apartments might be converted into condominiums. The list of illustrations could be extended indefinitely.

Basic economic principles explain why rent control can never be a means of making real rental prices lower and why rent control legislation leads generally to poorer housing within a society. At the same time, rent controls do exist in a number of places and from time to time are imposed in new places. Clearly they are not enacted out of lack of knowledge about their consequences: there has been too

---

30. The work on rent control is sizable. For a sample, see Charles W. Baird, *Rent Control: The Perennial Folly* (Washington, D.C.: Cato Institute, 1980); Joel F. Brenner and Herbert M. Franklin, *Rent Control in North America and Four European Countries* (Washington, D.C.: Potomac Institute, 1977); *Verdict on Rent Control* (London: Institute of Economic Affairs, 1972); and Steven N. S. Cheung, "Roofs or Stars: The Stated Intents and Actual Effects of a Rents Ordinance," *Economic Inquiry* 13 (March 1975): 1–21.

much scholarship on this topic for legislators to plead ignorance of the consequences of rent control, just as there has been on minimum wage and similar legislation. It is far more likely that this type of legislation has been enacted precisely because of a knowledge of their consequences or at least of certain types of consequence, as Chapter 7 will explore. A satisfactory explanation for such regulations of the welfare state as minimum wage legislation and rent controls must rest on the incentives within prevailing political institutions, incentives that revolve around the short-run gains to particular people from appropriating someone else's property for their own benefit.

THE PROBLEM OF INDUCTION AND GENERALIZATION

The preceding illustrations of the actual operation of the police or regulatory component of the welfare state could easily be expanded into a multivolume compilation. However, there would remain the task of developing the central implications of the lengthy and varied list of divergencies between the rationalizations advanced in support of the welfare state and its actual accomplishments. To a significant degree that divergence is a matter of intent, reflecting the operation of self-interest within a system of majoritarian democracy, rather than a matter of accident and unforeseeable events.

Of course, a selection of studies of the consequences of the regulatory policies of the welfare state such as those presented in this chapter cannot be the sole basis for judging the failings of the welfare state to be significant—significant in the sense that something better is attainable. Policy failures will always be present when those judgments about failure are made from historical hindsight. Even in a market system, after all, mistaken entrepreneurial choices are continually being made and rescinded. So far no exhaustive study has been made of the consequences of the regulatory and budgetary programs of the welfare state. Nonetheless, the persistence of policies that clearly run contrary to the rationalizations advanced in their support suggests that something systematic is at work. This suggestion is reinforced by the recognition that those policies are commonly advantageous to many important groups of people, such as members of the welfare bureaucracy, labor unions, or professional associations. No single empirical study can serve as the basis for making this inference, but the presence of a pattern that results from a large and growing number of such studies increases the strength of such an inference. The conceptual underpinnings of this inference will be explored in the next chapter.

In any event, comparisons of prefisc and postfisc distributions of income provide no evidence about the welfare state's impact on the distribution of income or on the creation or destruction of wealth. The prefisc distribution of income reflects the immense variety of government-imposed restrictions on competitive markets and on the ability of people to employ their talents through contractual processes. Therefore, the prefisc distribution does not represent the outcome of a contractarian state. The essential characteristics of the distributional outcome of a contractarian state must remain a matter of speculation. The extent of poverty under existing institutions gives no insight into what the extent of poverty might be in a contractarian state.

Poverty in a contractarian state, however, would not result from artificial incentives of the sort created by the present welfare state. Nor would it result through restrictions on the ability of people to exploit their talents, for in a contractarian state people could employ their talents as they chose, subject only to the normal rules of property and contract. Poverty in a contractarian state would arise either because people choose leisure over labor or because the skills they possess are valued so little by others that earnings would be low even in the presence of great effort. For the most part, the wages of common labor would represent the minimum rate of earnings, though just what the earnings of common labor would be in a contractarian state is unknown. Physical or mental handicaps would doubtlessly prevent some people from earning at the rate of common labor.

In *The Myth of Mental Illness,* Thomas S. Szasz argues, as his title suggests, that "mental illness" is mythological in character.[31] A natural extension of his perspective would raise the question of to what extent poverty would be mythical, perhaps particularly in a contractarian state without legal obstacles to the cultivation and employment of people's talents. For instance, Carolyn L. Weaver presents evidence suggesting that there was little dependency among the aged in the period before social security.[32] In New York State in 1929, nearly

---

31. Thomas S. Szasz, *The Myth of Mental Illness* (New York: Harper & Row, 1961).

32. Carolyn L. Weaver, *The Crisis in Social Security* (Durham, N.C.: Duke University Press, 1982), pp. 41–44. For further elaboration, see Carolyn L. Weaver, "Support of the Elderly before the Depression," *Cato Journal* 7 (Fall 1987): 503–25.

95 percent of people over age 65 were self-supporting. Moreover, in a number of surveys of the elderly in different cities over the 1925–1929 period, less than 10 percent were regarded by government commissions as in need of assistance. Moreover, most of the source of low standards of living among the elderly was attributed not to failures to exercise foresight but to low incomes throughout their working lives. If disability and shortsightedness are rewarded while self-reliance and farsightedness are taxed, appearances of disability and incompetence in the earning of livelihood will increase in relative significance among the population. Relatedly, Donald O. Parsons has examined how the relative increase in disability benefits under social security since the late 1960s led over the next decade to a doubling of the percentage of low-wage workers who left the labor force.[33] The number of people who truly could not provide for themselves within a contractarian state might be few indeed. In any event, the experience with the present-day combination of welfare state and neomercantilistic, restricted economy surely provides no valid evidence to the contrary.

33. Donald O. Parsons, "The Decline in Male Labor Force Participation," *Journal of Political Economy* 88 (February 1980): 117–34.

7

THE MARKET FOR LEGISLATION IN A REPUBLICAN POLITY

The developing literature on public choice has important implications for the conduct of the welfare state and indeed for the conduct of public policy in general. In most discussions of public policy, failings such as reductions in rates of saving and of labor-force participation, increases in crime and in teenage pregnancies, and increased dependence on transfer programs are treated as reflecting some combination of inadequate knowledge and unforeseeable events impinging on good intentions. The main contribution of the public choice literature has been to explain why a substantial portion of those policy failings are likely to reflect not so much inadequate knowledge as the understandable consequences of the incentives faced by participants in political processes. To the extent that this is so, those "failures" are not failures from the point of view of those people who exercise control over the policies, but instead are by-products of self-interested choices within a system of majoritarian democracy.

The character of contemporary policy is generally a product of the interplay of people rationally pursuing opportunities within a particular constitutional-institutional order, with that order serving to constrain and channel that pursuit in certain general directions. The present constitutional order is far removed from that established in the United States in 1776 and 1787. The original idea of government under law has been transformed into a system of what can be called majoritarian democracy, in which legislative majorities are essentially unconstrained in making rules for others, rather than being constrained to operate by the same rules as other persons and organizations in society.

The central characteristics of contemporary public policy in general—and that subset that is called the welfare state in particular—can be seen as a natural consequence of such a system. Indeed, the outcomes that constitute the welfare state are one nonseparable component of policy outcomes in general. Such outcomes as the reduction in labor-force participation and the increase in teenage pregnancies are inseparable from such outcomes as sugar quotas and inflation; all are part of the incentives contained within a system of unlimited or majoritarian democracy. Better public policy, therefore, is not simply a matter of generating better information about how to do better within a majoritarian polity; it also requires some degree of political reformation. This chapter sets forth the central features of the theory of majoritarian democracy; Chapter 8 examines the welfare state in light of that theory.

CONSTITUTIONAL VERSUS MAJORITARIAN DEMOCRACY

The central idea of constitutional government is that a constitution is an antecedent agreement among a set of people to constitute a government. A constitution is most clearly *not* an act of government itself. People's rights are prior and superior to particular acts of government, and those rights limit the legitimate activities of government. Therefore, as the noted constitutional scholar Charles McIlwain observed in his historical survey of thought and practice on constitutional government, "Constitutional government is by definition limited government."[1] Government is regarded and treated as but one participant or institution among many within a society. Government governs, but it governs subject to the same rules of law that apply to all other persons and institutions in society.

This idea of constitutional or limited government raises the age-old question of how government's adherence to the rule of law can be policed and maintained, if government acts both as a participant in the division of labor in society and as a referee of the propriety of

---

1. Charles H. McIlwain, *Constitutionalism: Ancient and Modern*, rev. ed. (Ithaca, N.Y.: Cornell University Press, 1947), p. 21.

the participants' actions. This dual capacity always raises the issue of whether the refereeing will be impartial or discriminatory, whether the sphere of *gubernaculum* (government) can be kept subservient to the sphere of *jurisdictio* (law). The literature on constitutional theory and history shows that the task of maintaining this subservience can be exceedingly difficult, as reflected by the recognition that "eternal vigilance is the price of liberty."

Constitutional government is at base a compact or contract among people, in which the actions of government are supposed to reflect the consent of the governed. The idea of "no taxation without representation," which was certainly one of the guiding principles in the establishment of the American republic, originally meant no taxation without the consent of the person being taxed.[2] This outlook is certainly consistent with the idea that people and their personal rights are prior and superior to acts of government and that governmental action should therefore reflect the consent of the governed.

Yet it has long been recognized that democratic government has a two-sided character. It may genuinely reflect the consent of the governed, but it can also be despotic or tyrannical, as the phrase "tyranny of the majority" suggests. Students of political theory and history have long noted that while a democratic polity may support the liberty and the prosperity of those who live within its boundaries, it also has a latent tendency to replace the promotion of the general interest in liberty and prosperity with the promotion of particularized interests, with the common interest ultimately suffering in the process. Alexander Tytler, an eighteenth-century Scottish historian, generalizing from his study of democracy in ancient Greece, summarized the process by which unlimited, majoritarian democracy erodes liberty and wealth: "A democracy cannot exist as a permanent form of government. It can only exist until a majority of voters discover that they can vote themselves largesse out of the public treasury. From that moment on, the majority always votes for the candidate who promises them the most benefits from the public treasury, with the result that democracy always collapses over a loose fiscal policy."[3]

The danger to prosperity and liberty resulting from the tax-transfer

2. See Bruno Leoni, *Freedom and the Law* (Los Angeles: Nash Publishing Co., 1961), pp. 119–20.

3. As quoted in William A. Niskanen, "The Prospect for Liberal Democracy," in James M. Buchanan and Richard E. Wagner, eds., *Fiscal Responsibility in Constitutional Democracy* (Leiden: Martinus Nijhoff, 1978), p. 159.

politics that Tytler and other scholars saw as inherent in majoritarian democracy is what James Madison described as the "violence of faction" in his famous essay, *Federalist* No. 10. As Madison noted there, "By a faction I understand a number of citizens, whether amounting to a majority or minority of the whole, who are united and actuated by some common impulse of passion, or of interest, adverse to the rights of other citizens, or to the permanent and aggregate interests of the community."[4] *Faction*, then, refers to, among other things, the ability of the members of winning coalitions to use the power of government to enrich themselves at the expense of the other members of a nation.

Italian scholars in the late nineteenth century developed two alternative models of government in their writings on public finance.[5] One model focused on the cooperative aspect of governmental actions and emphasized government as a means of providing services of common value that could not be supplied efficiently through market transactions. The other model emphasized government as a means by which those who gain control over government exploit their position at the expense of the rest of society. The Italian writers described such an alternative model in terms of ruling class or oligarchy, but democracy can also result in the exploitation of some people by others through the use of political power to abridge some people's liberty for the benefit of others.

At base there are two models or categories of democratic government. One model—cooperative, concordant, or consensual democracy—describes a system of government in which choices concerning the use of resources tend to reflect the consent of the governed. In such a system, government itself must act within the constraints created by the rules of property and contract, much as was originally envisioned by the Fifth Amendment prohibition on government's taking of property without just compensation.[6]

4. Willmore Kendall and George W. Carey, eds., *The Federalist Papers* (New Rochelle, N.Y.: Arlington House, n.d.), p. 78.

5. See the discussion in James M. Buchanan, "'La scienza delle finance': The Italian Tradition in Fiscal Theory," in his *Fiscal Theory and Political Economy* (Chapel Hill, N.C.: University of North Carolina Press, 1960), pp. 24–74.

6. For a thorough examination of the Fifth Amendment from such a constitutional perspective, see Richard A. Epstein, *Takings: Private Property and the Power of Eminent Domain* (Cambridge, Mass.: Harvard University Press, 1985). See also the essays by Roger Pilon, Gale Ann Norton, Peter H. Aranson, and Richard A. Epstein in James D. Gwartney and Richard E. Wagner, eds., *Public Choice and Constitutional Economics* (Greenwich, Conn.: JAI Press, 1988).

In the second model those choices can at most be said to reflect the consent of a dominant subset of people, which could be only a minority subset. This category of democracy has been referred to as monopolistic, discordant, or majoritarian democracy. Legislative majorities are not constrained by the rules of property and contract, but rather are able continually to abridge those rules through legislation. The two models of collective choice in democratic regimes are not so much separate alternatives as differences in degree. Concordant or consensual democracies emphasize the positive-sum aspects of collective choice. Discordant or majoritarian democracies may well undertake various programs of a positive-sum nature, but in addition they place considerable emphasis on imposing burdens on some people so as to award benefits to others.

Classifying democracies as either cooperative or monopolistic cannot be easily done by inspecting their constitutions and related features of their political systems. The presence of majority rule as a means of making certain types of collective choices does not imply the presence of what might be called majoritarian democracy, which in turn would reflect a tyranny of the majority. Majority rule is a procedure for making collective choices that can be consistent with consensual democracy, though it can also be indicative of majoritarian democracy. In consensual regimes, majority rule is a low-cost way of making collective choices, with agreement about the need for or appropriateness of making the choices in the first place. This situation is one in which people generally agree that collective action is legitimate and subsequently resort to a procedure grounded in majority rule as a cost-effective means of making that choice.

But with majoritarian democracy, there is no consensus about the need or appropriateness for collective choice in the first place. In this case, majority rule can become a means by which some people expropriate the rights and wealth of others, rather than a means by which people exploit opportunities for mutually profitable trades that could not be exploited through ordinary market transactions because of various problems relating to externalities and public goods.

There is a way in principle to test whether a particular democratic regime is consensual or majoritarian. The consensual interpretation of majority rule implies that people will on average approve of the scope of government. In some cases they may prefer government to spend and do more and in other cases to spend and do less. But those two circumstances will roughly offset each other, and on average there will be a consensus that the overall scope and size of government are appropriate. No one will systematically support either expansions or contractions in the general range of governmental activities. By contrast, the presence of significant numbers of people who support either general expansions or contractions indicates that government is more majoritarian than consensual.

MAJORITARIAN DEMOCRACY AS REPUBLICAN DISEASE

In contrast to a system of consensual or concordant democracy, the majoritarian polity does not operate under the constraints of the rules of property and contract. In a system of majoritarian democracy, the members of winning coalitions are able to infringe upon the rights of others. This happens when a winning majority shifts much of the cost of the programs it favors onto nonsupporters, as well as when it uses government's police powers to benefit some people at the expense of others—for instance, by abridging and redefining rights of property. As a result, programs that shift resources from more valued to less valued uses can nonetheless be adopted through democratic processes.

Recent scholarship in public choice, stemming from the seminal work of James Buchanan and Gordon Tullock, has extended and deepened our knowledge of the operation of majority rule, reaffirming in the process the insights of Alexander Tytler and James Madison.[7] One of the major features of factional or majoritarian democracy is the use of government as a vehicle for transferring wealth. Government becomes an arena in which contending factions try to form winning coalitions in a competition to be net recipients of transfers. One result is an increase in the size of government, with this increase reflecting the transfer activities of government.

Those transfers are also accompanied by the imposition of even larger net costs on the remainder of the citizenry. A simple illustration will make this point. Suppose an entrepreneur, thinking that a nearby lake offers valuable opportunities for recreation and camping, proceeds to assemble the necessary resources—the land, utility hookups, boats, water slides, and so on. All of these resources could have been

---

7. James M. Buchanan and Gordon Tullock, *The Calculus of Consent* (Ann Arbor, Mich.: University of Michigan Press, 1962).

used in different employments, but the entrepreneur has, by outbidding other possible users, chosen to commit them to camping and water-oriented amusement. If the entrepreneur is correct in his judgment that this use of resources will be profitable, he will have succeeded in shifting resources from less valued to more valued uses, thereby making the other members of society better off at the same time he becomes wealthier. Should the entrepreneur's choice prove wrong and he takes a loss, the entrepreneur's use of resources will generate services of lesser value than some other employment could have yielded, and the other members of society will be worse off because of the entrepreneur's error. It is in no one's power to guarantee that a particular use of resources will prove profitable—that is, that it will shift resources from less valued to more valued uses. However, the existence of residual claimancy or profit and loss does serve to concentrate the entrepreneur's attention on his choices more strongly than if he did not bear this responsibility.

An entrepreneur's choice of the kind of facility to create depends on his judgment about how willing people will be to pay for different types or sizes of facilities. The more he thinks they are willing to pay, the larger the investment that will seem warranted. Suppose it turns out that people will support a 200-acre facility, but not one of 400 acres; this means that users will not be willing to contribute in admission fees enough to bid away the resources required for the second 200 acres from others who would choose to employ those resources differently. The creation of the 200-acre facility where none had existed before would represent a value-enhancing shift of resources, but the creation of a 400-acre facility in place of the 200-acre facility would represent a value-diminishing shift in the use of resources.

Suppose, however, that an external party offered to pay 40 percent of the admission fee so that a $5 ticket could be bought for $3. Under this arrangement, the greater use of the facility might justify a 400-acre facility. But where does the $2 subsidy come from? Within a system of majoritarian democracy, it can come from nonusers of the facility. Assume for purposes of illustration that 60 percent of the population enjoys camping and water-related recreation, while the other 40 percent has little, if any, use for such activities. Further assume, to simplify the illustration, that the average income is the same for both categories of people. This simplification means that if government is financed by an income tax, the users will pay 60 percent and the nonusers will pay 40 percent of the funds budgeted for the facility.

In this case, users are receiving a 40 percent subsidy from the taxes paid by nonusers. The 60 percent majority is able to place 40 percent of the cost of the facility upon the minority. In such a situation it is easy to understand why the winning coalition on the issue of how much campground and park to provide will choose a larger facility than if its members had to bear the full cost themselves. As compared with a 200-acre facility, the 400-acre facility represents a shift of resources from more valued to less valued uses. But there is no entrepreneur who loses wealth as a result of making the choice to commit resources to the larger facility, because the loss of wealth is diffused over the nonuser minority of taxpayers whose tax payments to finance the facility exceed the value they place on the facility.

Majoritarian democracy leads to an increase in the size of government, because this increased size reflects the transfers of wealth that take place between the winners from a particular legislative enactment and the losers. If campgrounds are paid for fully by those who use them, people might use them an average of, say, ten days per year. But if part of that cost can be put off on others who do not use them, the fall in price to the users will mean that the average use will exceed ten days per year. When a winning coalition of campground users is able to secure governmental subsidies through its ability to impose taxes on others, there will be a greater investment in campgrounds than if users had to pay the full cost of their use.

There is, of course, nothing exceptional about the proposition that beneficiaries will choose a larger project when they can impose part of the cost on others than when they have to bear the full cost themselves. At first glance, however, such transfers in a system of majoritarian democracy might seem to represent just that—that is, *transfers* of wealth and not erosions or destructions of wealth—because the winners become wealthier precisely to the extent that the losers become poorer. However, these transfers destroy wealth in several ways. They reduce the gains, both to the winners and to the losers, from the productive employment of their labor and capital. As working and saving become taxed more heavily, the reward for such productive activity is lessened. At the same time, it becomes relatively more rewarding to people to pursue wealth by engaging in a political search for transfers through government's budget and police powers than by engaging in productive activity. All of the resources invested in such activities reflect a cost of a type of civil warfare. These resources could otherwise be turned to productive use, were it not for the individually productive, though socially wasteful, incentives to engage in transfer-seeking activity under a system of majoritarian or factional democracy.[8]

Moreover, democracy is an ongoing process characterized by logrolling on issues. People who win on the campground issue will lose on other issues. A person who secures a subsidy on campgrounds may live in an area where flooding is no threat and so may lose on flood control subsidies. In general, people who are recipients of subsidies on some issues will be providers of subsidies on other issues. It would be a mistake, however, to think that the wins and losses cancel out, thereby negating the excessive expansion in the size of government. The income effects do cancel out; there is no general increase in income that leads people to desire more government services. But there remains a substitution effect that lowers the relative price of government services and that is responsible for the general expansion in the size of government.

A related situation will illustrate the point. Instead of the guests in a restaurant each paying their own checks for their individual orders, suppose the bills of all the guests are aggregated, and each then pays an equal share of the total. Normally, someone who chooses an entrée of beef Wellington for $30 over one of broiled red snapper with shrimp and crabmeat stuffing for $20 will pay the extra cost of $10. But if the aggregate bill is to be divided evenly among 100 guests, the cost to the person ordering the more expensive entrée is only $0.10—$10 divided by 100 people. In this setting, the total amount that people spend will exceed what they would choose to spend if they were each responsible for their own orders. Under a regime of individual responsibility, people may tend to order the two entrées with equal

---

8. For careful surveys of the literature on rent seeking and legislation, see Robert D. Tollison, "Rent Seeking: A Survey," *Kyklos* 35 (No. 4, 1982): 575–602; and Robert D. Tollison, "Public Choice and Legislation," *Virginia Law Review* 74 (March 1988): 339–71. For a historical examination of the growth of the rent-seeking majoritarian polity, see Terry L. Anderson and Peter J. Hill, *The Birth of a Transfer Society* (Stanford, Calif.: Hoover Institution Press, 1980). For a wide-ranging survey of pertinent scholarship on majoritarian democracy, see William C. Mitchell, "Fiscal Behavior in the Modern Democratic State: Public-Choice Perspectives and Contributions," in Larry L. Wade, ed., *Political Economy: Recent Views* (Boston: Kluwer-Nijhoff, 1983), pp. 69–114.

frequency. But under collective responsibility they will increase the frequency with which they order beef Wellington, say to 80 percent. On any given night, those who order the red snapper will be subsidizing those who order the beef Wellington, for all will pay a $28 bill.

However, to maintain the governmental analogy, suppose the guests are compelled to return to the restaurant night after night. On any particular night some of the people who ordered red snapper the night before will order beef Wellington, and vice versa. As this process continues, there will be no systematic losers or winners if everyone orders beef Wellington 80 percent of the time. Everyone would, in this case, pay $28 per meal. Yet, over time, the total amount that it would cost those people to eat would exceed what it would have cost them had people individually been responsible for their own choices. Each would have preferred the 50–50 mixture at an average cost of $25, but they end up paying $28 for the 80–20 mixture. And just as the growth in the costliness of dining out is a natural response to changing from a system of private to collective choice, so the growth in government more generally, including the subset of programs that constitute the welfare state, is a response to a system of majoritarian democracy.

One of the most trenchant summarizations of the essential conclusions of the theory of majoritarian democracy that has emerged from the scholarly literature on public choice was offered, from a different point of departure, by the noted French theologian, Jacques Ellul.

For most men today the involvement which is most useful and which best expresses Christian freedom, is involvement in anarchy . . . What leads me in this direction is the constitution and development of the modern state. All specialists agree that we now have to speak of the nation state, i.e. the state which absorbs into itself the entire life of the nation. They also agree that the state is . . . authoritarian, even when democratic. It is arbitrary, for no state observes rules and constitutions. It is universal. . . . It knows neither limit nor humanity. . . . The state in any country, no matter what may be its form, whether democratic or dictatorial, new or popular, is in fact the chief danger known to man, whether from the material standpoint or from the spiritual standpoint. . . . Every modern state is totalitarian. It recognizes no limit either factual or legal. This is why I maintain that no state in the modern world is legitimate. However, I do not believe that it is possible to destroy the modern state. It is pure imagination to think that some day this power will be overthrown. . . . Furthermore, I do not believe that anarchist doctrine is the solution to the problem of organization in society and government. I do not think that if anarchism were to succeed we should have a better or more livable society. . . . On the other hand, it seems to me that an anarchist attitude is the only one that is sufficiently radical in face of a general statist system.[9]

It might be worthwhile, before continuing further, to reconsider some of the strictures made earlier about the difficulty of distinguishing between majority rule as a cost-effective means of reaching collective choices in a consensual democracy and majority rule as an instrument of majoritarian democracy.

If people generally had similar preferences for parks, the use of majority rule might be a cost-effective method of reaching a concrete choice on how much to spend. People would then be choosing to pledge part of their wealth to support the expenditure on parks that the collectivity then makes by majority rule. But this consensual interpretation implies that people who might have preferred less spending on parks will prefer more spending on other items, such as schools. It also implies that the overall, aggregate outcome would be that people would have no systematic desire to support either general increases or general decreases in the size of government. Nor would they have any systematic disagreement about what was the appropriate scope or range of governmental activities.

The presence of systematic disagreement among people over whether the range of collective activities is appropriate or legitimate and the aggregate size of government is desirable means that the models of majoritarian democracy do have explanatory significance. Expansion in the size of government is the means by which wealth transfers take place between the members of winning and losing coalitions.[10] The winning majority will tend to receive a dominant share of the benefits of the spending programs it enacts, while the minority will bear

9. Jacques Ellul, *The Ethics of Freedom*, trans. by Geoffrey W. Bromiley (Grand Rapids, Mich.: William B. Eerdmans, 1976), pp. 395–97, as quoted in Richard E. Wagner, "Christianity and the Problem of Political Economy," in Ronald W. Hansen, ed., *Economics, Theology, and the Social Order* (Rochester, N.Y.: Center for Research in Government Policy and Business, University of Rochester, 1986), pp. 23–45.

10. For an exposition, along with supporting evidence, of the thesis that politicians are essentially brokers in this wealth transfer process, see Robert E. McCormick and Robert D. Tollison, *Politicians, Legislation, and the Economy* (Boston: Martinus Nijhoff, 1981).

most of the taxes. The illustration of the campground and park has general validity as an illustration of majoritarian democracy, particularly when this illustration is combined with revolving majorities through logrolling.

Majoritarian democracy must be distinguished from a system of government that uses majority voting but is constrained by a rule of law. Under a rule of law, government cannot modify rights of ownership but can act only within the basic confines of those rights as one participant among many in society. Within a system of majoritarian democracy, however, government is able to change these relationships without the consent of the affected parties; government is not constrained by the same rules of law as are individual citizens, but rather it makes those rules of law to which others must conform.

MAJORITARIAN DEMOCRACY AND MINORITY DOMINANCE

Madison's apprehension about faction within a system of majoritarian democracy reflected a concern with what Alexis de Tocqueville in *Democracy in America* labeled the "tyranny of the majority." Madison was not worried about a possible tyranny of the minority, because he assumed that it would be prevented by majority voting. The problem he wrestled with in his essays in the *Federalist* was how to prevent majority tyranny.[11] One of the major developments of the newly emerging literature on political economy and public choice has been an understanding of some of the ways minority factions, a tyranny of the minority, can be successful within systems based on majority voting.

Within a system of representative democracy, how much support is required to enact legislation? The support of a majority within a legislature need not imply the support of a majority within the population at large. It is possible for the support of as little as one-quarter of the citizenry to translate into a legislative majority. All that is required is a bare majority of supporters in a bare majority of districts. Minority factions can thus secure legislative majorities.

To illustrate this point, suppose the population of the nation falls

11. For a careful treatment of the *Federalist* from a public choice perspective, see Vincent Ostrom, *The Political Theory of a Compound Republic*, 2d. ed. (Lincoln, Neb.: University of Nebraska Press, 1987).

into two categories. A little more than one-quarter of the population is employed by producers of products for which prices are higher than average; wages are also higher than average. A little less than three-quarters of the population is employed by producers of products for which prices are lower than average; wages are also lower than average. To some extent there is competition between the two types of producers, as once existed between high-cost textile plants in the Northeast and low-cost textile manufacturers in the South. Suppose the high-priced producers and their associated labor are located so that they comprise a slim majority in 218 of the 435 congressional districts, as well as in 26 of the 50 states, and are found hardly at all in the other congressional districts and states.

A legislative proposal that established a minimum wage somewhat higher than the wage presently being paid by the low-cost producers would be able to secure majority support. Such legislation would increase the prices of the products produced by the low-cost producers and would reduce employment among those producers. The legislation would not affect the cost of labor to the high-cost producers. Thus, the differential in price between the high-cost and the low-cost producers would narrow, which would shift some business from the low-cost to the high-cost producers. Wealth would be transferred from the comparatively low-priced producers and labor, who constitute nearly three-quarters of the population, to the comparatively high-priced producers and labor, who are little more than one-quarter of the population.

Furthermore, through logrolling, legislation supported by a minority of people in a minority of legislative districts can still be enacted within a system of majoritarian democracy. Suppose there are three bills: A, B, and C, each of which imposes costs on the majority for the benefit of a minority. If each bill were considered independently, as through a referendum, each would fail. But with logrolling they can all pass. Those who want A passed can agree to support B, in exchange for support of A; moreover, the supply of potential bills can be expanded indefinitely. Through logrolling, minority dominance can emerge within a majoritarian democracy.

Majority rule is no guarantee against a tyranny of the minority. Contemporary scholarship has developed an understanding of how some significant asymmetries operate within prevailing political processes. These include asymmetries in the locus of the costs and benefits of government programs and in the knowledge held by the gainers and losers of public programs. If the benefits of a program are more concentrated than the costs, the gainers will have a stronger incentive to support the program than the losers will have to oppose it. The loss to the low-wage workers might be $100 on average, which implies an average gain to the high-wage workers of nearly $300. The concentrated gains will generally offer stronger incentives to action than will the diffused losses. At the same time, the beneficiaries can be more easily convinced of the benefits they will get from the program than the losers can be convinced of the costs they will bear.

The average gain to domestic automobile producers from a limitation on Japanese imports will be considerably larger than the average loss to the other members of society. A 10 percent increase in the price of automobiles will yield a 10 percent increase in income for producers, but the increase in the cost of living for consumers will be much less. How much less depends on the relative importance of automobile expenses in a consumer's budget. If this share is 10 percent, the 10 percent rise in price will translate into only a 1 percent increase in the consumer's cost of living. And since the incentive to learn about something varies directly with the gain from doing so, it will be easier to cultivate the support of those who will gain from such legislation than that of those who will be harmed, even though the aggregate amount of loss to consumers may substantially exceed the gain to producers. It is surely easier to get a mule's attention with one swat of a two-by-four than with 1,000 swats of a long toothpick, even though those 1,000 toothpicks contain more wood than a single two-by-four.

The creation of an egg marketing board may transfer $50,000 to each of 1,000 growers.[12] But the $50 million loss suffered by the general public will impose a per-capita loss of only $5 in a state with 10 million people. People must invest some effort in finding out enough about the issue to reach this determination. It may not be worthwhile for many people to make that effort when the stakes are relatively small. Even if someone were to invest sufficient effort to acquire knowledge about the loss to consumers from the creation of an egg marketing board, it would be impossible to prevent the loss without

---

12. On this topic, see Thomas E. Borcherding and Gary W. Dorosh, *The Egg Marketing Board* (Vancouver, British Columbia: Fraser Institute, 1981).

convincing a sufficient number of other people of the loss. Unless people have a concentrated interest in proposed legislation, it is rational for them to know less about its cost than they would about the cost of private options from which they would gain directly. Consequently, legislators will generally gain little in trying to oppose such programs as the creation of egg marketing boards, because it will be difficult at best for them to convince their constituents that they would gain from such opposition. Majoritarian democracy can suffer from a dominance of a minority on any particular issue when the minority's interest is relatively intense (for instance, involving heavy subsidies per capita) and the majority's interest is relatively weak (for instance, involving much lower tax losses per capita).

Furthermore, so long as legislators tend not to oppose bills for which there is no organized opposition and interest groups allocate their resources more effectively to secure passage of the bills they desire than to secure the defeat of the bills that others desire, such special or minority interests will tend to dominate legislative outcomes. William A. Niskanen argues that existing political processes do not reflect the general interest of the citizenry because representatives and citizens face a difference in incentives: representatives bear most of the costs of reaching decisions, but citizens bear most of the external costs of those decisions.[13] Consequently, Congress will adopt voting rules and parliamentary procedures that promote minority rule as a by-product of its efforts to economize on the costs of decision making that its members bear. Related to this bias within legislatures is the fact that the costliness of political participation adds to the control of the bureaucracy over budgetary outcomes.[14] Both the bureaucracy and the legislature generally will be biased toward an expansion in the size of government, because this expansion is the vehicle by which wealth is transferred from losers to winners—notwithstanding the wealth that is dissipated in the process.

The asymmetries that have been noted here are all reflections of the one fundamental asymmetry that inheres in the absence of a quid

---

13. William A. Niskanen, "The Pathology of Politics," in Richard T. Selden, ed., *Capitalism and Freedom: Problems and Prospects* (Charlottesville, Va.: University Press of Virginia, 1974), pp. 20–35.

14. See, for instance, Robert J. Mackay and Carolyn L. Weaver, "Monopoly Bureaus and Fiscal Outcomes," in Gordon Tullock and Richard E. Wagner, eds., *Policy Analysis and Deductive Reasoning* (Lexington, Mass.: D. C. Heath, 1978), pp. 141–65.

pro quo relationship between the claims government places on citizens and the services it renders in return. The negative-sum expansion of government becomes possible and actually results, because there is no contractual relationship between government and individual citizens. Those people who have no use for the campground and park must pay for it anyway, and those who would like to use it can do so—to the extent they are able to place the cost on others—without paying for it. One important incentive that characterizes majoritarian democracy is the incentive to design policies that take from some citizens to give to others, with wealth being dissipated in the process. The contemporary literature on public choice has added new insights to our understanding of majoritarian democracy. The central principles of its operation have, of course, been known for ages.

LEGISLATION AND THE MARKET FOR PUBLIC POLICY

The production of public policy, including those policies that constitute the welfare state, clearly has economic aspects; the production of legislation can be examined in terms of the categories of demand and supply. Some people desire various types of policies, and other people are in the business of producing those policies. What results is a "market" for legislation or public policy.

Some legislation may be demanded by all or most citizens, while other legislation may be demanded by only a few. Instances of universal or general demand correspond to the common descriptions of the theory of public goods. A desire to be free from attack by a foreign nation is surely one instance of such a demand, and a desire to be free from attack by a member of one's own nation is another. One portion of the market for legislation relates to the provision of such common or general demands.

Other legislation deals with the provision of the specific wants of a subset of citizens, with the satisfaction of those wants often coming at the expense of the remainder of the citizenry. In this case, legislation is not so much a means of increasing the general level of well-being as it is of transferring income or wealth from some people to others. Sometimes those who benefit in this process of transferring (as contrasted with creating) wealth may constitute a majority of the citizenry, as a literal interpretation of the notion of majoritarian democracy might suggest. At other times they may constitute only a minority. In both cases the legislation provides gains to only a subset of citizens and not to all citizens, although the cost of that legislation may be borne by all taxpayers. If the residents of an area threatened by flooding are able to secure legislation that provides for a flood control project, paid for by people who do not live in the floodplain, then the residents of the floodplain gain at the expense of the remainder of the citizenry. And because of this lowered cost to beneficiaries of the project, they will choose a larger investment in flood control than they would choose if they had to bear the full cost themselves. An important feature of this large class of legislation is its ability to transfer wealth from the general citizenry to groups whose demands are satisfied by the legislation.

Demand for Legislation

Some central features of the demand for legislation for transfer-seeking purposes can be explored by reconsidering the gains made by a set of producers from forming a cartel. Although producers gain from the higher prices that come with agreeing not to compete, the cartels' inherent contradiction causes them to break down. To sustain the rise in price, the members of the cartel must all restrict their output so that the sum of the outputs of the individual producers equals what a monopolist would produce. However, any single member of that cartel would do even better by chiseling on that cartel agreement; by slightly lowering its price to undercut the cartel, any single member can increase its sales and profits.

Such a cartel arrangement would be inherently unstable. For example, suppose there were 1,000 producers of eggs in a market, each producing 100 dozen eggs per day at a price of $1 per dozen. Industry output is 100,000 dozen eggs daily at a revenue of $100,000 daily. Suppose, if a cartel could be formed, it would cut output by 30 percent, to 70,000 dozen eggs daily. At this lower output, suppose the price rises to $1.42 per dozen, a price that keeps total revenue unchanged at $100,000 per day. Although revenue is unchanged, total cost of production is lower because output is lower. Suppose that cost fell by $30,000. This drop in cost would indicate the increased profit created by the cartel. In the simplest case, this cartel outcome would be achieved by having each producer reduce output by 30 percent to

70 dozen eggs daily.[15] Each producer is now making a cartel-created profit of $0.42 per dozen when eggs are sold for $1.42. But by selling more than 70 dozen eggs, which might be done by lowering the price to $1.40, any single firm could increase its profits still further. The very incentive that led to the formation of the cartel, the search for profit, also makes the cartel an unstable arrangement, because the members have an incentive to cheat. Moreover, the cartel produces incentives for newcomers to enter the industry. Since they have not agreed to the terms of the cartel, they are free to offer a lower price.

Successful, sustained cartels require acts of public policy to create an enforcement agency. Such legislation is valuable to the members of the industry. What would be the gains to the egg producers from the creation of an egg marketing board that regulated the production and sale of eggs? For the members of the cartel, the gain would be $30,000 per day, or $30 per day per producer and about $11,000 per producer per year. Each egg producer gains $11,000 per year from an effective cartel, which requires an act of legislation. The opportunity to capture this gain is one source of the demand for legislation.

Supply of Legislation

Legislation is utility- or wealth-enhancing—sometimes for citizens generally and sometimes for only a subset of the citizenry. The gain to one subset may come at the expense of the rest of the polity, as when consumers pay higher prices for eggs because legislation creates a monopoly over what would otherwise be the competitive provision of eggs. The supply of legislation, like the supply of any product or service, can be understood largely in terms of its ability to yield a return to the suppliers. Political parties and the individual legislators the parties comprise are suppliers of legislation, and they receive returns from their activities as suppliers. Political parties supply their members to legislatures, and those members, as legislators, supply legislation to the citizenry.

The individual politicians who belong to a party and a legislature have much in common with the individual members of a business

---

15. "Simplest case" means constant costs of production. With U-shaped cost conditions, the cartel would close down 30 percent of its plants, for otherwise it would not produce its output in the least costly manner.

partnership.[16] As with partnerships, some of the legislators are senior to others and more influential within the party and the legislature. The electoral system provides the rules by which someone becomes a partner—that is, joins the legislature as a member of a particular party. In the United States, legislators are distributed according to geography, and the legislator for some designated geographical territory is elected by the people who live in that territory.

The returns to legislators from being elected can have many dimensions. Some of these are directly pecuniary, as are basic salary, expense allowances, and bribes. Others are less directly pecuniary, such as business for a law firm in which a legislator is a partner or the enhanced value of postlegislative employment in a business that has extensive dealings with government. Other returns are nonpecuniary—for instance, a fascination with politics and the use of power, or a sense of vocation in helping people deal with problems. The reasons legislators run for office are not important here, any more than with the reasons accountants or lawyers choose their professions. Regardless of reasons or motivation, all of them will be engaged, to a large extent, in satisfying or supplying the demands of their clients.

A legislator must be involved in producing legislation that clients wish to have, or he or she will find it difficult to continue being a legislator. The relationship between legislators and clients is not, of course, a formal one, like the relationship between accountants or lawyers and their clients. Nonetheless, legislators are also in the business of promoting the interests of their clients. Legislators get elected because a sufficient number of people in their geographical territories think they will best serve their interests. Legislators must maintain this support to get reelected, which means they must follow through in promoting the interest of a sufficient number of their constituents more effectively than those constituents think some alternative candidate would do.

The market for legislation operates, for the most part, tacitly rather than explicitly. Those who gain from the legislation will "buy" it from "sellers," but there is generally no open market for votes on various pieces of legislation. The tacit nature of the market for legislation does not deny that those who gain from individual pieces of

16. See, for instance, Arleen Leibowitz and Robert Tollison, "A Theory of Legislative Organization: Making the Most of Your Majority," *Quarterly Journal of Economics* 94 (March 1980): 261–77.

legislation dissipate part of their gains by making payments to suppliers. Rather it suggests that the payments take such tacit forms as campaign contributions, support of favored causes, the use of particular law firms, and the like.

To speak of a market for legislation is not to deny that legislation may reflect a concern with promoting the general welfare. It does suggest, though, that a substantial component of legislation can be understood as serving special interests, even if this is to the detriment of the general interest. The survival value of such legislation can be understood in terms of the pattern of costs and gains produced by a system of majoritarian democracy.

THE WELFARE STATE AND THE MARKET FOR LEGISLATION

The activities of the welfare state can be examined from within the purview of the economic theory of legislation. This theory treats public policy outcomes as resulting from the rational pursuit by legislators and bureaucrats of their self-interest, as this interest is channeled through a particular set of institutional constraints. As seen from this perspective, the governmental programs represented by the welfare state grow, at least in part, because this growth facilitates a transfer of wealth to the members of a winning coalition. Those transfers are accompanied by the imposition of even larger costs on the remainder of the population.

As noted earlier, minimum wage legislation clearly illustrates both the wealth-transfer outcomes of majoritarian democracy and dissonance between justifications for the welfare state and the welfare state's actual accomplishments. Intent seems a more plausible explanation for such outcomes than does ignorance. Furthermore, the conjunction of minimum wage legislation and Aid to Families with Dependent Children (AFDC), as examined by Keith B. Leffler in the study discussed in Chapter 6, is a particularly instructive illustration of the political economy of the welfare state, for its description of logrolling shows that many outcomes are understandable in terms of a set of policies even though they may not be understandable individually.[17]

As noted in Chapter 6, minimum wage legislation fits sensibly within

---

17. Keith B. Leffler, "Minimum Wages, Welfare, and Wealth Transfers to the Poor," *Journal of Law and Economics* 21 (October 1978): 345–58.

the emerging economic theory of legislation, in that it aids some people and harms others. The harm is often concentrated on the poor, the group that welfare state rationalizations portray as the beneficiary of the minimum wage. For instance, minimum wages have significant differential effects among adults, as Peter Linneman's work on this topic demonstrates.[18] Linneman found significant differences in the impact of minimum wage legislation among different categories of adults. Men gained and women lost: 76 percent of white men gained and 62 percent of black men gained; 72 percent of black women lost and 73 percent of white women lost. Union membership made a difference: 85 percent of union members gained while 56 percent of nonmembers lost. For the 10 percent of the general population that Linneman estimated as the subminimum population, 69 percent lost from the minimum wage. In contrast, 52 percent of the wealthier remainder of the population gained through imposition of the minimum wage.

Taken by itself, minimum wage legislation clearly harms the poor on average; it represents a transfer of income from people with lower to people with higher incomes, along with the other types of transfers noted above. But legislators from low-income districts generally support minimum wage legislation. This might seem anomalous, except that, as Leffler has shown, those who are rendered employed by minimum wage legislation do not lose income. They lose wage income, but that loss is replaced by transfers from such programs as AFDC. The welfare state, at least in this instance, demonstrates certain features that are apprehensible within the framework of the economic theory of legislation. Minimum wage legislation in conjunction with AFDC, for instance, represents a coalition of high-cost industries and labor along with certain segments of the low-wage population. By reducing the rate of accumulation of human capital through diminishing the ability of people to acquire initial job experience, minimum wage legislation reduces the lifetime earnings of the recipients of the offsetting transfers, though it may not reduce their lifetime consumption. It does, however, clearly promote transgenerational welfare dependency.

A welfare state that discourages work and capital accumulation and

---

18. Peter Linneman, "The Economic Impacts of Minimum Wage Laws: A New Look at an Old Question," *Journal of Political Economy* 90 (June 1982): 443–69.

encourages instead the reliance on transfer payments for support complements transfer-seeking legislation that also tries to maintain the value of particular investments in human and physical capital by seeking to curtail sources of competition. Any creation of an entitlement or sheltered status concomitantly entails either a limitation on the ability of someone else to earn a livelihood or a taking of some of the results of previous effort. If the position of high-cost garment manufacturers is sheltered by legislation that prevents people from manufacturing garments in their homes for sale, the ability of other people to earn a livelihood, in this case by sewing, is impaired. Alternatively, because of regulations sheltering existing owners of taxis, others who might be willing to support themselves by driving people around town are prevented from doing so. Similarly, minimum wage legislation, in conjunction with child labor laws and restrictions on apprenticeship, serves to reduce the options available to people who lack the interest or ability to prepare for various professional and white-collar careers. The licensing required in more than 1,000 occupations also has the effect of foreclosing options.[19] Moreover, if some people are entitled to food, shelter, and medical care without payment, others must be compelled to work to provide those services; the factor market equivalent of the awarding of entitlements in the product market is, after all, duressed or servile labor.

19. On the proliferation of occupational licensing, see Janet Kiholm Smith, "Production of Licensing Legislation: An Economic Analysis of Interstate Differences," *Journal of Legal Studies* 11 (January 1982): 117–37.

8

THE TRANSFER SOCIETY AND THE WELFARE STATE

To the extent that the creation and implementation of public policy follows an economic logic, the legislative creation and the bureaucratic implementation of public policies can be understood within the framework of economic analysis. An important basis for this understanding is the recognition that people's motivations are fundamentally the same regardless of the type of public policy with which they are concerned.[1] People are the same whether they are producing the policies that constitute the welfare state or approving pork-barrel projects. It makes little sense to say that while transfer seeking might manifest itself in agricultural marketing orders, charity comes to the fore in the programs that constitute the welfare state. All policy outcomes are a product of the interaction of people who are pursuing their diverse interests, and that interaction is shaped and constrained by the opportunities offered and limitations imposed by a particular institutional-constitutional order.

Within a system of essentially unlimited, majoritarian democracy, legislative majorities are able to award entitlements and impose restrictions as they choose. The legislature is not bound by the rules of property and contract in relating to the other members of society.

1. For a clear statement of this universality, see William H. Meckling, "Values and the Choice of the Model of the Individual in the Social Sciences," *Schweizerische Zeitschrift fuer Volkswirtschaft und Statistik* 112 (December 1976): 545–60.

Because it is outside of or beyond those rules, it is able to amend them as it chooses. If the legislature wants to gain control of someone's property or just wants to restrict its use, it does not have to buy that property or purchase some form of easement; it can simply take the property through eminent domain or restrict its use through zoning, announcing some public purpose in the process. Likewise, if the legislature wants to provide food and shelter to someone, it can compel, through taxation, other people to labor to provide that food and shelter. The legislature can tell potential landlords and tenants that they cannot make a contract that calls for a price above some amount. The legislature can prohibit potential employers and employees from contracting for services at less than some hourly rate or on a piece rate basis or for work to be done at home. The outcomes of the welfare state are but a subset of the outcomes of a system of unlimited, majoritarian democracy, under which in myriad ways competition can be, in effect, a tort. The forces at work in producing the outcomes that constitute the welfare state are the same that are at work in producing all of the other regulatory and budgetary activities of government.

TRANSFER SEEKING IN THE WELFARE STATE

It is conventional to view the transfer programs of the welfare state, as well as other governmental programs, in a partial equilibrium context, so that a policy market is examined in isolation from other policy markets. Educational policies are viewed independently from agricultural policies, which are viewed independently from housing policies, and so on. This approach leads naturally toward a tendency to view the programs of the welfare state as reflections of charitable interests, whereas other governmental programs are viewed as reflecting the operation of self-interest. Yet it is well recognized by economists that many conclusions from partial equilibrium analysis do not hold up under general equilibrium analysis. For instance, an excise tax on a single product may increase the price of that product, but an excise tax applied to all products—a sales tax—will not increase the prices of all products but rather will lower the incomes that producers receive for their services.[2]

---

2. See the discussion in Peter Mieszkowski, "On the Theory of Tax Incidence," *Journal of Political Economy* 75 (June 1967): 250–62.

In similar fashion, a general equilibrium perspective on the collective choice of policy measures leads to a recognition that one policy cannot be examined independently of other policies. All programs and policies are produced by the same legislative institutions operating under the same constitutional rules. The mix of legislation that maximizes the value to a controlling set of politicians will be adjusted to equalize support at the margin from different programs. While people may be charitable, Gordon Tullock is surely correct in observing that they are not massively charitable.[3] This observation in conjunction with a general equilibrium perspective on legislation would suggest that the welfare state does not reflect the operation of the charitable side of human nature, while people revert to their normal selves when considering other governmental activities, such as military spending, highway construction, and safety regulation.

The central characteristics of contemporary public policy in general—and that subset that is called the welfare state in particular—are a natural and inescapable consequence of a system of majoritarian democracy. Under that system legislative majorities are essentially unconstrained in making rules for others, rather than being constrained to operate by the same rules as all other persons and organizations in society.[4] A system of unlimited or majoritarian democracy produces a wide variety of wealth transfers, some of which are the programs constituting the welfare state. Those programs arise out of a particular political system, through the operation of the incentives contained in that system.

It is misleading to assess the welfare state without considering whatever else is produced by the same constitutional framework, so it is inappropriate to assess transfer programs by looking only at that subset of programs commonly referred to as the welfare state. Those programs are produced not in isolation but as part of a process that produces all the other programs as well. The outcomes that constitute the welfare state are simply one inseparable component of policy outcomes in general; the reduction in labor-force participation and

3. Gordon Tullock, "The Charity of the Uncharitable," *Economic Inquiry* 9 (December 1971): 379–92.

4. The theme that legislative majorities are essentially unconstrained is developed with respect to taxation in Gale Anne Norton, "The Limitless Federal Taxing Power," *Harvard Journal of Law and Public Policy* 8 (No. 3, 1985): 591–625; reprinted in James D. Gwartney and Richard E. Wagner, eds., *Public Choice and Constitutional Economics* (Greenwich, Conn.: JAI Press, 1988), pp. 253–84.

the increase in teenage pregnancies are produced by the same forces that fill caves with cheese and milk—all are products of the incentives contained within a system of unlimited or transfer-seeking democracy.

The theory of transfer seeking or rent seeking has explained how a wide variety of regulations and market restrictions are a natural outcome of majoritarian democracy.[5] These restrictions arise as part of a process in which legislation is sold to highest bidders. The rules by which this is done tend to give strong survival value to outcomes that diminish the average level of wealth as a by-product of transferring wealth to the subset of people favored by that legislation. The outcome is an economy riddled with protection, which is also an economy filled with obstacles and encumbrances to people's employment of their talents. After all, a protected position for one person must be an obstacle to improvement for someone else.

Transfer seeking will be present even if the only item for collective choice is the size of the public assistance budget; but when there are many items subject to collective choice, opportunities for the further pursuit of transfer seeking will also arise through logrolling. In this more complex setting, classifying people as either net taxpayers or recipients is not sufficient for a thorough analysis of transfer seeking. Some taxpayers may also own long-established industrial enterprises that are losing their position of prominence due to some combination of high production costs and strong foreign competition. Other taxpayers may own relatively new, high-technology enterprises and may find themselves highly competitive in international markets.

Those taxpayers who are losing out may be able in a number of ways to strengthen their position at the expense of the taxpayers who are in the more progressive industries. One way might be developing tax provisions that shift the tax burden from the older to the newer enterprises—for instance, by giving more favorable tax treatment to investments in plant and machinery than to investments in inventory or new products. Another way would be imposing equally stringent

5. The seminal work is Gordon Tullock, "The Welfare Costs of Tariffs, Monopolies, and Theft," *Economic Inquiry* 5 (June 1967): 224–32. For a selection of papers on rent seeking, see James M. Buchanan, Robert D. Tollison, and Gordon Tullock, eds., *Toward a Theory of the Rent Seeking Society* (College Station, Texas: Texas A & M University Press, 1980). For a survey of scholarship on rent seeking, see Robert D. Tollison, "Rent Seeking: A Survey," *Kyklos* 35 (No. 4, 1981): 575–602.

and costly requirements for pollution control, even though pollution is much more severe in the areas where the older enterprises tend to be located than where the newer enterprises are. Still another way might be imposing minimum wage requirements and restrictions on working at home. This might have little effect on older enterprises that are highly unionized and geared to factory workplaces, but it could have a negative effect on the newer enterprises that might offer much scope for working at home. And yet another way might be imposing quotas on foreign products that are competitive with those produced by the older enterprises. This action would in turn increase the prices that people who own and who are employed by the newer enterprises must pay for the products produced by the older enterprises.

Regardless of the particular method such taxpayers might choose to boost their otherwise sagging fortunes, they may find that the achievement of their objectives requires the support of some people who are not recipients. An increase in payments for public assistance in exchange for import quotas or minimum wage legislation might be a price that those taxpayers must pay to get the legislation they want. If they did not have to pay any such price, they might be even better off. But minority interests generally receive majority support only through logrolling. As George Meany, late president of the American Federation of Labor-Congress of Industrial Organizations (AFL-CIO) asserted in 1980, "Every piece of social welfare legislation in the last two decades carries a union label."[6] Such legislation may well represent not so much the operation of charity as a price of pro-union legislation. Unemployment insurance, for instance, may be a product of the political process of securing pro-union legislation and hence may be one component of the cost of the welfare state and our system of majoritarian democracy.

The recipients can differ among themselves just as much as can the taxpayers. Some recipients may live in states that are suffering economic stagnation or decline, while others may live in states that are making rapid economic progress. Those who live in the former states may find the taxpayers who reside there becoming less generous, in contrast to the situation confronting recipients in the other

6. Quoted in Morgan O. Reynolds, *Making America Poorer: The Cost of Labor Law* (Washington, D.C.: Cato Institute, 1987)

states. Recipients in the declining states may well support some greater nationalization of public assistance, either directly or through grants-in-aid, even though such a program would harm the recipients in the more progressive states. But to secure passage of such a program, the recipients in the stagnant states might need to support some programs desired by the taxpayers.

Numerous illustrations could be given of the relation between transfer seeking and the welfare state. The existence of logrolling negates the significance of any inferences about votes on any single issue. People in low-income areas may well support minimum wage legislation even though it reduces their work-related income. But it would be misleading to infer from looking at such votes that they are acting stupidly or perversely. The more accurate interpretation would be that they are voting for such a measure to acquire support for something else. But because it is impossible meaningfully to treat issues in isolation from one another (as if voting by secret ballot in a referendum), the welfare state must be viewed as simply one manifestation of a transfer-seeking polity.

WEALTH, POVERTY, AND THE WELFARE STATE

The primary question of knowledge about the welfare state is determining whether the activities of the welfare state represent a response to natural conditions or whether those activities themselves represent the man-made creation of those conditions: is poverty a natural or a self-inflicted problem? If the former, the welfare state provides people with income that they could not have earned in an enterprise economy operating within a contractarian state. If the latter, the welfare state serves largely as a substitute for income that people alternatively could have earned within such an economy. To make this latter statement is not, however, to imply that such income could have been earned within the strongly restricted economy that presently characterizes the United States.

Moreover, poverty can be man-made or self-inflicted for two quite different reasons. On the one hand, poverty can result because of the choices made by the impoverished—for instance, choosing to drop out of school at age sixteen, having children outside of marriage, or refusing to save money.[7] On the other hand, poverty can result from

---

7. For men, the completion of high school reduces the chance of being impoverished to less than one-half of 1 percent for whites and less than 5 percent for blacks. For women, the

the very absence of such choices, often because of the constraints imposed by others. For instance, the person who dropped out of school at age sixteen might have had a difficult time getting started in the world of work because of the minimum wage requirement; but in the absence of that requirement he or she might have found work at $3.15 per hour, learned the qualities that it takes to get along in the world, and subsequently earned a decent livelihood. Alternatively, someone might have been hit by a drunken driver running a red light and been confined to a wheelchair, unable to work, ever after. The reason for poverty surely makes a great difference in any normative evaluation, though public policy is complicated by the recognition that an increase in the amount of aid granted for specific conditions will generally increase the prevalence of those conditions within the population. For instance, the number of people who are out of the labor force because of disability has increased sharply as disability has become more lucrative.[8]

Efforts to formulate canons of distributive justice typically take for granted that the natural distributional outcome of a contractarian state will necessarily violate those canons and that some supplementary distributive activity by the state is required. Yet this central presupposition might be wrong. As was noted in Chapter 6, many public policies promote inequality rather than equality; they also promote the erosion of wealth. It seems clear that public policies relating to the distribution of income do not generally have the character of policies designed to offset any maldistribution that results from a market economy. To a substantial degree, poverty may be a consequence of the restrictions on freedom of contract that are part of a transfer-seeking society, rather than an inherent attribute of an enterprise economy.

The poor may be victims or they may be responsible for their own fate, and they may be either for two different reasons. They may be victims of the very nature of a well-working enterprise economy, or they may be victims because the operation of that enterprise economy is constrained, shaped, and distorted by a variety of laws and regu-

---

conjunction of high school graduation and the avoidance of having children outside of marriage was sufficient to reduce the chance of impoverishment to 2 percent for whites and 9 percent for blacks. See Charles Murray, "Have the Poor Been 'Losing Ground'?" *Political Science Quarterly* 100 (Fall 1985): 427–45.

    8. Donald O. Parsons, "The Decline in Male Labor Force Participation," *Journal of Political Economy* 88 (February 1980): 117–34.

lations that in turn have been "purchased" by others to insulate their own wealth positions. People may be poor because other people were able politically to secure restrictions on their ability to employ their talents. Someone may have been born with a physical disability or raised in a family setting where the values and attitudes taught by the parents—perhaps by negative example—clashed with requisites for economic success. But someone else who suffered no such handicaps may have been fully able and willing to usher in a theater for $3 per hour, but was prevented from doing so by the minimum wage requirement.

And insofar as the poor may be regarded as responsible for their own fate, this may be because they have actively sought the programs of the welfare state, or it may be because they have responded rationally to the options they have faced but have had little hand in creating. Some recipients of Aid to Families with Dependent Children (AFDC) may have actively sought transfers in that form because of its offer of support without work. But others may simply have responded to what was made available and, as a result of the incentives contained within that offer, found themselves and their families saddled with transgenerational welfare dependency.[9] While different specific talents would doubtless bring different returns in different institutional orders, many talents are fairly interchangeable. To a great extent people who would do well in a free-enterprise economy would also do well in a socialist or communist economy. This suggests that the poor are more likely to be rational responders to circumstances others have created than to be active seekers of those circumstances.[10]

Experience since the mid-1960s confirms the elementary principle that people's incomes are not independent of their choices. People do not make choices regarding the formation and use of their human capital and then take the activities of the welfare state into account without revising those initial plans. Rather, the offer of welfare payments will prompt some substitution of those payments for the earning

9. The transgenerational rate of welfare dependency has been found to be about 40 percent; this means that 40 percent of adult recipients were recipients as children. See Morley D. Glicken, "Transgenerational Welfare Dependency," *Journal of Contemporary Studies* 4 (Summer 1981): 31–41.

10. See the development of this theme in Dwight R. Lee, "The Politics of Poverty and the Poverty of Politics," *Cato Journal* 5 (Spring 1985): 17–35.

of income. As was discussed in Chapter 5, the evidence on this point is compelling. Since the late 1960s, when the working poor became increasingly eligible for recipient status while working, the number of people whose earnings lead to their being classified as poor has increased about 50 percent.

Despite the explosion in transfer spending over the past two decades—or perhaps even because of it—the number of people whose money income would place them below the poverty line has generally increased.[11] Throughout the postwar period, poverty was declining due to general economic growth. But since 1968, the overall rate of poverty has increased by around 20 percent. Although it is commonly presumed that the activities of the welfare state represent efforts to alleviate natural conditions that epitomize a free economy, there are grounds for thinking that those activities may be a means of creating those very conditions. This alternative possibility is made more plausible by the recognition that foreclosed opportunities are an inescapable component of a state that has the ability to award entitlements. If this were the case, the welfare state would serve largely as a substitute for income that could have been earned, rather than a provider of income that could not have been earned. Poverty would be not so much a natural feature of a free economy as a by-product of a substantially restricted economy, of which the welfare state is one component. The experiments with negative income taxation, discussed in Chapter 5, bear this out. Those experiments had a limited duration, and the impact would have been even stronger had the program been permanent.

People clearly have substantial interest in bringing some measure of security to their futures. People can reduce the uncertainty they face by trying to gain control of sources of uncertainty, such as those that arise from the actions of competitors in introducing new products, new techniques of production, or new approaches to business conduct.[12] The creation of sheltered or protected wealth positions and the awarding of entitlements or transfers are complementary facets of the existing welfare state. The welfare state, as one manifestation of a transfer-seeking polity, operates within the market for legislation by

11. See, for instance, James Gwartney and Thomas S. McCaleb, "Have Anti-poverty Programs Increased Poverty?" *Cato Journal* 5 (Spring 1985): 1–16.

12. See Jack Wiseman, "Uncertainty, Costs, and Collectivist Economic Planning," *Economica* 20 (May 1953): 118–28.

awarding subsidies and entitlements and by imposing taxes and limiting options. The state is involved in the extension of principles of status rather than in the expansion of principles of contract and opportunity. The status-extending welfare state operates by trying to prevent the erosion of wealth positions through retarding the operation of forces for change within a society.

A status-oriented approach is dominant in a system of majoritarian democracy because of transfer seeking, the market for legislation, and time horizons based on elections. The formation of status positions through the creation of sheltered positions and entitlements confers an immediate gain to recipients, while the costs are vague and to a large extent deferred. When viewed from a short-run perspective, the programs of the welfare state seem primarily to concern the distribution of income and wealth. Any proposal to expand transfer spending appears to revolve around questions of whether or not some people should be taxed more heavily so that other people can be given higher benefits. But when viewed from a long-term perspective, those programs and possible alternatives to them primarily concern the creation—and the destruction—of wealth. However, because there is no political equivalent to a capital market to evaluate present choices with future consequences, the political impact of the wealth destruction will be weaker than its magnitude might seem to warrant.

SAMARITAN'S DILEMMA AND PERSONAL CHOICE

Thomas Szasz noted in *The Myth of Mental Illness* that people can use incompetence and lack of foresight as instruments for getting something from someone else. This possibility in a different vein has been called the "Samaritan's dilemma" by James Buchanan.[13] This dilemma refers to the problem of moral hazard associated with the welfare state: the presence of insurance against an accident may reduce the care people take to avoid an accident, thereby making an accident more likely. In the biblical story, the Samaritan came across a man who had been robbed and beaten by thieves while traveling from Jerusalem to Jericho, and the Samaritan aided the beaten traveler. The story described a unique event to which the Samaritan re-

13. Thomas S. Szasz, *The Myth of Mental Illness* (New York: Harper & Row, 1961); James M. Buchanan, "The Samaritan's Dilemma," in Edmund Phelps, ed., *Altruism, Morality, and Economic Theory* (New York: Russell Sage, 1975), pp. 71–85.

sponded. The Samaritan's dilemma arises when the conduct of the Samaritan is generalized as a rule of conduct for all such situations.

If the condition of being in need of aid is truly beyond the victim's control so that the condition has a zero supply elasticity, the Samaritan faces no dilemma, but only the consequence that the choice to render aid, rather than pass by as did the Levite and the priest, entails a sacrifice of time and money. A dilemma arises when the generalization of the Samaritan's conduct is seen to increase the number of cases requiring aid. Whether the elasticity of supply of people's exposing themselves to such dangers would be zero or positive would be an empirical matter.

At first glance, a positive elasticity of supply might seem to be unlikely in the strict setting the Samaritan faced; even if Samaritans traveling between Jerusalem and Jericho were to aid all victims of thieves they came across, it might seem unlikely that people would choose to increase their exposure to such thievery—for instance, by traveling alone more frequently. But if the potential victims did not have a great deal of money to be taken in the first place, if they generally had to work quite hard to earn a relatively meager living, and if the lodgings provided by the Samaritans, along with the respite from work that was offered, seemed sufficiently pleasant, a positive elasticity of supply would seem quite likely. If so, the offering of aid by Samaritans would reduce the caution that people would exercise in traveling between Jerusalem and Jericho.

As the principle behind the Samaritan's choice is expanded from offering aid to beaten travelers between Jerusalem and Jericho to offering aid to people in a variety of unfortunate circumstances, supply elasticities are likely to become more elastic. In the context of the welfare state, the Samaritans are those who feel themselves to be relatively fortunate, and who wish to aid those whom they regard as unfortunate. The recipients of aid, those in the lower levels of the income distribution, are analogous to the beaten traveler. Suppose the donors wish to supplement the earnings of those with relatively low incomes, with the amount of the supplement increasing as the income earned by the recipient falls. If labor-supply elasticities were zero, the recipients would earn what they could through work, and the Samaritan-donors would supplement those earnings through charitable contributions. However, once recipients recognize that the amount of the donation they receive varies inversely with the amount they earn on their own, they will face an incentive to reduce their own earnings to elicit larger contributions from the Samaritan-donors.[14]

One formulation of this situation is illustrated in Figure 8–1. The line E represents the idea that there is some natural distribution of earnings or income in a contractarian state. The lowest income would be $a. Suppose Samaritan-donors were to think that $b represented the lowest acceptable income or standard of living. Samaritans would want to help all people whose standard living was lower than $b. For an outlay of abc, the Samaritans would be able to bring everyone whose rank on the earnings distribution was below r_1 up to the income level $b, *if the recipients continued to work and earn the same as before.* But why should the recipients do this? If the Samaritans offer to supplement all earnings below $b to bring the standard of living up to $b, why would the people below rank r_1 continue to supply labor as described by E? The answer, of course, is that they would not, for the return to work is zero, which in turn means the cost of leisure is zero. The labor supply of the first r_1 people would no longer be characterized by the segment ac of E, but rather would lie along the abscissa. They would supply no labor; therefore, the cost to the Samaritans of guaranteeing the lowest r_1 earners a standard of living of $b would require an outlay of $Obcr_1$, which is $Oacr_1$ more than abc.

Furthermore, people whose earnings place them just above r_1 would have the same incentive to reduce their supply of labor. Suppose $b is $6,700 per year, which is what would be earned by working 40 hours per week for 50 weeks at the minimum wage of $3.35 per hour. Consider someone who ranks just above r_1, who is earning, say, $6,900. Compared to someone who earns nothing and is supported by the Samaritan, this person is, in effect, working for $0.10 per hour. His options are to earn nothing and to receive $6,700 from the Samaritan or to earn $6,900 by working 2,000 hours for the year. Only $200 is gained by choosing to work. And even someone who could earn $8,700 per year is really working for only $1 per hour, when the alternative to working is being supported by the Samaritan.

A related formulation of the Samaritan's dilemma is illustrated in

14. This perspective about moral hazard and the Samaritan's dilemma is applied to governments in Roland Vaubel, "The Moral Hazard of IMF Lending," in Allan H. Meltzer, ed., *International Lending and the IMF* (Washington, D.C.: Heritage Foundation, 1983), pp. 65–79.

Figure 8–1. Earnings by Rank, and Cost of Income Guarantees.

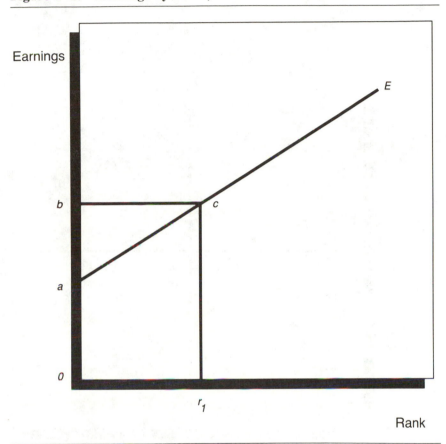

Figure 8–2, which describes Buchanan's model of the Samaritan's dilemma using Gordon Tullock's nomenclature.[15] The donor has two options: to offer aid or to refrain from offering aid. The potential recipient, Idler in Figure 8–2, likewise has two options: to work or to be idle. The latter option represents the reduction in work effort in response to the negative relationship between the amount of gifts offered by donors and the amount of income earned by recipients. In each of the four cells in Figure 8–2 the Samaritan's ranking of the

15. Gordon Tullock, *Economics of Income Redistribution* (Boston: Kluwer-Nijhoff, 1983), pp. 59–61.

Figure 8–2. Samaritan's Dilemma.

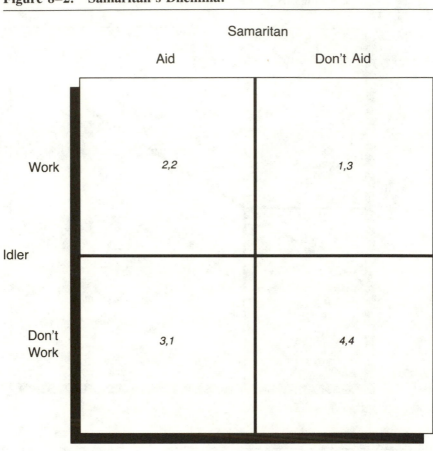

preferred options is given first and the Idler's ranking is given second.

The Samaritan's most preferred outcome is not to give aid and to have Idler work and be self-supporting. This would describe a situation in which Idler's earnings were sufficient to erase the Samaritan's charitable sentiment. The Samaritan's second preference is to give aid while Idler still works. In this case, despite strenuous work effort, Idler cannot earn enough to fully erase the Samaritan's charitable sentiments. The Samaritan's least preferred option is to refrain from giving aid while Idler remains idle; the Samaritan would prefer to aid the idle Idler than to let him go hungry or homeless. Idler's most preferred option is to receive aid from the Samaritan while remaining idle. But remaining idle while receiving no aid from the Samaritan is Idler's least preferred option, for going hungry and homeless is more unpleasant than is working. And if Idler chooses to work, Idler would surely prefer to receive aid from Samaritan than not to receive aid.

The Samaritan's dilemma is simple to understand. If Idler remains idle or generally does not provide for himself, the Samaritan will give aid, which is Idler's most preferred outcome and Samaritan's second-lowest outcome. The Samaritan ends up aiding an idle Idler. The only way the Samaritan can get Idler to work is to withhold aid. However, if Idler's earnings in this case are sufficiently low so that Samaritan has some wish to aid Idler, the granting of such aid will lead Idler to become idle again. While this illustration cannot capture all the subtleties confronted in reality, it surely does account for an important element of that reality: the granting of aid threatens to promote the conditions that bring forth such aid. But to negate this threat, Samaritan must be willing to withhold aid, and this possibility must be regarded as credible by Idler. Samaritan may have to tolerate some hunger and homelessness today to gain the credibility that is necessary to prevent Idler from dictating the outcome. Doing so would represent, in Buchanan's terms, the dominance of "strategic courage" over "pragmatic compassion."

A particularly colorful illustration of the point of the Samaritan's dilemma was penned by Simon Newcomb in 1885 in his *Principles of Political Economy*:

> Let us first take up the familiar case of a beggar. A gentleman is implored for relief by a repulsive piece of humanity, enshrouded in rags and covered with dirt. Moved by pity, he gives him a dime and passes on. What is the economical nature of this transaction? We reply that the transaction is one of supply and demand, belonging to the same class as the supply of and demand for personal services. The combined willingness and ability of a number of persons in the community to give dimes to beggars constitutes a demand for beggary, just as much as if an advertisement, "Beggars wanted; liberal alms guaranteed," were conspicuously inserted in the columns of a newspaper. If there is any difficulty in seeing the truth of this statement, it should disappear when the reader reflects that nothing is necessary to constitute an economic demand except readiness to make payments on certain conditions. Among a crowd of children fond

of music, an ability and a willingness to give pennies to organ-grinders constitute a demand for their services. . . .

So in a community where there is a demand for beggars a certain number are sure to become beggars, and to study the professional accomplishments which will be most likely to draw money from the pockets of the benevolent. Hence, in the case supposed, mendacity will exist according to the same laws that govern the existence of other trades and occupations.[16]

THE SAMARITAN'S DILEMMA AND COLLECTIVE CHOICE

The Samaritan's dilemma as originally formulated by Buchanan described a choice faced by an individual. The dilemma the Samaritan faces is, of course, the problem of moral hazard, which in this case means that the willingness of the Samaritan to offer aid will increase the "need" for aid. While individual Samaritans may face such dilemmas, they also have incentives to prevent the recipients from taking advantage of their willingness to aid. In the world of private charity described by the Samaritan's dilemma, the offer of aid will surely elicit some increase in the conditions that bring forth an offer of aid. However, individual donors are residual claimants. Since the aid comes directly out of a particular Samaritan's pocket, the Samaritan will not be likely to continue to increase the amount given as recipients ever more fully manifest the conditions for which the Samaritan has been giving aid.

But these charitable incentives are weaker in a setting of collective choice, largely because of the absence of residual claimancy or personal responsibility. This weakened incentive to combat moral hazard holds for both donors and recipients. Donors and recipients can have identical or different preferences. In the case of different preferences, problems concerning a form of adverse selection arise. With respect to recipients, *adverse selection* means that, of all people at any particular standard of living, applicants for aid are on average likely to have above-average preferences for leisure. They are, in Szasz's terms, more likely to seek an excuse for avoiding work and receiving aid and are less likely to "play hurt." While some people proudly declare

16. As quoted in George J. Stigler and Claire Friedland, eds., *1985 Engagement Calendar of Great Economists* (Chicago: University of Chicago Press, 1984).

they "won't take charity," others actively campaign for welfare rights, guaranteed incomes, and the like.

Some donors will be more willing to "bite the bullet" than others. While some will cut off aid and let the recipients choose between working and going hungry, recognizing that without the donors' willingness to do this they will be controlled by the recipients, other donors will continue to give aid. Some people may adopt a hard-nosed response to the Samaritan's dilemma, while others are soft touches. Potential recipients who do not like the terms of aid offered by the hard noses will seek out soft touches. Some type of equilibrium will result, with hard noses giving less aid than the soft touches and imposing more stringent requirements upon the recipients. The recipients clearly prefer dealing with the soft touches. The soft touches will perhaps look upon the hard noses as cold and uncaring. If recipients of aid cannot vote, the outcome of the collectivization of charity will depend on the relative numbers of hard noses and soft touches. But when recipients can vote, they will support the soft touches and increase the expected value of the aid offered, as well as increasing the extent of the conditions that bring forth aid.

This conclusion follows from a straightforward model in which charity is subject to market provision. In this situation some people have relatively high incomes and others have relatively low incomes; those who have high incomes have some wish to act charitably toward those with low incomes. When acting individually, each donor will respond in one way or another to the Samaritan's dilemma. When collective action is introduced, the participants do not change in any relevant aspect; however, the outcomes can change, and how they change will depend, among other things, on their relative numbers.

Compare a world of competitive private charities with one of state provision. The preferences of donors are the same in both cases, but the recipients can vote when charity is provided collectively. The introduction of such a right to vote should by itself strengthen the force of the Samaritan's dilemma. Recipients understandably would want larger transfers than the donors would choose to grant. The recipients would also generally want easier eligibility and fewer work requirements. Simple electoral considerations would suggest a strengthening of the Samaritan's dilemma and the moral hazard problems of the income guarantees of the welfare state.

But even if recipients could not vote, the force of the Samaritan's dilemma would seem to be stronger when charity is supplied through the state than when it is supplied privately, for there are sources of differences in incentives other than the interest of recipients in receiving transfers. Under collective provision the individual Samaritan-donors are taxed, with the proceeds distributed as charity. Under private provision various charitable organizations solicit contributions from the Samaritan-donors. The argument that charity has some characteristics of a public good suggests that private donations will be too small, as judged by the donors themselves. This amounts to the prediction, perhaps untestable, that a parliament of donors would agree to contribute more to charity than would be forthcoming in a competitive market. It's not at all clear that this is so, and even the experimental literature on the free-rider proposition generally finds a comparatively small amount of free riding, particularly in settings that approximate real-world institutions.[17]

In a competitive system, recipients who reduced their own efforts would probably find less favor in the form of increased transfer payments. In a collective system, the recipients' reduction in effort immediately confronts the Samaritans with the concern that the recipient will go hungry or the recipient's child unclothed. But in a competitive system, potential donors do not face this dilemma nearly so directly, because no single donor can be regarded as the source of the marginal dollar to the recipient.

Suppose the basic minimum level illustrated by Figure 8–1 is $600 per month, and recipients can earn $400 on their own. Consider a charity that has a level of support from donors that allows it to offer total assistance of $6,000 per month. With this budget the charity could support ten recipients who reduced their own efforts at self-help to zero. Alternatively, it could support thirty recipients who maintained their efforts to support themselves. To the extent that the competitive process among charities leads donations to flow toward those that make the largest amelioration of need, those charities that require recipients to help themselves will prosper over those charities that do not. Whereas the latter type of charity aids ten people, the former is able with the same budget to help three times as many people to secure the same level of living.

17. See the survey assessment in Thomas S. McCaleb and Richard E. Wagner, "The Experimental Search for Free Riders: Some Reflections and Observations," *Public Choice* 47 (No. 3, 1985): 479–90.

In the world of private charity, no particular charity or Samaritan is responsible for letting someone who refuses to work in the hope of getting a larger donation go hungry. This strengthens the credibility of the donor's imposition of self-help requirements as a condition of aid. But in the case of state charity—or in the related case of a world of private charity in which the state acts as a "charity of last resort,"—the Samaritan's dilemma reinforces itself because there is some particular agency that possesses marginal responsibility.

This comparison of collective and private organization of charity relates to the discussion in Chapter 2 of the justification for wealth transfers as the price of domestic tranquillity. This justification, like the others discussed in Chapter 2 and examined in Chapters 4–6, confronts a disjunction between the setting envisioned by the justifications and the actual setting for the pertinent choices regarding wealth transfers. Democratic governments seem less likely than privately established organizations to deal effectively with the Samaritan's dilemma, mainly because those who make the choices bear a minuscule share in the cost resulting from their choices, whereas private parties bear the entire cost.

BUREAUCRACY AND THE WELFARE STATE

While the legislature enacts the various budgetary and regulatory programs that constitute the welfare state, the implementation of those programs rests with a variety of executive departments and independent agencies. Such public bureaus differ from profit-seeking firms both in the form of ownership and in their method of financing.[18] With respect to ownership, bureaus, unlike firms, possess no residual claimant status. As a result, any profits or losses are diffused among taxpayers rather than concentrated on those who make the choices that produce those profits or losses. Bureaus, unlike firms, rarely derive their revenues from payments made by their customers. Most of their revenues come instead from appropriations from the legislature. These differences in the form of ownership and the source of financing lead to some significant differences between public bureaus and private firms.

18. The contemporary economic literature on bureaucracy stems from Gordon Tullock, *The Politics of Bureaucracy* (Washington, D.C.: Public Affairs Press, 1965); and William A. Niskanen, *Bureaucracy and Representative Government* (Chicago: Aldine, 1971).

The impact of institutional framework on organizational performance has been an important part of economics at least since Adam Smith enunciated the principle that "public services are never better performed than when their [public officials'] reward comes only in consequence of their being performed, and is proportioned to the diligence employed in performing them."[19] A corollary of this principle is, of course, that the manner in which public services are performed depends on the way in which performance is rewarded. The stronger the connection between payment and performance, the more intensely public officials will exert themselves to perform effectively.

Officials who administer public assistance programs will work more strenuously to overcome the Samaritan's dilemma if their own compensation somehow varies directly with their success in doing so. This might happen, for instance, if such officials were compensated in proportion to the work-related earnings of recipients. But if the compensation of public officials were unrelated to the work performance of recipients and instead were based on such considerations as the number of years they have been on the job, public officials would surely make less effort to promote self-support among recipients.

Consider again the illustration of private and public charity, and suppose that for each $6 million distributed each month among recipients, charitable activity incurs administrative expenses of $2 million. Consider a public assistance bureau that receives an appropriation from the legislature of $96 million per year, of which $24 million goes for salaries and other administrative expenses, leaving $72 million to be distributed among recipients. The bureau can be operated in one of two ways, "hard" and "soft." When operated in the soft form, the bureau would spend the budget with as little hassle as possible for administrators. It would distribute the $6 million per month among 10,000 recipients, who in turn would be subject to little if any active enforcement of self-help requirements. When operated in the hard form, the bureau would seek actively to maximize the living standards of recipients. It would distribute the $6 million among

19. Adam Smith, *The Wealth of Nations*. 1776 (New York: Modern Library, 1937), p. 678. On this characteristic of Smith's approach to economics, see Nathan Rosenberg, "Some Institutional Aspects of the *Wealth of Nations*," *Journal of Political Economy* 68 (December 1960): 557–70.

30,000 recipients and make a serious effort to enforce self-help requirements.[20]

It is easy to see why officials of the public charity prefer the soft form of approach. The bureau receives $2 million per month for distributing $6 million, regardless of whether it deals with 10,000 or 30,000 recipients. The bureau's budget is the same regardless of the contribution it makes to the living standards of the potential set of recipients. If the bureau enforces no self-help and distributes the $6 million among 10,000 recipients, those recipients reduce their market earnings to zero. But each recipient could continue to earn $4,000 per year through market activity if the bureau enforced self-help requirements. Hence, the charity alleviates only $2,000 worth of deficiency with an outlay of $6,000, at an efficiency rating of 33 percent. So long as the return to officials is invariant to their performance in alleviating income deficiency, those officials will generally make little effort to monitor recipients and to enforce self-help requirements.

Suppose, by contrast, that the bureau and its officials are paid not a fixed sum but a percentage of the income deficiency it truly eliminates—assuming this figure can be determined with reasonable accuracy. For instance, if the bureau eliminates $6 million of income deficiency with their budget, bureau officials will receive $2 million. But if it eliminates only $2 million of income deficiency, bureau officials will receive only $667,000. This alternative form of compensation will give public officials a $1 bonus for each $4 of income deficiency they eliminate and will surely elicit a stronger effort to induce self-help by recipients than does the present system of compensation.

But a system of residual claimancy, which characterizes a world of private charities, contains even stronger incentives. In large part this is because data on the true amount of income deficiency that is elim-

---

20. In an interesting and valuable book, Lawrence Mead argues not that government should be less involved with transfer payments and welfare programs, but rather that government should become less permissive and more authoritarian. Government should force people to develop the competencies that would allow them to become self-supporting, much as private charities might be motivated to do. The possible incompatibility between such a program and the dominant incentives within our political system is not addressed by Mead. See Lawrence Mead, *Beyond Entitlement: The Social Obligations of Citizenship* (New York: Free Press, 1986).

inated can never be fully known, although it is information that people can seek to discover. Private charities competing for donations from Samaritans would be largely engaged in demonstrating their efficiency in the elimination of deficiencies, which in the simplest case could be income pure and simple, but more likely would be a complex combination of characteristics, including attitudes and values. But, in any event, charities would compete for donors and their donations. A charity that stood pat with distributing $6 million over 10,000 recipients and made no effort to alleviate a greater amount of income deficiency would be likely to lose out in the competition to charities that were more successful in developing ways of monitoring the activities of recipients and eliciting their full efforts at self-help.

A number of illustrations could be given to show the absence of any direct link between the compensation of members of the welfare bureaucracy and the efficiency of their performance. If the Samaritans wish to provide support for the unfortunate without inducing people to take on those characteristics that increase their eligibility for aid, they must develop some way of relating the compensation of public officials to the work-related earnings of recipients.[21]

THE WELFARE BUREAUCRACY AND THE LEGISLATURE

The incentives in public bureaus generally and the welfare bureaus in particular have some significant features that impede efforts to promote self-reliance. In part this is because the ordinary expansionary interests of the bureaucracy run contrary to the promotion of genuine self-reliance. AFDC, for instance, originally began as a program for widows only and was a part of Aid to Dependent Children (ADC). The thesis that bureaus have a strong interest in expansion is certainly consistent with the evolution of ADC into AFDC. The AFDC program presently serves few widows; it serves mostly divorcées and single mothers.

Despite the expansionary interests of public bureaus, it is the leg-

---

21. For a succinct statement of the problems of developing an approach to compensation that contains incentives for good performance, see Gary S. Becker and George J. Stigler, "Law Enforcement, Malfeasance, and the Compensation of Enforcers," *Journal of Legal Studies* 3 (January 1974): 1–18. See also William M. Landes and Richard A. Posner, "The Private Enforcement of Law," *Journal of Legal Studies* 4 (January 1975): 1–46.

islature that chooses to create bureaus instead of alternative forms of organization. For instance, the legislature could have chosen to award grants to private charities or to have left charity completely to private organizations. The legislature generally can implement legislation either by awarding appropriations to public bureaus or by giving contracts to private firms. The legislature chooses to deal with bureaus because the legislature can more easily make transfers to those people who purchase the relevant legislation. If legislation is implemented by private firms and contracts for implementation are awarded through competitive bidding, the ability of the legislature to sell legislation may be diminished by the open nature of the competitive process. The use of bureaus in place of firms can increase the value of the legislation that the legislature is able to sell.

Legislators are usually assigned to oversight committees within the legislature according to their personal interests, so that there is a congruence of interest between the legislature and the bureau. Employees of the bureau generally fare better as the bureau's budget expands. At the same time, the legislators on the committee will generally have a particularly strong interest in the enactment of legislation that will be implemented by the bureau. Consequently, bureaus and the legislative committees with which they deal will generally have similar interests, and the two will tend to share in the profits that accrue from the production of legislation.

This congruence of interest does not preclude conflict over the division of the rents created by legislation.[22] The legislature may create a bureau rather than contract with a profit-seeking firm because this allows the legislature to designate the recipients of transfers more fully than could be done with competitive bidding. At the same time, however, the absence of residual claimancy means that a simple indicator such as a rate of profit cannot be used by the legislature to gauge the success of a bureau's performance. The task of monitoring is more complex in the absence of residual claimancy, and this complexity probably operates to increase the bureau's share in the profits from legislation.

The nonprofit status of bureaus means that monitoring of the bureau by the legislature often involves some confounding of inputs and

---

22. For a general examination of this situation, see Gary J. Miller, "Bureaucratic Compliance as a Game on the Unit Square," *Public Choice* 29 (Spring 1977): 37–51.

outputs. It is relatively easy to measure many of the inputs into the provision of police or fire services, but the outputs are not nearly as easy to measure. This difficulty is not inherent in the nature of the service but is created by the nonprofit status of bureaus. The primary difference between a public and a private service is that the profit-seeking status of the private firm provides an unambiguous indicator of the success with which the firm has used the resources at its disposal. With public bureaus there is a general inability to specify output, essentially because of the absence of a contractual relationship between the bureau and the users of its output. Resource cost therefore becomes by default a primary indicator of a bureau's output.[23]

The legislature could choose some different compensation scheme for public officials but chooses not to do so. The reason must be that the present form of compensation allows the legislature to charge more for its services than it would be able to charge otherwise. For instance, the use of a compensation scheme by which a welfare bureau was rewarded in proportion to the extent to which it induced recipients to become self-sufficient may come into conflict with the reasons for the recipients' dependency. Take, for instance, the case of minimum wage legislation as a way of reducing competition with high-priced union labor, the immediate result of which is unemployment (though there is little loss of consumption because the lost income is covered through expanded welfare payments). A welfare bureau that was truly successful in promoting the self-reliance of its clients would invariably clash with its central function as part of a transfer-seeking polity. The promotion of such self-reliance would necessarily involve such things as undermining minimum wage legislation, possibly through inducing recipients to work at home or in the underground economy. In other words, a welfare bureau that sought to promote self-reliance in place of reliance on the dole would necessarily be a bureau that would be injecting competitive forces into the economy. Yet the central driving force of the welfare state in a transfer-seeking polity is the slackening of those competitive forces.

23. On this theme with specific references to hospitals administered by the Veterans Administration, see Cotton M. Lindsay, "A Theory of Government Enterprise," *Journal of Political Economy* 84 (October 1976): 1061–77.

9

THE WELFARE STATE VERSUS
THE GENERAL WELFARE

The theory of public choice explains why there is a considerable clash between the constitutional charge to "promote the general welfare" and the actual conduct of the welfare state. This clash is a natural product of the institutional order of majoritarian democracy that has evolved in the United States. With the erosion of constitutional limits on the ability of the legislature to legislate, a market for legislation emerges, and the legislature becomes an arena within which wealth is transferred from losing to winning interest groups. Politics increasingly centers on giving-and-taking and taxing-and-transferring and deemphasizes helping people to organize the activities of general benefit that they cannot organize effectively by other means.

The result of such tax-transfer politics is a destruction of potential wealth; people's energies are turned away from productive activities into various transfer-seeking activities. The process of competing through legislation for larger shares of the pie means that less effort and attention are given to the baking of pies. These negative-sum aspects of government are a by-product of the pursuit of self-interest within the institutional order that characterizes contemporary majoritarian democracy. While the market order is so constituted that people increase their wealth by engaging in positive-sum actions, a political order of majoritarian democracy is so constituted that self-interest is advanced significantly by transferring wealth, ultimately a negative-sum activity.

This chapter explains why the clash between the welfare state and the promotion of the general welfare is endemic to the system of unlimited majoritarian democracy in the United States. Since this clash is due less to electoral choices people make than to the incentives within the institutional setting from which policy outcomes emerge, effective reform is less a matter of electing better candidates than of developing a better institutional or constitutional framework. Such a framework would be one in which government, rather than being unrestrained, is bound by the same rules that apply to other participants in society. Furthermore, effective reform cannot so much be addressed to the welfare state per se as to the constitutional order through which the welfare state emerges as a natural outcome. Chapter 10 explores political reform; this chapter focuses more directly on welfare and its reform.

SOCIAL SECURITY AS DEMOCRATIC FRAUD

The social security programs provide one of the sharpest illustrations of the clash between the natural outcomes of the welfare state and those outcomes that would promote the general welfare. Until the mid-1980s, social security indisputably enjoyed widespread popularity, and its popularity remains substantial. At the same time, however, social security has increasingly undermined the very basis for the provision of security in a society. That provision requires the accumulation of capital within a well-integrated capital structure, but the social security program discourages saving and diminishes capital accumulation.

Several scholars have referred to social security as a "paradox," an "inherent contradiction," the "fraud" in our future, and a portent of a "coming revolution."[1] Social security is paradoxical because,

1. William C. Mitchell, *The Popularity of Social Security: A Paradox in Public Choice* (Washington, D.C.: American Enterprise Institute, 1977); Warren Shore, *Social Security: The Fraud in Your Future* (New York: Macmillan, 1975); Peter J. Ferrara, *Social Security: The Inherent Contradiction* (Washington, D.C.: Cato Institute, 1980); and A. Haeworth Robertson, *The Coming Revolution in Social Security* (Reston, Va.: Reston, 1981). For a historical examination of how social security arrived at its present state, see Carolyn L. Weaver, *The Crisis in Social Security: Economic and Political Origins* (Durham, N.C.: Duke University Press, 1982). Weaver shows that the underlying process of dissipation is primarily due to political incentives and not to a lack of knowledge.

though it is eroding wealth, it is widely popular. The inherent contradiction is that social security, although characterized as an insurance program, is really a welfare program, and the effort to blend the two types of programs into one will never have a satisfactory outcome. The fraud results because legislators have enacted programs whose promises cannot be kept. The promises to beneficiaries of what they can expect to receive are inconsistent with the promises to taxpayers on how much they will have to pay. The revolution is threatened because people who are relatively young will fare poorly with social security, compared to what they could get from the private purchase of retirement annuities.

Social security is not an insurance program, despite the denials that people are paying taxes and the repeated insistence that they are making "contributions" to their "accounts." If social security were an insurance program, those contributions would be credited to people's accounts, and the contributions plus accumulated interest would be converted at retirement into annuities people would receive for the remainder of their lives. But social security does not work this way, because it is essentially a welfare program. The taxes people pay go not into individual accounts to earn interest but immediately as payments to people now retired.[2]

That this welfare program has proven to be a bonanza for most people goes far toward explaining its popularity. This bonanza, a natural product of the start-up phase of this type of welfare program, becomes a fraud when the returns that people receive on their taxes during the start-up phase cannot be even remotely sustained during its mature stage. Until now, retirees have been able to receive full benefits despite having paid social security taxes only part of their working lives or, in the case of more recent retirees, having paid quite low rates of tax for most of their working lives. Not until early in the next century will people retire who had to pay high social security taxes throughout their working lives.

Considering that as late as 1947 the maximum social security tax was $60, it is no wonder that some retirees could receive benefits that repressed phenomenal rates of return on their earlier tax payments,

2. There are presently plans to run a large surplus until the year 2015 to help finance the retirement of the baby boom generation, but this promised surplus does not change the essential pay-as-you-go nature of social security. Moreover, it remains to be seen whether the projected surpluses will truly accumulate and not be dissipated at least in part.

even in excess of 1,000 percent. Those large "returns" resulted because the retirees paid little tax, and yet the tax base grew rapidly—rates of tax were being increased and an ever larger number of people were being subjected to the tax. Until the late 1980s, the United States has been in the initial phase of its pay-as-you-go system, as present retirees have spent less than a full working life paying taxes and have had the advantage of reaching retirement age during a period when the grasp of the tax was being widened and its rate increased.

The United States is now starting to enter the mature phase of its pay-as-you-go system. In the 1990s significant numbers of people will begin retiring who will have spent their entire working lives paying social security taxes. And another generation must pass before the pay-as-you-go system reaches full maturity. Then the predominant number of retirees will have spent their entire working lives under the system and will have done so at relatively high rates of tax. They will not be able to secure unearned gains by enacting further expansions in the number of people covered by the tax. Some projections see social security tax rates of around 40 percent within half a century.[3] The point of such projections is not that such rates will actually come to pass but that the present course of social security cannot be maintained, precisely because those rates of tax are not likely to be tolerated by even the most quiescent of taxpayers.

Under the pay-as-you-go form of social security, people who enter the system in its early years benefit from a transitory period of high rates of return. However, the rate of return that eventually can be sustained is much lower than under a true insurance program, in which a person's contributions would be placed in an investment fund that on retirement would be converted along with accumulated interest into an annuity. Under a pay-as-you-go system, retirees can receive a return equal to the rate of growth in real wages per worker. Historically, this potential rate of return has been about 3 percent, although the rate may be lower in the future if trends such as declining fertility rates and a slower rate of economic growth continue.

With a funded system, the rate of return to participants depends on the yield from investment. Historically, this yield has ranged from 10 to 12 percent before tax, which indicates that a funded system could offer a rate of return that is several times higher than a pay-as-you-

3. Robertson, *Coming Revolution*, p. 51.

go system can offer on a sustained basis. However, retirees could not actually receive this superior return, at least at present, because the yield on saving is heavily taxed. Although the rate at which saving is taxed varies, depending on the circumstances of individual savers, a rate of around 75 percent has not been uncommon in the past. At such a rate, the posttax yield that people could receive from their saving is in the same range as what they could receive under a mature pay-as-you-go system. On the other hand, should the taxation of saving be eliminated, thereby treating saving and consumption equally, taxpayers would be treated identically under the two systems and retirees would be in a superior position under funding.

Compared with a true system of retirement insurance, the pay-as-you-go or welfare approach to social security is likely to reduce people's incentive to save. This diminishes investment and the capital stock, which in turn reduces future standards of living. There has been considerable controversy over the efforts to measure the actual magnitude of this reduction in saving and real income. Martin S. Feldstein, for instance, estimated that the welfare approach to social security reduced the national capital stock by 40 percent and real income by about 15 percent.[4] The reason the welfare approach to social security is likely to reduce saving, capital formation, and real income is straightforward. With genuine retirement insurance, people save and this saving is invested in capital goods, the yield on which is the interest that savers receive. With a pay-as-you-go form of social security, the government guarantees people the same retirement benefits, but instead of investing the taxes it collects, it gives those revenues to present retirees to finance their consumption.[5]

From the perspective of people who are currently working, the two approaches to retirement insurance are identical. What they would have saved under genuine insurance is instead taxed away under the present system of retirement welfare. In either case, though, they are

---

4. Martin S. Feldstein, "Social Security, Induced Retirement, and Aggregate Capital Accumulation," *Journal of Political Economy* 82 (October 1974): 905–26. For disagreement with Feldstein's estimated magnitudes but not about the qualitative impact of social security on saving, see Alicia H. Munnell, "The Impact of Social Security on Personal Savings," *National Tax Journal* 27 (December 1974): 553–67.

5. This negative impact on saving would not result if people increased their private savings and bequests sufficiently to fund the future taxes necessary to finance the benefit payments. This line of argument is explored in Robert J. Barro, "Are Government Bonds Net Wealth?" *Journal of Political Economy* 82 (December 1974): 1095–1117.

promised support during their retirement. Under retirement insurance, their savings are invested to provide productive capital goods. But under retirement welfare, their taxes are used to finance the consumption of current retirees. The amount of saving is reduced, as a first approximation, by the amount of social security taxes, which are about half of total personal saving in the United States. The effect of the reduction in saving upon the reduction in income is small in any one year; a 50 percent fall in saving for one year would reduce the overall capital stock around 2 or 3 percent, assuming an average life of twenty years for capital goods. But a continued, sustained reduction of 50 percent in the rate of saving would reduce the capital stock by this same amount.

Social security of the welfare variety, then, appears to have been responsible for a substantial reduction in the standard of living, compared to what it could otherwise have been. This reduction will become larger in future years. And yet the program has enjoyed strong support to date; it has allowed politicians to buy support by subsidizing retirees at the expense of ever larger burdens on the future. For those retired or close to retirement, changes in social security benefits are a substantial and often dominant element in their future income. For the workers being taxed to support those who are retired, an increase in social security taxes involves a smaller percentage of their present and future income. For them, changes in earnings from work affect their net incomes more strongly than changes in social security taxes. An increase of 10 percent in social security taxes will increase by 5 percent the disposable income of a retiree for whom social security payments represent 50 percent of retirement income. But that tax increase would reduce the disposable income of an average worker by only about 1 percent. Moreover, one adult in seven is age 65 and over, and the over-65 share of the population will rise in the future.

Furthermore, people in this age category, for whom the opportunity cost of time is relatively low, vote more frequently than other people. About one-half of the total eligible electorate have voted in recent presidential elections, but around two-thirds of those over age 65 have voted. It is perhaps no accident that average social security benefits have grown considerably more rapidly than average hourly industrial earnings over the past two decades. And it is difficult to blame the recurrent discussions of problems with social security on the continual appearance of unforeseeable, exogenous events. To some extent the reappearance of financial problems is an inherent, inescapable product of the tax-and-transfer system that social security has become, as Carolyn L. Weaver has explained with particular clarity in her study of the historical development of social security.[6]

STATUS VERSUS CONTRACT IN THE PROVISION OF PERSONAL SECURITY

People clearly have substantial interest in bringing some measure of security to their future. And although the proliferation of activities such as the awarding of entitlements and the conferral of sheltered statuses can be examined from a transfer-seeking perspective, much of the underlying interest that produces the welfare state nonetheless is a variation on the insurance motive discussed in Chapter 2. One way that people can reduce the uncertainty they necessarily face is by trying to gain control of sources of uncertainty that might arise from the actions of competitors in introducing new products, new techniques of production, new approaches to business conduct, and the like.[7] The creation of sheltered or protected wealth positions and the awarding of entitlements or transfers are complementary facets of the existing welfare state.

Sir Henry Maine's famous statement that the history "of the progressive societies has hitherto been a movement from status to contract" as the basis for social relations, leads naturally to a comparison of status-oriented and contract-oriented approaches to the welfare state and its safety net for personal security.[8] The present welfare state represents a status-oriented approach to the provision of personal security. The status-oriented welfare state operates by awarding subsidies and entitlements and by imposing taxes and limiting options; it is a manifestation of the servile state. Security is dispensed through the taxing-and-transferring apparatus of the state and its bureaucracy. The status-oriented welfare state tries to prevent the erosion of wealth positions through retarding the operation of forces for change, such as entrepreneurial activity outside of established channels.

---

6. Weaver, *Crisis in Social Security.*
7. This theme is developed in Jack Wiseman, "Uncertainty, Costs, and Collectivist Economic Planning," *Economica* 20 (May 1953): 118–28.
8. Henry Sumner Maine, *Ancient Law,* 5th ed. (New York: Henry Holt, 1864), p. 165.

Yet the only way that security can truly be provided, to the extent it can be provided at all, is through capital accumulation within a well-integrated capital structure.[9] The status-oriented welfare state actually impedes the accumulation of capital and undermines its own justification. Nonetheless, prevailing political processes seem biased toward the programs of the status-oriented welfare state, perhaps in part because the very shortsightedness that is sometimes used as justification for the welfare state actually operates more fully in the polity than in the economy. The benefits of the welfare state are concentrated in the present, whereas an important part of the costs accrue only in the future—a future that lies beyond the time horizons bounded by elections that seem to epitomize democratic political processes.[10]

Viewed from a short-run perspective, the programs of the welfare state seem primarily to concern the distribution of income and wealth. Any proposal to expand the welfare state appears to revolve around questions of whether or not some people should be taxed more heavily so that other people can be given higher benefits. The outcome depends on the political strengths of the various affected parties as these relate to what appears essentially to be a zero-sum, purely distributional choice. But from a long-term perspective, those tax-and-transfer programs and their possible alternatives primarily concern the production—and the destruction—of wealth. Both the tax and the expenditure sides of the status-oriented welfare state promote the consumption of capital: the taxation of productive activity to finance the transfers of the welfare state reduces the incentives to accumulate capital, and the subsidization of various consumption activities by the welfare state likewise reduces that incentive for recipients. As a result, people generally will be less wealthy in the future than they would have been had the tax-and-transfer programs of the welfare state not been extended.

Although the outcome is negative sum and not merely zero sum, the negative consequences for wealth and security lie in the future

9. The significance of the "well-integrated" attributes of a capital structure is noted especially clearly in Ludwig M. Lachmann, *Capital and Its Structure*. 1956 (Kansas City: Sheed, Andrews, and McMeel, 1978).

10. This thesis about time horizons is explored in James M. Buchanan and Dwight R. Lee, "Politics, Time, and the Laffer Curve," *Journal of Political Economy* 90 (August 1982): 816–19.

and are not realized in the present, which makes its political impact weaker than its magnitude would seem to warrant. An illustration developed by Irving Fisher and Herbert W. Fisher can be adapted to explain this point.[11] Suppose capital yields an annual return of 20 percent, with that yield being taxed at 50 percent to finance transfer payments; the implicit policy alternative in this illustration is one of simultaneously reducing taxes and transfer payments.[12] Further suppose that the after-tax yield on investment is reinvested. If $10,000 is invested at the start of year one, $2,000 is earned at the end of the year; $1,000 of this is taxed away and $1,000 is reinvested. The capital stock at the start of year two, $11,000, yields $2,200 at the end of the year, $1,100 of which is taxed away and $1,100 of which is reinvested. In like manner, the capital stock at the start of year three will be $12,100, which will yield $2,420 at the end of the year; $1,210 is taken by the government and $1,210 is reinvested. Consequently, the capital base at the start of year four is $13,310.

Each year the budgetary process seems essentially to concern how much income to transfer from savers and investors to the recipients of transfer payments. In year one, the central budgetary question appears to be whether to impose a tax of $1,000 on investment income, with the revenues being used to expand various transfer programs. It is the same in years two and three, except that the amounts in question are $1,100 and $1,210 respectively. In any event, the essential nature of the budgetary process appears to be whether or not to raise taxes on investment income so as to raise the level of support for transfer or entitlement programs.

This simple zero-sum appearance vanishes, however, when the entire process is examined over a sequence of years. If investment income were not taxed, $2,000 would have been reinvested at the end of year one. The resulting capital base of $12,000 would, in turn, have yielded $2,400, which would have made possible a capital base of $14,400 at the start of year three. This base would have yielded $2,880, which would have left a capital stock of $17,280 at the start of year four.

This longer term perspective shows that the tax-and-transfer pro-

11. Irving Fisher and Herbert W. Fisher, *Constructive Income Taxation* (New York: Harper, 1942).

12. In other words, the illustration assumes that the taxes are devoted to consumption and not to capital formation, which illustrates more sharply the point about time horizons.

grams of the status-oriented welfare state have been responsible for the destruction of capital and, thereby, have weakened the means of achieving security. Moreover, the value of the capital destroyed exceeds the amount of taxes collected and revenues spent. Only $3,310 of capital is accumulated in the presence of the welfare state, whereas $7,820 would have been accumulated otherwise. Hence, $4,510 of capital has been destroyed through the resulting nonaccumulation. Furthermore, the size of this capital destruction relative to the size of the taxes and expenditures increases sharply with the passage of time. With the same assumptions about yield, accumulation, and taxation, wealth will be $453,000 at the end of year forty, and total tax collections over the forty years will have been $442,000. But in the absence of tax, wealth would have been $14,800,000 at the end of year forty. Therefore, the collection of $442,000 in taxes to finance the transfer programs was responsible for the destruction of $14,358,000 of capital. However, this strongly negative-sum character of the status-oriented welfare state asserts itself only with the passing of time, time that would seem at most to have a minuscule impact on the conduct of electorally dominated democratic politics.

In contrast to a status-oriented approach to the provision of security, with its contradiction between the requirements for security and the incentives it contains, a contract-oriented approach would seek to promote the personal accumulation of capital within a well-integrated capital structure. There are many forms this approach might take, and in all cases security would be sought in the extension of the domain over which property and contract operate. All such contract-oriented approaches—which might be thought of, in current parlance, as a privatization of welfare—are grounded in personal responsibility and the ownership of assets.

If the development of characteristics such as self-reliance and personal responsibility can be nurtured or discouraged, depending on whether the approach to security in society is contract oriented or status oriented, the ownership of property and the responsibility for it may be important in supporting social relations grounded in reciprocity and contract, just as the lack of ownership and responsibility may reinforce social relations grounded in status and compulsion. If so, the approach to the provision of security, by influencing knowledge and incentives and their political expression, might exert some influence over whether society will be more or less servile in the future, as well as more or less secure. However, the creation of such an alternative approach also clashes with the central imperatives of a system of majoritarian democracy.

Economists treat perspectives toward time as a matter of preference, as represented by the concept of *time preference*. Thus, someone who discounted the future relatively heavily and therefore made little provision for the future would be characterized as having a high rate of time preference. By contrast, someone who made little or no discount of the future and acted now to make considerable provision for the future would be characterized as having a low rate of time preference. When faced with the same initial conditions, people with low rates of time preference would save more and consume less than people with high rates and would tend to become wealthier over time. Many scholars have noted that people with low incomes seem to have high rates of time preference; their budgets and choices are heavily oriented toward what offers rewards now instead of what offers rewards sometime in the future.[13]

To some extent, what appears to be a matter of time preference may be a matter of rational conduct under institutional arrangements that do not hold people accountable for the consequences of their actions. Under an institutional arrangement of private property, people have strong incentives to manage resources, including themselves, in ways that maximize their present values. Someone who owns a forest and harvests it prematurely—so soon that the rate of growth in the value of the forest would have exceeded the rate of interest—will bear that reduction in the forest's value. The sale price of the forest (or the land where the trees once stood) will fall by more than the sale price of the trees in the form of prematurely harvested timber. However, if there were no private property in forests, someone who harvested the trees prematurely would gain the income from that harvest but would not bear the reduction in the sale price of the forest.[14]

These considerations of time preference and institutional arrangements are relevant to an examination of alternative approaches to welfare because different types of constitutional orders entail very dif-

13. Perhaps the best-known work in this vein is Edward C. Banfield, *The Unheavenly City* (Boston: Little, Brown, 1965).

14. This point is illustrated in Ronald N. Johnson and Gary D. Libecap, "Efficient Markets and Great Lakes Timber: A Conservation Issue Reexamined," *Explorations in Economic History* 17 (October 1980): 372–85.

ferent approaches to the responsibility for the future consequences of present choices. The central idea of a constitutionally limited democracy is that government is not a source of rights but a reflection of people's use of their rights. But a majoritarian democracy becomes a source of rights, with rights in turn being brokered through legislative processes. In such a setting the security of ownership claims weakens. It then becomes rational to discount more fully the future consequences of present actions, because the likelihood of bearing those consequences is lessened.[15]

A contract-oriented approach to the provision of personal security seems clearly to be consistent with a constitutional regime of limited democracy. Indeed, this approach is but one manifestation of the operation of such a constitutional order. However, a status-oriented approach seems much more consistent with the imperatives of a constitutional regime of majoritarian democracy, in which legislative majorities are essentially unlimited in what they can do. Indeed, a contract-oriented approach would seem fundamentally inconsistent with a system of majoritarian democracy. After all, a legislature that is able to redefine and rearrange rights at will can hardly be expected to restrain itself when it deals with that subset of human activities and concerns that are the welfare state.

STATUS, CONTRACT, TRANSFER SEEKING, AND RACE

To be sure, problems of welfare are as prevalent in racially homogeneous nations as they are in contemporary America, as the English experience with the Poor Laws shows.[16] Perhaps one of the most significant illustrations of the conflict between status-oriented and contract-oriented approaches concerns some of the racial aspects of the welfare state. This conflict appears regularly, for instance, in the assertion that one is an "equal opportunity/affirmative action" employer. One can be an affirmative action employer or an equal opportunity employer, but surely not both.

---

15. One little-noted but exceedingly important consequence of the shortened time horizons that rationally characterize a regime of majoritarian democracy is a reduction in the ability to deal with adversaries on a sustained, long-term basis. See, for instance, Robert Ayanian, "Nuclear Consequences of the Welfare State," *Public Choice* 49 (No. 3, 1986): 201–22.

16. For an examination of this experience between 1750 and 1850, see Gertrude Himmelfarb, *The Idea of Poverty* (New York: Alfred A. Knopf, 1984).

Affirmative action, in giving preferential treatment to favored groups, represents the extension of status relationships—hiring, retaining, and promoting on the basis of minority status and not on the basis of performance relative to other competitors.[17] *Equal opportunity*, by contrast, treats everyone the same and elevates contract or opportunity over status. Status is represented by the affirmative action award of privileged status positions and as such is a further manifestation of transfer seeking. By contrast, contract or opportunity is reflected in the equal opportunity abolition of restrictions on the ability of people to employ their talents, and as such would represent a restriction of the scope for transfer seeking.

It cannot be claimed that a regime of free competition will eliminate racial differences in income and wealth, because there might be other reasons for systematic differences in, for instance, birthrates and average ages. If so, racial groups with higher birthrates and lower average ages will have lower average incomes than other racial groups with opposing characteristics.[18] One can, however, ask whether a regime grounded in contract or one grounded in status offers a more rapid means of narrowing the presently large black-white income differentials. There are several economic reasons why the granting of a favored status, which might appear to be a means of speeding those accomplishments along, might actually retard those accomplishments.[19]

Suppose that several newcomers join a running club. None of them is in particularly good shape to start, and initially they finish far behind the other members of the club. Is affirmative action (the extension of status and transfer seeking) or equal opportunity (the curtailment of status and transfer seeking) the better approach to making the newcomers competitive with the oldtimers? The oldtimers may want to impose restrictions on the ability of the newcomers to train on weekends and evenings or for more than forty hours per week or by running uphill. The equal opportunity approach will allow the newcomers to train as hard as they choose, free of restrictions on their

17. Affirmative action as applied to universities is examined in Thomas Sowell, *Affirmative Action Reconsidered* (Washington, D.C.: American Enterprise Institute, 1975).
18. For a wide-ranging examination of these types of questions, see Thomas Sowell, *Ethnic America* (New York: Basic Books, 1981).
19. For further elaboration of this line of reasoning, see Richard E. Wagner, "Wealth Transfers in a Rent-Seeking Polity," *Cato Journal* 6 (Spring 1986): 155–71.

ability to train. The affirmative action approach, by contrast, will develop a set of handicaps and head starts. In a 5-mile run, for instance, the newcomers can be given a 1-mile head start and the oldtimers can have 4-pound lead weights strapped to their ankles. The lengths of the head starts and the weights of the lead anklets can be adjusted until the desired composition of newcomers and oldtimers in the various finishing brackets is attained.

Alternatively, suppose some of the newcomers live under the equal opportunity rules while the others live under the affirmative action rules. Under which set of rules will the newcomers more quickly come to be competitive with the oldtimers? Which set of rules is more consistent with the fuller and quicker development of people's talents? Economic principles suggest that it would be the equal opportunity regime; but at the same time public choice principles warn of the prevailing biases toward transfer-seeking regimes. Compared with an equal opportunity regime, the affirmative action regime diminishes the incentives of the newcomers to become competitive quickly, because it becomes possible for them to win races without expending as much effort on training.

An additional problem arises once it is recognized that the newcomers will differ in their own interests and abilities. In the equal opportunity regime, those who are best suited for racing, because they have the ability and the interest, will train hard and catch up with the others. But those who are weak on talent or interest will probably tire of finishing in the rear and will move on to some other activity. But the affirmative action regime diminishes the ability of such self-selection to reveal comparative advantages. If the newcomers with lesser interest or talent are given longer head starts than the other newcomers, self-selection processes will work less strongly to ensure that those newcomers who are best suited to racing will continue to engage in it. Not only does affirmative action reduce performance levels, it may also reduce the extent to which the self-assignment of people to activities reflects comparative advantage.

Affirmative action policies are essentially equivalent to infant industry policies for protecting domestic industries against foreign competition. In both cases there is an argument for granting preferential positions of a temporary nature. And both types of policy seem likely to fail for the same constellation of reasons: a protected status weakens incentives for performance, government has little ability to distinguish winners from losers among the competing claimants, and ordinary processes of self-selection are enfeebled. Walter E. Williams, in assessing ways that opportunities to gain initial experience are foreclosed, offered the following conjecture:

> I would guess that if we abolished the minimum wage law, reduced licensing restrictions, changed labor legislation and reorganized the delivery of education, in twenty to thirty years hence there would be no "Negro problem" as there is no Japanese, Chinese, Jewish or other earlier-immigrant problem. Those people were able to start off poor and progress because they did not face the market restrictions that today's minorities face.[20]

PRINCIPLES FOR WELFARE REFORM

It seems fairly straightforward to lay out general principles for a welfare system that are generally consistent with the promotion of the common welfare, though the strength of the clash between the measures this implies and the incentives contained in our existing political order should not be underestimated. At base the central principles have not changed drastically since the English discussions of Poor Law reform in the early nineteenth century, although prevailing attitudes and political incentives have changed. These principles were described by Charles Murray: (1) people respond to incentives, (2) people are *not* inherently moral and hard working, and (3) people must be held responsible for their actions if society is to function.[21]

The application of such principles in our contemporary setting would reaffirm the validity of the essential characteristics of the English Poor Law reforms of 1834, even if it would not endorse their concrete implementation. In any event, these principles argue against providing for "comfortable" guarantees, and argue in favor of removing impediments to people's efforts to provide themselves with such guarantees. They also argue against the erection and maintenance of obstacles to the efforts of people to help themselves. Welfare should not allow people to live as comfortably as people could live by working in relatively low-paying jobs. But this sort of negative injunction, which translates into the positive refrain "get a job," clashes strongly with the protectionist element of contemporary rent-seeking legisla-

20. Walter E. Williams, "Government Sanctioned Restraints that Reduce Economic Opportunities for Minorities," *Policy Review*, No. 2 (Fall 1977): 7–30, at p. 30.
21. Charles Murray, *Losing Ground* (New York: Basic Books, 1984), p. 146.

tion. If people are expected to support themselves when able, they must be free to use their talents to that end, unencumbered by the presence of obstacles such as the minimum wage laws or licensing restrictions.

The Poor Law discussions and the actual legislation distinguished between the deserving and the undeserving poor. While this distinction is not currently fashionable, it does recognize that people are not inherently moral and hard working. Rather, the extent to which those virtues manifest themselves in a population depends to an important extent on the incentives people face. Institutions and practices that reduce the returns to morality and effort, while increasing the returns to immorality and sloth, will promote the replacement of virtue with vice. The higher the level of support someone who earns nothing or little can get through welfare, the greater will be the number of people who give up work and seek leisure through welfare.

The English Poor Laws dealt with this natural consequence of human nature by imposing a wedge between the deserving and the undeserving poor. In order to receive welfare support, people had to live in workhouses. This was called indoor relief, as distinct from outdoor relief, which was assistance to the sick, the aged, and children in their own homes. Other people who lived at home could not receive support from public charities; they may have been poor but they were independent. To receive support, people had to give up their independence and move into the workhouses. They were stigmatized as paupers. The modern sensitivity finds the idea of stigmatizing the poor offensive. But if stigmatizing is abandoned and replaced by an idea of providing "decent and humane" levels of support, the problem of moral hazard erupts, and many people will choose to replace work with welfare as a means of support.

Rather than seeking to avoid stigmatizing welfare, one could move in the opposite direction. Why not, for instance, aim to create conditions under which penury becomes a sign of moral failing? It is doubtful if these conditions could ever be secured, but consider the implications of doing the opposite. If the stigmatization of welfare were to be fully avoided, the receipt of welfare would have to be anonymous. To the outside world, recipients of welfare could be people who worked at home as consultants or independent contractors. The more fully such anonymity was combined with "decent and humane" levels of support, the more often people would choose this form of living. But the ever-increasing tax burdens imposed on those who continued to work would with increasing intensity induce those tax suppliers to seek alternatives to supporting people on welfare.

Stigmatization is an important element in curbing the substitution of welfare for work as a source of support. Welfare represents a living off of others, in contrast to the mutual benefit that characterizes exchange and the division of labor. The less costly it is to live off of others, the more people will choose to do it. The two main costs are the nonmonetary stigma of welfare and the monetary differential between support through public assistance and support through working. It has been documented with increasing frequency that people can receive public assistance at levels that are commensurate with working at unskilled jobs and can sometimes do even better. The monetary differential between public assistance and work is apparently quite low and is sometimes negative. This differential could, of course, be widened through lowering support under public assistance.

Considerations such as stigmatization and the reduction of real levels of support will doubtless be seen as inhumane. Humaneness is, to be sure, an elusive concept. It is commonly used to argue for higher levels of welfare support. But why isn't one component of the humane thing a duty to try to avoid being a burden on others?[22] In his book *Pauperism* Henry Fawcett tells the tale of Robinson and Smith, who work in the same place for the same wages. Robinson is frugal and saves enough to provide an annuity to support himself in his old age. By contrast, Smith spends an amount equivalent to Robinson's savings in drink and entertainment, has no annuity to support him in his old age, and applies for public assistance.[23] One can generalize from this tale that the fact that one person has a capital account does not necessarily make the person without the account more deserving of support. Whether or not Smith is more deserving depends on the circumstances by which his situation came to be. He could have been someone whose frugality was equal to or possibly even greater than

22. The acceptance of such a duty is surely an important attribute of self-respect, the erosion of which is clearly fostered by the welfare state. See in particular Charles Murray, *In Pursuit of Happiness and Good Government* (New York: Simon and Schuster, 1988), especially pp. 112–57.

23. Henry Fawcett, *Pauperism: Its Causes and Remedies* (London: Macmillan, 1871), pp. 33–34. This tale is similar in thrust to Charles Murray's later tale of Harold and Phyllis in *Losing Ground*.

Robinson's, but the supplier of his annuity went bankrupt or perhaps embezzled the funds.

Would the humane action be to aid Smith? Or is the humane act Smith's avoidance of his course of life in the first place? If actions like Smith's are rewarded, they will multiply, and concomitantly the frugal actions of people like Robinson will diminish. If the goal of social policy is one of fostering dependence and servility, the present form of the welfare state works in that direction. But if what is desired is the promotion of autonomy and independence, an alternative approach is required, one similar in its central foundation to the English Poor Law of 1834. This approach would largely amount to an abandonment of the welfare state or perhaps, equivalently, to the privatization of welfare.

The principal obligation would not be on the Robinsons of the world to support the Smiths, but rather on the Smiths to provide for their own support. But requiring this would entail more than abandoning the public assistance programs of the welfare state. A massive reformation would be needed in other areas that give sheltered status positions to prevailing practitioners and thereby block or at least impede the ability of others to provide for their own support.

Suppose that a person with little skill might be willing to support himself by doing lawn and yard maintenance work. However, if that person does not carry insurance, the homeowner who hires him may be held liable for any injury the worker might suffer. In part, these insurance requirements benefit established landscaping companies by restricting the terms on which newcomers can compete. Moreover, this sort of liability is generally treated as inalienable, in that the worker cannot agree with the homeowner to waive liability. Even if the two agreed to waive liability, had the uninsured worker subsequently been injured while working in the yard, the homeowner would have been liable. Hence, even rules of legal liability may impede the ability of people to support themselves, by giving an advantage to more highly capitalized companies over individual, relatively poor people.

The idea of discarding the welfare state and relying instead on networks of private support might seem like the "sink-or-swim" approach to teaching people to swim. Some people thrown into a lake will make it to shore, but others will not. This approach to the teaching of swimming seems brutal, and recognition of the analogy between the sink-or-swim method and the abandonment of the welfare state may seem strong grounds for maintaining the welfare state.

The validity of the sink-or-swim analogy is subtle, and, on consideration, that subtlety shows that the abandonment of the welfare state is a far more reasonable step than at first appears. Swimming *is* usually taught on a sink-or-swim basis, subtly applied. A mother wants to teach her child to swim. At first the mother will hold her hand under the child's stomach and teach the child how to stroke, kick, and breathe. As the child begins to master these elements, the mother may take her hand away for an instant as her child moves through the water. But the mother will also be alert to replace her hand quickly, before the child becomes frightened and loses the confidence that she has been trying to instill in her child.

Soon the child will be swimming several strokes without her mother's support, but only if Mother is close by, ready to provide support if the child flounders. But if the mother is always close by in the water, the child may never learn to swim with confidence. When the mother knows the child is ready, she must convince her child to take the plunge without Mother standing by, ready to catch her. This is sink or swim. If the mother has done her job well and understands her child, the child will swim and not sink. At the same time the child must know or believe that mother will not provide assistance, for otherwise the child will continue to rely upon Mother for support. To be sure, should the mother have to rescue her child, the result may be traumatic and the child may never learn to swim. Nonetheless, swimming is largely taught in a context of sink or swim subtly applied.

The welfare state, however, is not a superparent. It seems unreasonable to expect the state to possess the intensity of personal caring that parents have and the detailed knowledge that is necessary to deal effectively with individual cases. Public bureaus must operate through rules and general categories, making use of formal knowledge that can be made explicit. Tacit or intuitive knowledge about particular circumstances and cases will appear largely to be arbitrary and capricious if used by bureaus.[24] A parent can more readily and legitimately tailor programs to fit the needs of different children than can the state.

24. The importance of tacit knowledge and its distinction from explicit knowledge is developed in Michael Polanyi, *Personal Knowledge: Towards a Post-Critical Philosophy* (Chicago: University of Chicago Press, 1962). For an important application of this distinction to alternative forms of economic organization, see Don Lavoie, *Rivalry and Central Planning: The Socialist Calculation Debate Reconsidered* (Cambridge: Cambridge University Press, 1985).

The private institutions that would organize networks of support in the absence of a welfare state would surely be closer to parents than to the state in this regard. There is nothing arbitrary or capricious about a charity's making more stringent demands on some potential recipients than on others, say in the form of work requirements. When done privately, such differences in treatment of particular cases are legitimate uses of rights of property and contract. Private institutions are able to make better use of particularized knowledge about people and situations than can state bureaus. They can also handle the Samaritan's dilemma better, as explained in Chapter 8, because no one charity occupies the position of deciding whether a particular person receives support.

The Samaritan's dilemma is unavoidable. Regrettably, but inescapably, misfortune has didactic value. The failure to allow misfortune impales the Samaritan on one horn of his dilemma. But to accept misfortune as part of a process of education and incentive creation does not lead easily to a good conscience, and it threatens to impale the Samaritan on the other horn. This situation and the problems it poses are, of course, an essential and ineradicable aspect of life.[25] While these problems are ineradicable, the welfare state is surely a less capable institutional arrangement for dealing with them than is the complex network of privately organized institutions that would flourish in its absence.

---

25. See, for instance, Thomas Sowell, *A Conflict of Visions* (New York: William Morrow, 1987), for a comparison of "constrained" and "unconstrained" visions of human nature and social order. The perspective adopted here clearly falls within the constrained vision.

10

WELFARE REFORM, CONSTITUTIONAL REFORM, AND THE GENERAL WELFARE

Once policy outcomes are recognized as resulting primarily from the interplay of people's pursuing their interests within an institutional or constitutional regime, it becomes difficult to attribute to ignorance, error, or exogenous and unforeseeable events the observed disparities between what policies are rationalized as being necessary to accomplish and what those policies actually accomplish. Rather, policy outcomes are understandable consequences of the pattern of costs and rewards contained in an institutional or constitutional regime. For this reason, any effort to narrow the gap between justification and reality is more a matter of changing the incentives within which the market for public policy operates than of producing better studies of the consequences of different policy options. Accordingly, this chapter emphasizes the reformation of the political system out of which the programs that constitute the welfare state emerge.

WELFARE REFORM OR POLITICAL REFORM?

If the welfare system is viewed in isolation from other policy outcomes, it is relatively easy to articulate the types of reforms that would move toward mitigating the conflict between the welfare state and the common welfare, as Chapter 9 noted. Security can be provided only through capital accumulation within a well-integrated capital structure. However, the welfare state, in its status-oriented manifestation, acts in contradictory fashion by awarding entitlements, conferring sheltered wealth positions, and generally attenuating and abridging ownership rights. In consequence, people are discouraged from working, saving, and accumulating capital and are encouraged to be less responsible in the conduct of their lives. A welfare state that is consistent with the provision of security cannot rest upon a foundation of taxing-and-transferring. Such a foundation undermines the requisites for genuine security for all participants. Those who are taxed are discouraged from working and saving, as are those who are subsidized for not working and not saving.

Genuine security requires creation of the opposing incentives: working, saving, and accumulating capital must be encouraged and not discouraged. This alternative approach, however, would seem to run afoul of the incentives of legislators within a transfer-seeking polity. The status-oriented welfare state would seem to be a natural component of a system of majoritarian, transfer-seeking democracy. The award of support for not working and not saving is a natural concomitant of a set of policies that prohibit people from working for less than $3.35 per hour or in their homes, using their vehicles for carrying passengers or freight, pruning trees, selling home-baked bread, or installing lawn sprinkling systems. These types of programs, as an inherent by-product of creating protected statuses for certain groups, make it more difficult for people to support themselves.

Although it is possible to articulate a general principle about the nature of a contract-oriented welfare state whose modus operandi would be congruent with the underlying conditions for security within a society, political problems of consistency and sustainability emerge. Consistency is difficult to attain because of the clash between the types of policies that would be required and the types that are compatible with the incentives in the prevailing institutional order of majoritarian democracy. As has been noted in earlier chapters, the dominant political system has become one in which government is a maker of rules for others, rather than being bound by the same rules as all other participants in society. Because government is able to make the rules to which others must adhere, a market naturally arises to secure favorable rules and favorable interpretations of those rules. Welfare reform of the contract-oriented type seems inconsistent with the system of incentives in the existing institutional-constitutional order.

But suppose for purposes of discussion that some type of contract-oriented welfare state were created. The problem of sustainability arises because strong incentives would still exist to enact legislation that would subvert the contract-oriented welfare state and replace it with features of the status-oriented welfare state. Even though everyone may be likely to be wealthier and more secure in a contract-oriented state than in a status-oriented welfare state, individual members and groups in the society can further improve their positions by securing special treatment that would reintroduce elements of the status-oriented welfare state. So long as the constitutional order is a majoritarian democracy, such reintroduction should be expected.

Legislatures cannot be expected to bind themselves. Congress has adhered to the requirements of its own Budget Control Act of 1974 only twice since its enactment. What one legislature does can be undone at will by a succeeding legislature. A contract-oriented welfare state does not seem sustainable within a regime of majoritarian democracy, in which the legislature serves as a marketplace where people compete to secure transfers and other favorable treatment by imposing taxes and other forms of disability on others. Such a regime features a status-oriented welfare state as a natural component, despite the incongruity between its mode of operation and the underlying requisites for wealth and security. Institutional-constitutional reform seems of more fundamental importance than welfare reform per se, primarily because of the problems of consistency and sustainability.

CONSTITUTIONAL REMEDIES FOR MAJORITARIAN DEMOCRACY

So long as government is organized according to majoritarian principles, its participation in economic life will contain important forces tending to erode liberty and prosperity, because successful politicians and special interests can profit from the supply of legislation that has these effects. The problem of constitutional design is determining how to accentuate the positive activities of government while restricting the negative activities. This requires the development of an *appropriate* set of constraints on government that will allow the positive activities to filter through the net of constraints while the negative activities are screened out. This problem, which the Constitutional Convention dealt with in 1787, is likewise central to the contemporary interest in constitutional controls on government.

In numerous situations in the absence of constraining constitutional rules, the individual pursuit of interest will lead to generally undesirable outcomes, and yet it will be in no one's interest to prevent those outcomes. This property of a system of unlimited or majoritarian democracy was examined in Chapter 7. A regime of majoritarian democracy would be expected to produce policies such as high license fees for taxicabs, cartels for the marketing of milk, prohibitions on working at home, and so on, as aspects of the "market for legislation." Although such transfer seeking is rational within the prevailing constitutional framework, it might not be rational under an alternative framework. In any event, the prevention of such waste requires some form of constitutional constraint to overcome the prisoner's dilemma that the participants face. Legislative enactment is not sufficient, because legislators are the prisoners in the dilemma: they are doing what politically yields profit within a system of majoritarian democracy.

James Madison thought—mistakenly, as judged from the hindsight of history and the insights of public choice theory—that the problem of minority faction could be controlled by the use of majority rule. Madison thought majority faction could be controlled through the republican form of government that the constitution he supported would establish. The system of concurrent majorities that would be created by the proposed constitution would mitigate if not solve the problem of majority faction, thereby allowing government to control itself.[1] Madison took the supremacy of the legislature as inescapable within a republican government and looked to the organization of the legislature within the overall federal system as the focus for the control of government through concurrent majorities.

To the extent that the two legislative branches are selected on different bases of representation, concurrent majorities in the two branches would imply greater support in the society at large than if the two branches were similar. Indeed, in the event of a total dissimilarity between the two branches, majority support in each branch could even result in unanimous support. This concern with legislative organization shows clearly Madison's recognition of the problem of majori-

---

1. See Vincent Ostrom, *The Political Theory of a Compound Republic*, 2d ed. (Lincoln, Neb.: University of Nebraska Press, 1987), and Vincent Ostrom, "Why Governments Fail: An Inquiry into the Use of Instruments of Evil to Do Good," in James M. Buchanan and Robert D. Tollison, eds., *The Theory of Public Choice—II* (Ann Arbor, Mich.: University of Michigan Press, 1984), pp. 422–35.

tarian democracy and his understanding that its control was a matter of constitutional design. With respect to this principle of dissimilarity between legislative branches, the evolution of the federal legislature has reduced the degree of dissimilarity—as represented, for instance, by the shift to the direct election of federal senators.

Madison also saw the federalist form of government as central to controlling majority faction. The Constitution dealt with this problem by delegating different powers to state governments than it delegated to the federal government. As Madison noted in *Federalist* No. 45:

> The powers delegated by the proposed Constitution to the federal government are few and defined. Those which are to remain in the State governments are numerous and indefinite. . . . The powers reserved to the several States will extend to all the objects which, in the ordinary course of affairs, concern the lives, liberties, and properties of the people, and the internal order, improvement, and prosperity of the State.[2]

In the case of the minimum wage, as discussed in Chapter 7, a faction of one-quarter of the population was dominant because it formed a bare majority in 218 congressional districts located in 26 states. Madison would have presumed that any such power to set wages was clearly not delegated to the federal government. It would have been a state matter, if, indeed, it had been a matter suitable for legislation at all. If minimum wage legislation were the province of the states, half the nation would have had minimum wage legislation and half would not. The effect of faction would have been more tightly controlled than when such legislation was a national matter. And to the extent that such legislation truly weakened the general prosperity, those states that did not enact it would have become wealthier. As a result of the differences in standards of living that would ensue, processes of learning and emulation would to some extent have been set in motion and led to a revision of such harmful legislation. The subsequent adoption of the Ninth and Tenth Amendments reflected Madison's understanding of the division of powers between the federal government and the state governments that the Constitution clearly called for. Those amendments have been effectively repealed through an ongoing process of constitutional erosion.

In a federal form of government, the ability of different jurisdic-

---

2. Willmore Kendall and George W. Carey, eds., *The Federalist Papers* (New Rochelle, N.Y.: Arlington House, n.d.), pp. 292–93.

tions to pursue different policies and to choose different institutional regimes for implementing policies creates a type of laboratory for experimentation, in which valuable knowledge about the properties of different policy measures and institutions can be acquired. One jurisdiction might use progressive income taxation, another regressive taxation, and still another value added taxation. One jurisdiction might require mandatory participation in elections, another might restrict the franchise to property owners, and yet another might weight people's votes in proportion to the taxes they pay. Innumerable possibilities for institutional variation exist. Other things being equal, people who live in governments that possess or manage to find positive-sum institutions will become wealthier than those who live in governments that have negative-sum institutions.

Such a competitive order would create conditions and incentives favorable to the development of knowledge about the merits of different institutional orders. By contrast, as government becomes increasingly centralized, the options for choice become more restricted. The scope for experience to be applied to assessing different options is narrowed because of the decreasing availability of varied experience. In a truly centralized regime it would be impossible to determine whether a particular institutional order was positive sum or negative sum, for this determination can be made only in the presence of competing options. After all, what makes it possible to form a judgment about the quality of different options is precisely the availability of those options. The simultaneous existence of competing sources of supply, along with the ability to compare and choose, enables someone to make a reasonable judgment about whether or not one supplier's product is more valuable than another's. As competition among suppliers is restricted, it becomes less possible for people to make reasonable judgments.

When governments operate in a truly competitive or federal system of government in which there is wide autonomy for people to choose their own institutional arrangements, policies created by one government compete with policies created by other governments in the federation. The simultaneous existence of governments that differ in their approaches to policy issues provides a setting in which claims about different policies, as well as about the institutional regimes, will be tested by experience.

But as the scope for different institutions and policies is narrowed through an increasing nationalization of what was once a truly federal system of government, the ability of people to apply their experiences in determining the survival properties of those different policies and regimes is weakened. Negative-sum institutions will thus acquire greater survival power as the options are narrowed, because an essential aspect of the production of knowledge—the ability to compare and choose among competing options—is weakened. In the limiting case of total centralization, no meaningful options for choice would exist, for the policies and the regimes in which they were made in the different states would have little scope for variation because of the dominance of federal pressures for homogeneity. As a result, experience could not produce knowledge relevant to the options for choice. One option would no longer have to stand up to direct comparison with an alternative option; it would have to stand up only to conjecture. Science fiction would still exist, but history would have been sterilized.[3]

NORMATIVE PRINCIPLES FOR CONSTITUTIONAL CONSTRUCTION

It is common to speak of equity and efficiency as distinct normative principles, as well as to think in terms of some trade-off between these principles. The principle of *efficiency,* typically formulated as the benefit principle of public economics, states that public outcomes should reflect the valuations of the people who constitute the polity. By this criterion, budgetary outcomes should reflect the willingness of people to pay for the programs being undertaken. In turn, the evidence for the fulfillment of this criterion is consensus about budgetary outcomes. In contrast, the principle of *equity* is commonly related to some notion of ability to pay, as represented by the idea that the larger people's income or wealth, the larger the claims government should make on them.[4]

The idea that taxes should be based on *ability* to pay conflicts with

---

3. For further insightful considerations of the value of a federal system of government, see Gottfried Dietze, *The Federalist: A Classic on Federalism and Free Government* (Baltimore: Johns Hopkins University Press, 1960); and Martin Diamond, "The *Federalist's* View of Federalism," in *Essays in Federalism* (Claremont, Calif.: Institute for Studies in Federalism, Claremont Men's College, 1961), pp. 21–64.

4. For a clear description of the benefit and ability-to-pay principles and their intellectual background, see Richard A. Musgrave, *The Theory of Public Finance* (New York: McGraw-Hill, 1959), pp. 61–115.

the idea that taxes should be based on the *willingness* of people to pay. The latter is based on individual evaluations of budgetary outcomes, whereas the former expressly denies the propriety of such a basis. In the latter case, public outcomes are evaluated in terms of a consensus among the governed, constrained by the legitimacy of rules of property and contract. In the former case, public outcomes are evaluated in terms of an external criterion that expressly denies the normative status of consent. The common descriptions of a trade-off between efficiency and equity would in many cases seem to call for a mixing of two incompatible principles: one evaluates outcomes by a standard of consensus among the participants and the other evaluates those outcomes against some standard that is independent of what the participants might or might not consent to do.

But in a regime that takes seriously the dictum that government should reflect the consent of the governed, the only possible norm would seem to be the contractarian one of consent. People and their rights are prior to government within such a regime, so the standard of evaluation for policy outcomes must ultimately be a standard of consent among the participants. There can be no conflict between principles of efficiency and equity, because within a liberal democratic regime the only possible approach to normative evaluation is contractarian or consensual.

Under such a regime, people have their rights of person and property, and government accordingly acts as one participant among many in the society. Government must itself operate within the same general principles as all other participants in society. Indeed, the ageless problem of self-government has always been how government can maintain a kind of schizophrenia: in one capacity government is a participant in the economic life of a society, playing by the same rules as others; in the other capacity government is an umpire. But if in this latter capacity government is able to become a maker of rules for others to play by, it is likely to use its legislative powers to bias the game by changing the rules to favor some at the expense of others.

The raison d'être of constitutional government is that government is subject to limits that reside in people's prior rights of person and property and is itself neither the source of those rights nor the arbiter of those limits. If two people acting privately cannot legitimately take the property of a third, neither should they be able to do so when they form a political majority and invoke the name of government on their behalf. For to do otherwise would make government the source of people's rights, rather than merely a reflection of people's use of their rights.

Yet there are tendencies, latent if not manifest, for postconstitutional opportunism to emerge through democratic political processes, eroding those gains in the process of violating some people's rights for the benefit of others. For instance, suppose some people in a city own developed property while others own undeveloped property. If the owners of the developed property could prevent the owners of the undeveloped property from developing their property, they could enrich themselves at the expense of the owners of the undeveloped property.

The only legitimate way this could be done privately would be for the owners of the developed property to buy the undeveloped property. But they could accomplish the same thing at lower personal cost if they could enact a zoning ordinance, as illustrated by *Agins v. City of Tiburon.*[5] By restricting the supply of developed land, the zoning ordinance increases the value of the developed property, while lowering the value of the undeveloped property. It enables the owners of the developed property effectively to rob the owners of the undeveloped property, just as surely as if they had forcibly prevented the owners of the undeveloped land from developing their land. In this case the police power of government is being used as an instrument of plunder within a regime of majoritarian democracy.[6]

ECONOMIC CALCULATION AND THE CONDUCT OF GOVERNMENT

An important source of insight for a constitutional order is the theory of economic calculation. This theory originated in the 1920s as a result of various socialist proposals to replace markets with planning as the means of resource allocation. However, Ludwig von Mises showed that in such a socialist system the structure of production could not reflect consumer wants efficiently, because the knowledge necessary

---

5. 477 U.S. 255 (1980).

6. These normative principles of constitutional order and the difficulties in implementing them are surveyed in Richard E. Wagner, "Morals, Interests, and Constitutional Order: A Public Choice Perspective," *Oregon Law Review* 67 (No. 1, 1988): 73–92.

for economic calculation could not be generated.[7] The subsequent socialist literature retreated from the abolition of markets and proposed instead some variant of "market socialism," which, as Paul Craig Roberts noted, was hardly socialism at all and instead represented "a polycentric system with signals that are irrational from the standpoint of economic efficiency."[8]

The theory of economic calculation explains that the pattern of resource usage can efficiently reflect consumer wants only if economic activity takes place within the central institutional elements of property, contract, and residual claimancy. Thus, the theory meshes well with the normative principles discussed earlier. The theory of economic calculation explains why it is impossible to determine what would constitute an efficient set of policy or budgetary outcomes independently of a competitive market process operating in a framework of property and contract. This theory explains that the structure of production cannot possibly adapt efficiently to people's wants in the absence of prices and the information and incentive that they convey. Rational economic conduct depends upon an institutional order that allows for the ownership of property, that uses contract or consent to choose how property is used, and that holds people liable for the value consequences of their choices. To the extent that the sphere covered by this institutional order expands, the scope for effective economic conduct is widened. Prices are an important source of the knowledge necessary for effective conduct; they are also an important source of incentive, for in conjunction with residual claimancy they provide a means of rewarding effective actions and penalizing ineffective actions. Within such an institutional setting, choices concerning the use of resources actually reflect a consensus, within the prevailing rules of law that order economic activity, on the anticipated value consequences of alternative uses of resources.

Market and *democracy* are abstractions that become concrete only as they are cloaked in specific rules governing the relations among people. But what particular rules are to govern those relations? The

---

7. See the essays collected in Friedrich A. Hayek, ed., *Collectivist Economic Planning* (London: Routledge and Kegan Paul, 1935). For von Mises's particular contribution, see "Economic Calculation in the Socialist Commonwealth," pp. 87–130.

8. Paul Craig Roberts, *Alienation and the Soviet Economy* (Albuquerque, N.M.: University of New Mexico Press, 1971), p. 84. See also, by Roberts, "The Polycentric Soviet Economy," *Journal of Law and Economics* 12 (April 1969): 163–79; and "Oscar Lange's Theory of Socialist Planning," *Journal of Political Economy* 79 (June 1971): 562–77.

premise of a liberal society is that the use of resources should reflect individual valuations. But what does this mean, both in principle and in concrete implementation? This is the problem of economic calculation, and its solution requires, in a liberal framework, some consensus, which in turn can only be achieved within an appropriate set of rules. Growing bananas can be judged a better use of resources in North Dakota than growing wheat, either because the crop is selected by some nonliberal value system or because the participants agree that growing bananas is better than growing wheat. A market economy ordered around property and contract contains a set of rules that produces such an agreement in an economical fashion.

Thus, a single principle—consensus—enables resource utilization to reflect individual valuations. The problem of contemporary policy, in this perspective, is that the state and market are presently organized according to different principles. The state and market do not simply represent different reflections of the same principle, with each reflection appropriate to a different task. These different organizing principles create contradictions that are revealed by policy failures. Removal of those contradictions requires recognition that *all* choices concerning resource usage must be made within a unified institutional order that reflects in its particular features a general principle of consensus.

Hence, a unified approach to economy and polity—political economy—is called for in place of the current approach, in which the economy is organized by market transactions that take place through contract while the polity is organized through impositions and infringements upon contract. If the "consent of the governed" is to be taken seriously, the theory of economic calculation sets forth some general principles that must obtain. Yet there are many different ways of applying any set of principles to a concrete situation.

KNUT WICKSELL, ECONOMIC CALCULATION, AND CONSTITUTIONAL PRINCIPLE

Knut Wicksell published in 1896 what has proven to be a seminal work on the concrete implementation of principles of consensual or constitutionally limited government under a rule of law.[9] Wicksell

---

9. Knut Wicksell, *Finanztheoretische Untersuchungen, nebst Darstellung und Kritik des Stuerwesens Schwedens* (Jena: Gustav Fischer, 1896). For further consideration of Wicksell, see Richard E. Wagner, "*The Calculus of Consent*: A Wicksellian Retrospective," *Public Choice* 56 (February 1988): 153–66.

took for granted, as did Madison, that government's choices should reflect the consent of the governed and then showed how this principle could be used to construct actual institutional rules. Wicksell sought to describe institutions that would promote consensual or concordant democracy, as against factional or majoritarian democracy, and to do so within the Swedish context of his time. Sweden was a constitutional monarchy, so the two main institutions Wicksell studied were the Crown and Parliament.

The Crown, like any executive agency, Wicksell thought, would be generally interested in expanding its operations. But it could do so only by receiving larger appropriations from Parliament. Wicksell recognized that, should Parliament act by majority rule, government would become excessively large, according to the principle of consent of the governed. But Wicksell also saw Swedish society as essentially consisting of a relatively small number of homogeneous groups, a feature that meant the Parliament could be organized so as to give proportional representation to those groups. With different parties representing the groups, a system of proportional representation would bring about a fairly complete representation of Swedish society in a Parliament that contained a small number of homogeneous parties.

To implement a general principle of consensual or concordant democracy and to control factional or majoritarian democracy, Wicksell proposed to allow each party in Parliament to withhold the tax payments that would otherwise be due from its constituency, if it did not think its supporters were getting adequate value in exchange for their taxes. This feature of Wicksell's proposal is referred to as a rule of near unanimity. Wicksell proposed that taxing-and-spending choices require substantial consensus, on the order of 75 percent to 90 percent, among the parliamentary representatives. This type of near unanimity among the representatives of a small number of homogeneous groups within a Parliament selected by proportional representation is not, of course, anything like a rule of near unanimity applied to the contemporary U.S. Congress, which is based on single-member constituencies.

Wicksell gave little attention to the rules of procedure that might be required to conduct business in the Parliament he envisioned. The rules of procedure as we know them, as reflected in *Robert's Rules of Order,* are predicated on simple majority rule. Other parliamentary principles would call for different procedural rules. Wicksell did, however, note a few pertinent considerations. If groups are able to withhold their share of tax payments when they judge particular projects as not worthwhile, particular spending packages must be tied to particular sources of revenue. Any proposal to spend would have to be accompanied by a proposal to tax to cover the cost. Only in this way could people know how much they were being asked to pay for particular programs; without this knowledge they could not form reasonable judgments of the programs.

The withdrawal of the consent of one group would not mean that the proposed project would fail to be undertaken. Those who supported the project could always develop an alternative proposal to cover the cost of the project. Wicksell's specific suggestions for implementing a principle of consent were not designed to prevent people from undertaking beneficial programs. They were intended to prevent some people from undertaking projects only because they were being paid for through costs imposed on others—projects that would not have been undertaken, or would have been carried out on a smaller scale, had the beneficiaries had to bear the costs themselves.[10]

Wicksell recognized the negative-sum properties of majoritarian democracy, and he attempted to spell out an alternative institutional order of consensual democracy that would embody a quid pro quo relationship between citizens and government. The replacement of majoritarian democracy with consensual democracy would represent the creation of a contractual relationship between citizens and government. As a result of this relationship, government would expand in size so long as people thought the value of the services they were receiving in return for their contributions exceeded the value of whatever else they might have bought with those contributions. And if people did not think they were getting good value for their contributions, government would shrink in size. In other words, government would become subject to the same rules of economical conduct as private citizens, rather than being outside those rules as it is under majoritarian democracy.

Wicksell took as a general principle that government should reflect the consent of the governed and developed some particular institu-

---

10. Wicksell also recognized that a principle cannot be implemented de novo. Any state will have a menu of obligations it has incurred from its past. Wicksell included the public debt in this category and thought that majority rule was the proper way for dealing with these inherited obligations during the transition period while they were being discharged.

tional implications of that principle as he thought these would apply to Sweden in 1896. Wicksell's enduring contribution has been his recognition that government can act as a value-enhancing participant in the division of labor in society only if both the polity and the economy operate within essentially the same consensus-oriented institutional order. In that order rights of ownership are well defined and protected, and resources get shifted from one use to another by agreement among the owners of those resources rather than through the use of the state by one subset of owners to abridge the rights of other owners. Wicksell's specific proposals showed, in a particular historical setting, how to eradicate the incongruity in the modes of operation of government and the market economy by placing them on the same contractual or consensual footing.[11]

CONTEMPORARY CONSTITUTIONAL OPTIONS

Certain immutable principles characterize human affairs and social organization. Such principles as the one that people will seek to give up what they value less to get what they value more are as unchangeable as gravity. Wise legislation operates within the framework of such a principle. In contrast, legislation that operates contrary to it will at best be ineffective and more generally will be outrightly harmful. The problem of economic policy is essentially a constitutional one, broadly understood: are there ways of constituting governments within democratic principles that will discourage policy outcomes that by their efforts to contradict immutable principles create general harm, while at the same time enabling governments to do those things of general benefit that the same economic principles explain will otherwise not be undertaken for reasons described by the theory of public goods?

The general principle of a contractarian state can be implemented in numerous ways. Whatever form such an implementation might take, the theory of economic calculation suggests that there must be rights of ownership, agreement or contract as the method of converting resources from one use to another, and some profit-and-loss status through

---

11. For a valuable examination of the essential equivalence of Wicksell's principle of just taxation and Pareto's principle of optimality, both of which were grounded in consent, see P. Hennipman, "Wicksell and Pareto: Their Relationship in the Theory of Public Finance," *History of Political Economy* 14 (Spring 1982): 37–64.

which people bear personal responsibility for the value consequences of their actions.

Within the central features of American republicanism, the control of faction must focus ultimately on the legislature. Madison recognized this and sought to control the legislature by having the Senate and the House based on different principles of selection. If the interests represented by a majority in one chamber did not constitute a majority in the other chamber, a concurrent majority in both chambers would require an expansion in the representation of the interest of the population at large. It would always be possible to pursue this line of thought by considering changes in the basis on which legislatures are selected, with the intent of reducing the similarity of the two chambers. The greater that diversity, the more nearly true it will be that the legislation that receives majority support in both chambers will have broad, general value rather than narrow, factional value.

The search for diversity need not be limited to the design of different ways of selecting legislators. Diversity of interest may also be instilled within individual legislators by changing the method by which they are compensated. The problem with faction is that legislation is enacted, despite its diminution of the common wealth, because the concentrated gains it offers to supporters dominates the diffused (though larger in the aggregate) losses elsewhere. To the extent that government undertakes those protective and productive activities that promote the general welfare while refraining from undertaking those activities that retard it, the total wealth of the society increases. But under the prevailing regime of majoritarian democracy, legislators can gain by supporting programs that transfer wealth to particular interests, even though aggregate wealth and personal liberty are diminished in the process.

This negative outcome is facilitated because legislators have a direct stake not in the common or aggregate wealth of the members of the nation, but only in the particular wealth positions of the members of the warring factions that contend for favors. Madison thought that concurrent majorities among bodies with differing interests would in the end promote the general welfare. In a different application of the principle that Madison sought to implement, legislators could perhaps be compensated through a balanced portfolio of stocks, bonds, and other assets. To the extent that this could be done, the incentive for each legislator to promote the general welfare could be strengthened.

A legislator who represented a significant number of unemployed youths and might support a job creation program despite its demonstrated ineffectiveness would be more inclined to support a reformation of minimum wage and child labor legislation as more effective overall. The reason is that the legislator who is compensated by the stock portfolio would share in all the gains *and* losses of legislation. To the extent that such a balanced portfolio could be put into effect, legislators would tend to be rewarded in direct proportion to the general increase in national wealth, rather than in proportion to the favors conferred upon the beneficiaries of particular legislation.[12]

A well-working or well-ordered state is, within a liberal or contractarian perspective, one that supports the peaceful pursuits of its members. To the extent that government conducts its productive and protective activities in a manner consistent with liberal norms, the aggregate wealth of the members of the nation will rise. In like manner, should government fail to conduct its protective and productive activities properly, as assessed by a principle of consensus—and with such failure resulting either from government's doing what it should not do or failing to do what it should do—there will be a diminution in the aggregate wealth. In either case, compensation geared to the value of a balanced portfolio of assets might be constructed to operate similarly to stock options and related incentive plans in corporations. A direct relationship between performance and reward might lead in turn to a greater congruence between the norms or justifications for public policies and the actual consequences of those policies.

The brief references here to constitutional reforms have been advanced only to illustrate the point that public choice scholarship locates reform at the constitutional level and not at the level of postconstitutional politics. Once political outcomes are seen as largely determined by the rules that constrain political processes, the use of welfare economics as a vehicle for rendering policy advice becomes incoherent. Political interventions into the economy will follow an economic logic that is independent of the dictates of welfare economics. How closely particular policy measures will correspond to those

---

12. In a quite different context, W. H. Hutt proposed a system of *shared entrepreneurship* between workers and owners as a way of overcoming the faction that often characterizes present labor-management relations. See W. H. Hutt, "Every Man a Capitalist," *Policy Review* No. 22 (Fall 1982): 141–53.

dictates will depend on willingness to pay, broadly speaking, and not on the analytical cogency of those dictates. With an analytical framework that renders political outcomes dependent on constitutional rules, the removal of pathological outcomes becomes much more a matter of securing constitutional reformation than of giving better economic advice to politicians.[13]

IN SUMMATION

This book has examined some of the insights that the theory of public choice can bring to bear upon the activities of the welfare state. If the welfare state is viewed in isolation from other policy outcomes, it seems natural to seek to articulate the types of reforms that would move toward mitigating the clash between the welfare state and the general welfare. A number of scholars, cited throughout this book, have advanced valuable suggestions to this end.

However, the most pertinent question raised by the public choice perspective concerns the possibility that effective reform must go beyond the technical merits of proposals for specific reform of the welfare state. The central message of this perspective is that the actual operation of those institutions that are called the welfare state will depend on the pattern of costs and gains that different courses of conduct offer. What gets produced is what rewards the producers the most—in politics, in the transfer programs of the welfare state, and in economic life generally.

A contract-oriented welfare state would seem to run afoul of the incentives of legislators; the status-oriented welfare state is a natural component of a system of majoritarian, transfer-seeking democracy. While it is possible to articulate a general principle about the nature of a contract-oriented welfare state whose modus operandi would be congruent with the underlying conditions for security within a society, welfare reform of the contract-oriented type seems in large measure inconsistent with the system of incentives of the existing institutional-constitutional order. Consequently, the problems associated with the

---

13. This fundamental contrast between a policy perspective and a constitutional perspective are explored in Geoffrey Brennan and James M. Buchanan, *The Reason of Rules* (Cambridge: Cambridge University Press, 1985); and Dwight R. Lee and Richard B. McKenzie, *Regulating Government* (Lexington, Mass.: D. C. Heath, 1987).

welfare state and its reform should be seen not in isolation from all other political outcomes but rather as part of a pattern produced in a system of unlimited majoritarian democracy.

The equivalent of some denationalization of welfare might be achieved through ordinary political processes; however, any such denationalization would be precarious in the absence of constitutional reformation. Deregulation of welfare, airlines, or anything else might be achieved in a transfer-seeking polity. For this to happen, the value of opposing policy measures must be equal for different sets of people, and those people must face equal costs of political organization. But this makes deregulation, the absence of regulation, or, still more generally, the maintenance of a free economy a matter of the accidental constellation of political forces and not a central "default setting" of a constitutional order. To achieve this latter position requires constitutional reformation.

When policy outcomes are seen as a result of people's interactions as they pursue their interests in an institutional or constitutional order, one cannot attribute the disparities between the rationalizations and the reality of policies to error or external events. Policy outcomes must be regarded instead as a natural outcome of the pattern of costs and rewards contained within any institutional or constitutional regime. The transfer programs of the welfare state, as just one subset of outcomes of a political process, will probably not diverge greatly from political outcomes in general. As political institutions come increasingly to reward transfer-seeking activities relative to genuinely productive activities, the prospects that those political processes will generate a welfare state that operates in contrary fashion weaken.[14]

The conditions that have prompted the growing interest in welfare reform are to an important extent the predictable product of a system of unlimited majoritarian democracy. In addition to better knowledge about the consequences of policy measures, a successful effort to narrow the gap between justification and reality must include some change in the incentives within which the market for public policy operates. The problem of controlling legislators so that their personal interest corresponds to the promotion of the common interest does not resolve

---

14. For historical documentation of the replacement of genuinely productive activities by rent-seeking transfer activities in the United States, see Terry L. Anderson and Peter J. Hill, *The Birth of a Transfer Society* (Stanford, Calif.: Hoover Institution Press, 1980).

itself naturally, but it can be resolved only through appropriately constructed constitutional constraints, as Madison recognized. The study of public policy must go beyond analyzing the consequences of different policy measures, actual and potential, and must also consider the institutional and constitutional requisites for producing policies supportive of the free society that the American constitutional order promises.

SELECTED BIBLIOGRAPHY

Anderson, Terry L. and Hill, Peter J. *The Birth of a Transfer Society*. Stanford, CA: Hoover Institution Press, 1980.

———— and ————. "Constraining the Transfer Society: Constitutional and Moral Dimensions." *Cato Journal* 6 (Spring 1986): 317–39.

Ayanian, Robert. "Nuclear Consequences of the Welfare State." *Public Choice* 49 (No. 3, 1986): 201–22.

Baird, Charles W. *Rent Control: The Perennial Folly*. Washington: Cato Institute, 1980.

Banfield, Edward C. *The Unheavenly City*. Boston: Little, Brown, 1965.

Blinder, Alan S. "Inequality and Mobility in the Distribution of Wealth." *Kyklos* 29 (No. 4, 1976): 607–38.

Brennan, Geoffrey and Buchanan, James M. *The Reason of Rules*. Cambridge: Cambridge University Press, 1985.

Browning, Edgar K. "The Trend toward Equality in the Distribution of Net Income." *Southern Economic Journal* 43 (July 1976): 912–23.

————. "Taxation, Capital Accumulation, and Equity." In *Taxation and the Deficit Economy*, ed. by Dwight R. Lee, pp. 19–47. San Francisco: Pacific Research Institute for Public Policy, 1986.

———— and Johnson, William R. "The Trade-off between Equality and Efficiency." *Journal of Political Economy* 92 (April 1984): 175–203.

Buchanan, James M. *Public Finance in Democratic Process*. Chapel Hill: University of North Carolina Press, 1967.

————. *The Limits of Liberty*. Chicago: University of Chicago Press, 1975.

————. "The Samaritan's Dilemma." In *Altruism, Morality, and Economic*

Theory, ed. by Edmund Phelps, pp. 71–85. New York: Russell Sage, 1975.

————. "A Hobbesian Interpretation of the Rawlsian Difference Principle." *Kyklos* 29 (No. 1, 1976): 5–25.

———— and Tullock, Gordon. *The Calculus of Consent.* Ann Arbor: University of Michigan Press, 1962.

————; Tollison, Robert D.; and Tullock, Gordon, eds. *Toward a Theory of the Rent Seeking Society.* College Station: Texas A&M University Press, 1980.

Cogan, John F. "Labor Supply and Negative Income Taxation: New Evidence from the New Jersey-Pennsylvania Experiment." *Economic Inquiry* 21 (October 1983): 465–84.

Cowen, Tyler, ed. *The Theory of Market Failure: A Critical Examination.* Fairfax, VA: George Mason University Press, 1988.

Danziger, Sheldon; Haveman, Robert; and Plotnik, Robert. "How Income Transfers Affect Work, Savings, and the Income Distribution." *Journal of Economic Literature* 19 (September 1981): 975–1028.

Darby, Michael R. *The Effects of Social Security on Income and the Capital Stock.* Washington, DC: American Enterprise Institute, 1979.

Eckert, Ross D. and Hilton, George W. "The Jitneys." *Journal of Law and Economics* 15 (October 1972): 293–325.

Epstein, Richard A. *Takings: Private Property and the Power of Eminent Domain.* Cambridge: Harvard University Press, 1985.

Fawcett, Henry. *Pauperism: Its Causes and Remedies.* London: Macmillan, 1871.

Feldstein, Martin S. "Social Security, Induced Retirement, and Aggregate Capital Accumulation." *Journal of Political Economy* 82 (October 1974): 905–26.

Ferrara, Peter J. *Social Security: The Inherent Contradiction.* Washington: Cato Institute, 1980.

Friedman, Milton. "Choice, Chance, and the Personal Distribution of Income." *Journal of Political Economy* 61 (August 1953): 277–90.

Fuchs, Victor R. *How We Live.* Cambridge: Harvard University Press, 1983.

Garfinkel, Irwin and Haveman, Robert. *Earnings Capacity, Poverty, and Inequality.* New York: Academic Press, 1977.

Gilder, George. *Wealth and Poverty.* New York: Basic Books, 1981.

Glicken, Morley D. "Transgenerational Welfare Dependency." *Journal of Contemporary Studies* 4 (Summer 1981): 31–41.

Gross, Stanley J. *Professional Licensure and Quality: The Evidence.* Washington: Cato Institute, 1986.

Gwartney, James D. and Wagner, Richard E., eds. *Public Choice and Constitutional Economics.* Greenwich, CT: JAI Press, 1988.

———— and McCaleb, Thomas S. "Have Anti-poverty Programs Increased Poverty?" *Cato Journal* 5 (Spring 1985): 1–16.

Hausman, Jerry A. "Labor Supply." In *How Taxes Affect Economic Behavior,* ed. by Henry J. Aaron and Joseph A. Pechman, pp. 27–72. Washington: Brookings Institution, 1981.

Hennipman, P. "Wicksell and Pareto: Their Relationship in the Theory of Public Finance." *History of Political Economy* 14 (Spring 1982): 37–64.

Himmelfarb, Gertrude. *The Idea of Poverty.* New York: Alfred A. Knopf, 1983.

Hochman, Harold M. and Rodgers, James D. "Pareto Optimal Redistribution." *American Economic Review* 59 (September 1969): 542–57.

Hoffman, Elizabeth and Spitzer, Matthew L. "Entitlements, Rights, and Fairness: An Experimental Examination of Subjects' Concepts of Distributive Justice." *Journal of Legal Studies* 14 (June 1985): 259–97.

Lave, Charles A., ed. *Urban Transit: The Private Challenge to Public Transportation.* San Francisco: Pacific Research Institute, 1985.

Lavoie, Don. *Rivalry and Central Planning: The Socialist Calculation Debate Reconsidered.* New York: Cambridge University Press, 1985.

Lee, Dwight R. and McKenzie, Richard B. *Regulating Government.* Lexington, MA: D.C. Heath, 1987.

Leffler, Keith B. "Minimum Wages, Welfare, and Wealth Transfers to the Poor." *Journal of Law and Economics* 21 (October 1978): 345–58.

Leland, Hayne E. "Quacks, Lemons, and Licensing: A Theory of Minimum Quality Standards." *Journal of Political Economy* 87 (December 1979): 1328–46.

Leoni, Bruno. *Freedom and the Law.* Los Angeles: Nash Publishing Co., 1961.

Lewis, H. G. *Union Relative Wage Effects.* Chicago: University of Chicago Press, 1986.

Lindsay, Cotton M. "A Theory of Government Enterprise." *Journal of Political Economy* 84 (October 1976): 1061–77.

————. "Real Returns to Medical Education." *Journal of Human Resources* 8 (Summer 1973): 331–48.

Linneman, Peter. "The Economic Impacts of Minimum Wage Laws: A New Look at an Old Question." *Journal of Political Economy.* 90 (June 1982): 443–69.

McCormick, Robert E. and Tollison, Robert D. *Politicians, Legislation, and the Economy.* Boston: Martinus Nijhoff, 1981.

McIlwain, Charles Howard. *Constitutionalism: Ancient and Modern,* rev. ed. Ithaca, NY: Cornell University Press, 1947.

Mead, Lawrence. *Beyond Entitlement: The Social Obligations of Citizenship.* New York: Free Press, 1986.

Meckling, William H. "Values and the Choice of the Model of the Individual in the Social Sciences." *Schweizerische Zeitschrift fuer Volkswirtschaft und Statistik* 112 (December 1976): 545–60.

Mitchell, William C. "Fiscal Behavior in the Modern Democratic State: Public-Choice Perspectives and Contributions." In *Political Economy: Recent Views*, ed. by Larry L. Wade, pp. 69–114. Boston: Kluwer-Nijhoff, 1983.

Munnell, Alicia H. *The Effect of Social Security on Personal Savings*. Cambridge: Ballinger, 1974.

Murray, Charles. *Losing Ground*. New York: Basic Books, 1984.

———. *In Pursuit of Happiness and Good Government*. New York: Simon and Schuster, 1988.

Niskanen, William A. *Bureaucracy and Representative Government*. Chicago, Aldine, 1971.

———. "The Pathology of Politics." In *Capitalism and Freedom: Problems and Prospects*, ed. by Richard T. Selden, pp. 20–35. Charlottesville: University Press of Virginia, 1974.

Nozick, Robert. *Anarchy, State, and Utopia*. New York: Basic Books, 1974.

Ostrom, Vincent. *The Political Theory of a Compound Republic: Designing the American Experiment*, 2nd ed. Lincoln: University of Nebraska Press, 1987.

———. "Why Governments Fail: An Inquiry into the Use of Instruments of Evil to Do Good." In *The Theory of Public Choice—II*, ed. by James M. Buchanan and Robert D. Tollison, pp. 422–35. Ann Arbor: University of Michigan Press, 1984.

Paglin, Morton. "The Measurement and Trend of Inequality: A Basic Revision." *American Economic Review* 65 (September 1975): 598–609.

Parsons, Donald O. "The Decline in Male Labor Force Participation." *Journal of Political Economy* 88 (February 1980): 117–34.

Pasour, E. C., Jr. "Pareto Optimality as a Guide to Income Redistribution." *Public Choice* 36 (No. 1, 1981): 75–87.

Pommerehne, Werner W. "Public Choice Approaches to Explaining Fiscal Redistribution." In *Public Choice and Public Finance*, ed. by Karl W. Roskamp, pp. 169–90. Paris: Cujas, 1980.

Posner, Richard A. "Taxation by Regulation." *Bell Journal of Economics* 2 (Spring 1971): 22–50.

Rawls, John. *A Theory of Justice*. Cambridge: Harvard University Press, 1975.

Reynolds, Morgan O. *Making America Poorer: The Cost of Labor Law*. Washington: Cato Institute, 1987.

——— and Smolensky, Eugene. *Public Expenditures, Taxes, and the Distribution of Income*. New York: Academic Press, 1977.

Roberts, Russell D. "A Positive Model of Private Charity and Public Transfers." *Journal of Political Economy* 92 (February 1984): 136–48.

————. "Recipient Preferences and the Design of Government Transfer Programs." *Journal of Law and Economics* 28 (April 1985): 27–54.

Schiff, Jerold. "Does Government Spending Crowd Out Charitable Contributions?" *National Tax Journal* 38 (December 1985): 535–46.

Schiller, Bradley R. "Relative Earnings Mobility in the United States." *American Economic Review* 67 (December 1977): 926–41.

Smith, Janet Kiholm. "Production of Licensing Legislation: An Economic Analysis of Interstate Differences." *Journal of Legal Studies,* 11 (January 1982): 117–37.

Sowell, Thomas. *Affirmative Action Reconsidered.* Washington: American Enterprise Institute, 1975.

————. *Ethnic America.* New York: Basic Books, 1981.

————. *Conflict of Visions.* New York: William Morrow, 1987.

Stigler, George J. *The Citizen and the State: Essays on Regulation.* Chicago: University of Chicago Press, 1975.

Storing, Herbert J. *What the Anti-Federalists Were For.* Chicago: University of Chicago Press, 1981.

Stuart, Charles E. "Swedish Tax Rates, Labor Supply and Tax Revenues." *Journal of Political Economy* 89 (October 1981): 1020–38.

————, "Welfare Costs per Dollar of Additional Tax Revenue in the United States." *American Economic Review* 74 (June 1984): 352–62.

Tollison, Robert D. "Rent Seeking: A Survey." *Kyklos* 35 (No. 4, 1982): 575–602.

————. "Public Choice and Legislation." *Virginia Law Review* 74 (March 1988): 339–71.

Tullock, Gordon. *Economics of Income Redistribution.* Boston: Kluwer-Nijhoff, 1983.

————. "The Rhetoric and Reality of Redistribution." *Southern Economic Journal,* 47 (April 1981): 895–907.

————. "The Charity of the Uncharitable." *Economic Inquiry* 9 (December 1971): 379–92.

————. "The Welfare Costs of Tariffs, Monopolies, and Theft." *Economic Inquiry* 5 (June 1967): 224–32.

Vedder, Richard; Gallaway, Lowell; and Sollars, David. "The Tullock-Bastiat Hypothesis, Inequality-Transfer Curve and the Natural Distribution of Income." *Public Choice* 56 (March 1988): 285–94.

Wagner, Richard E. "Wealth Transfers in a Rent-Seeking Polity." *Cato Journal* 6 (Spring 1986): 155–71.

————. "Morals, Interests, and Constitutional Order: A Public Choice Perspective." *Oregon Law Review* 67 (No. 1, 1988): 73–92.

————. *"The Calculus of Consent*: A Wicksellian Retrospective." *Public Choice* (No. 2, 1988): 153–66.

Warren, Charles. *Congress as Santa Claus: National Donations and the General Welfare Clause of the Constitution*. Charlottesville, VA: Michie, 1932.

Weaver, Carolyn L. *The Crisis in Social Security: Economic and Political Origins*. Durham, NC: Duke University Press, 1982.

Weicher, John C., ed. *Maintaining the Safety Net*. Washington: American Enterprise Institute, 1984.

Welch, Finis. *Minimum Wages: Issues and Evidence*. Washington: American Enterprise Institute, 1978.

Williams, Walter E. *The State Against Blacks*. New York: McGraw-Hill, 1982.

————. "Government Sanctioned Restraints that Reduce Economic Opportunities for Minorities." *Policy Review*, No. 2 (Fall 1977): 7–30.

Wessels, Walter J. *Minimum Wages, Fringe Benefits, and Working Conditions*. Washington: American Enterprise Institute, 1981.

Yeager, Leland B. "Rights, Contract, and Utility in Policy Espousal." *Cato Journal* 5 (Spring 1985): 259–94.

Young, S. David. *The Rule of Experts: Occupational Licensing in America*. Washington: Cato Institute, 1987.

INDEX

ABOUT THE AUTHOR

Richard E. Wagner is currently Holbert R. Harris Professor of Economics at George Mason University. Professor Wagner has also held academic positions at the University of California at Irvine, Tulane University, Auburn University, and Florida State University. He received his Ph.D. in economics from the University of Virginia in 1966.

Professor Wagner has served on various academic advisory boards, among them the Center for the Study of Market Processes at George Mason University, the Independent Institute, the Institute for Research on the Economics of Taxation, and the James Madison Institute for Public Policy Studies. He currently serves on the Honorary Board of Scholars for the Liberty Park Foundation and is editor of *Constitutional Political Economy*.

Professor Wagner is the author of *The Fiscal Organization of American Federalism*, *The Public Economy*, and *Public Finance: Revenues and Expenditures in a Democratic Society*, among others. He has also coauthored several books including *Democracy in Deficit: The Political Legacy of Lord Keynes*, *Smoking and the State: Social Costs, Rent Seeking, and Public Policy*, and *The Federal Budget Process: Why it is Broken and How it Can Be Fixed*. His articles have appeared in *American Economic Review*, *Journal of Law and Economics*, *Policy Studies Journal*, and *Public Choice*.

OTHER STUDIES IN PUBLIC POLICY BY
THE PACIFIC RESEARCH INSTITUTE

FORESTLANDS
Public and Private
Edited by Robert T. Deacon and M. Bruce Johnson
Foreword by B. Delworth Gardner

URBAN TRANSIT
The Private Challenge to Public Transportation
Edited by Charles A. Lave
Foreword by John Meyer

POLITICS, PRICES, AND PETROLEUM
The Political Economy of Energy
By David Glasner
Foreword by Paul W. MacAvoy

RIGHTS AND REGULATION
Ethical, Political, and Economic Issues
Edited by Tibor M. Machan and M. Bruce Johnson
Foreword by Aaron Wildavsky

FUGITIVE INDUSTRY
The Economics and Politics of Deindustrialization
By Richard B. McKenzie
Foreword by Finis Welch

MONEY IN CRISIS
The Federal Reserve, the Economy, and Monetary Reform
Edited by Barry N. Siegel
Foreword by Leland B. Yeager

NATURAL RESOURCES
Bureaucratic Myths and Environmental Management
By Richard Stroup and John Baden
Foreword by William Niskanen

FIREARMS AND VIOLENCE
Issues of Public Policy
Edited by Don B. Kates, Jr.
Foreword by John Kaplan

WATER RIGHTS
Scarce Resource Allocation, Bureaucracy, and the Environment
Edited by Terry L. Anderson
Foreword by Jack Hirshleifer

LOCKING UP THE RANGE
Federal Land Controls and Grazing
By Gary D. Libecap
Foreword by Jonathan R.T. Hughes

THE PUBLIC SCHOOL MONOPOLY
A Critical Analysis of Education and the State in American Society
Edited by Robert B. Everhart
Foreword by Clarence J. Karier

RESOLVING THE HOUSING CRISIS
Government Policy, Demand, Decontrol, and the Public Interest
Edited with an Introduction by M. Bruce Johnson

OFFSHORE LANDS
Oil and Gas Leasing and Conservation on the Outer Continental Shelf
By Walter J. Mead, et al.
Foreword by Stephen L. McDonald

ELECTRIC POWER
Deregulation and the Public Interest
Edited by John C. Moorhouse
Foreword by Harold Demsetz

TAXATION AND THE DEFICIT ECONOMY
Fiscal Policy and Capital Formation in the United States
Edited by Dwight R. Lee
Foreword by Michael J. Boskin

THE AMERICAN FAMILY AND STATE
Edited by Joseph R. Peden and Fred R. Glahe
Foreword by Robert Nisbet

DEALING WITH DRUGS
Consequences of Government Control
Edited by Ronald Hamowy
Foreword by Dr. Alfred Freedman

CRISIS AND LEVIATHAN
Critical Episodes in the Growth of American Government
By Robert Higgs
Foreword by Arthur A. Ekirch, Jr.

THE NEW CHINA
Comparative Economic Development in Mainland China, Taiwan, and Hong Kong
By Alvin Rabushka

ADVERTISING AND THE MARKET PROCESS
A Modern Economic View
By Robert B. Ekelund, Jr. and David S. Saurman
Foreword by Israel M. Kirzner

HEALTH CARE IN AMERICA
The Political Economy of Hospitals and Health Insurance
Edited by H.E. Frech III
Foreword by Richard Zeckhauser

POLITICAL BUSINESS CYCLES
The Political Economy of Money, Inflation, and Unemployment
Edited by Thomas D. Willett
Foreword by Axel Leijonhufvud

WHEN GOVERNMENT GOES PRIVATE
Successful Alternatives to Public Services
By Randall Fitzgerald

For further information on the Pacific Research Institute's program and a catalog of publications, please contact:

PACIFIC RESEARCH INSTITUTE FOR PUBLIC POLICY
177 Post Street
San Francisco, CA 94108
(415) 989-0833

4687